A HANDBOOK TO
CHOPIN'S WORKS

BY

GEORGE C. ASHTON JONSON

FOR THE USE OF CONCERT-GOERS, PIANISTS
AND PIANOLA-PLAYERS

BOOKS FOR LIBRARIES PRESS
FREEPORT, NEW YORK

First Published 1905
Reprinted 1972

Library of Congress Cataloging in Publication Data

Jonson, George Charles Ashton, 1861–
  A handbook to Chopin's works.

  Reprint of the 1905 ed.
  Bibliography: p.
  1. Chopin, Fryderyk Franciszek, 1810–1849.
ML410.C54J8 1972   786.1'092'4   72–5428
ISBN 0–8369–6916–2

PRINTED IN THE UNITED STATES OF AMERICA

TO MY WIFE

WITHOUT WHOSE SYMPATHY, ENCOURAGEMENT,

AND ASSISTANCE

I COULD NEVER HAVE WRITTEN THIS BOOK

CONTENTS

CONTENTS

CONTENTS

CONTENTS

I.—WHAT THIS BOOK IS.

THIS book is not intended to be read straight through and then placed upon the shelf. It is a handbook, a kind of musical "Baedeker," a guide through the "Thoughtland and Dreamland" of Chopin's kingdom.

Students of Chopin have already written voluminously about him, and in their writings are many pearls of criticism and gems of sympathetic insight; but these are scattered through innumerable volumes, magazine articles, and newspapers, and are therefore inaccessible to all but the most devoted students.

I have tried to collect all such passages of the greatest value, and I have grouped them under the opus numbers of the works to which they refer, so that they are here presented for the first time in their natural connection, and are available for instant reference.

The main portion of the book consists of a brief account of each composition, its relative place amongst Chopin's works, its distinguishing features, notes of any special point of interest attaching to it and an epitome of the comments or criticisms that have been made upon it by all the great writers, critics, biographers, and virtuosi who have written about Chopin and his works.

Although I have begun with a brief sketch of Chopin's life, and short preliminary chapters on various aspects of the composer, this book is in no sense intended as a biography; whenever the events of Chopin's career exercised a palpable influence over his works, I have endeavoured in my comments to emphasise the fact, but any attempt to write a

biography when such a work as Professor Niecks'
Chopin is in existence would be lost labour.

Three years ago this book could only have met with
a very limited demand, owing to the fact that the
number of amateurs possessed of sufficient technique
to play Chopin's music (for the most part extremely
difficult) is very small.

But to-day, owing to the invention of the pianola and
the fact that all Chopin's works, including even the
least important of the posthumous compositions, are
now available for that instrument, the whole domain of
his music is for the first time open to all. Those who wish

may pass the portal hitherto guarded by the dragon of
technique, and roam at will in his entrancing music-land.

Nobody who has tried it will deny that the sensuous
enjoyment of music like Chopin's is enormously
increased by the intellectual interest that springs from
systematic knowledge. But life is short and art is long,
and there are few, even amongst those capable of doing
so, who can devote the requisite time to familiarising
themselves at the piano with the complete works of a
composer, when they are dependent on their own
unaided efforts. But now the pianola has rendered it
easy for any one sufficiently interested to acquire
quickly and systematically an intimate knowledge of
the works of the greatest masters.

Aided by the chronological table I have compiled of
the approximate dates of the compositions, the development of the composer's individuality can be studiously
followed, and whether for close study or for a passing
reference to a particular work, such an epitome of the
best critical opinions as is here contained must add
new zest to the enjoyment of music.

I have only reproduced such of the comments of the
writers I have quoted as are helpful to a fuller comprehension and appreciation of the music, and I have
omitted as unessential to the purpose of the work innumerable passages referring solely to finger technique.

The book will, I trust, be found equally useful and

helpful to concert-goers, for whom it forms a permanent analytical programme, to pianists, and to those
amateurs of music who can now, owing to the pianola,
pursue for the first time a systematic and co-ordinated
study of Chopin's works, a delight hitherto denied to
them owing to their inability to read or play the more
difficult compositions.

So great have been the pleasure and profit to myself
of the task of preparing this book, that whether it prove
successful or not, I intend, and have indeed already
begun, to write similar handbooks to the works of Beethoven, Schumann, Grieg, and other great composers.

Should there prove to be no demand for such a
series, I shall not conclude that such works are useless,
but rather that others have not realised, as I have, the
far-reaching educational value of the pianola, and the
vastly increased artistic pleasure to be obtained from
its intelligent use.

II.—CHOPIN'S POSITION AMONG THE GREAT MASTERS.

IN one of the numerous sketch-books in which
Beethoven used to jot down the first ideas for his
compositions, we find scribbled in the margin :
" Heaven knows why my pianoforte music always
makes the worst impression on me, especially when
it is played badly." To modern audiences who have
heard Godowsky play the " Appassionata " on a modern
concert grand, this little-known piece of self-criticism
sounds strange, and to understand it one must go back
for a moment to the history of the pianoforte. An
Italian named Cristofori made the first piano in
Florence in 1709. He called it the " pianoforte,"
because with the new hammer action it could play both
loud and soft. Previous to this, the tone of the harpsi-
chord, the keyed instrument then in general use, could

only be increased by means of a swell, or shutters, as now used on an organ.   Three years before his death the great Bach played on a German piano made by one Silbermann, but his Preludes and Fugues were written in 1722 for the clavichord.   It was not till three years after Beethoven was born that Clementi published his three Sonatas (Opus 2), which may be said to be the first music written specially for the pianoforte.   But the kind of piano for which Mozart wrote so much beautiful music at the end of the eighteenth century was very different from the magnificent instruments of to-day ; for instance, it was another hundred years before the loud and soft pedals were invented by John Broadwood.   The absence of these on the instruments of that time is the reason why the Sonatas of Mozart and Haydn can be played with very little loss of effect without using the pedals, and it was to compensate for the lack of singing power in the instrument that Mozart used to embellish his music with the endless turns, trills, and ornaments that helped to fill in the intervals between the notes of a melody.

With the improvement of the piano came a different style of playing ; the staccato method was abandoned, and the legato, of which Beethoven was the great exponent, came to the front.   His noble series of Sonatas will remain a priceless possession for all ages. But full as they are of the most noble and beautiful ideas, and abounding in sublime and inspiring melodies, Beethoven by no means exhausted the possibilities of the instrument.   There are many passages in his Sonatas which do not sound as if they were intended for the piano ; they are emphatically stringed instrument music, and many of his noblest melodies seem to demand an orchestra for their due expression.   It is, therefore, not surprising that, considering the value of their musical content, he found the renderings of his Sonatas on the instruments of the period unsatisfactory. The genius of Beethoven's contemporary, Schubert, that inexhaustible well of musical inspiration, found its

most perfect expression in song ; want of restraint
and concentration debarred him from perfection as
a writer for the piano ; but when we come to the
next great name in music, Frederic Chopin, we
have arrived at one of the culminating points of the
art.   Rubinstein, the greatest artist among pianists,
says,   "The   Pianoforte   Bard,   the   Pianoforte
Rhapsodist, the Pianoforte Mind, the Pianoforte Soul
is Chopin.   Whether the spirit of this instrument
breathed upon him, or he wrote upon it—*how* he wrote
for it, I do not know, but only an entire going-over of
one into the other could call such composition into life.
Tragic, romantic, lyric, heroic, dramatic, fantastic,
soulful, sweet, dreamy, brilliant, grand, simple, all
possible expressions are found in his compositions, and
are all sung by him upon this instrument in perfect
beauty."

In Chopin the romantic school found its highest
expression.   The only other name worthy to stand
beside his is that of Schumann, the genius whose
almost prophetic insight led him to acclaim his fellow
genius as the noblest poetic spirit of the age.

Than these two, said Rubinstein, the art of music
can no further go, and as far as regards pianoforte
music, there can be no gainsaying this dictum.   Writing
in 1850, a year after the death of Chopin, Liszt said
that posterity would rank him far higher than his
contemporaries had done, and the last fifty years have
seen a steady increase in his popularity.   Except in
the case of recitals devoted entirely to Beethoven, no
programme is complete without its group of Chopin
works ; whatever other composer is omitted, he is
always included, and yet out of his 214 works how
many can fairly be said to be familiar to the general
public.   A few of his easier compositions are perhaps
too well known as forming part of the *gradus-ad-
parnassum* of the young person.   Some others are
heard too often at concerts ; but there are many pieces,
perhaps not the most beautiful, but by no means the

b

least interesting, which are not heard from year's end to year's end. Even in his easier works there generally occur one or two rather difficult passages, as if Chopin had intended to warn off bunglers, and the greater number of his compositions are technically very difficult. It is not too much to say that 80 per cent. of his works are a sealed book to the average amateur, and the knowledge to be gained by hearing occasional isolated performances at concerts can give not the faintest idea of the range and power of Chopin's work.

There can be no greater mistake than to think that because Bach, Handel, Mozart, and Beethoven were great masters, therefore they must be superior to everybody in everything. Bach in his organ fugues, Handel in his choral writing, Wagner in music drama, Beethoven in his symphonies, each touched the highest pinnacles of art. Chopin in his pianoforte works, with the sole exception of Beethoven, stands as the unchallenged master. Even then it is a case of honours divided, for if in fundamental brain-stuff and majesty of musical material Beethoven is the superior, in the actual expression and in the choice of subject most fitly to be expressed on the piano, Chopin has the decided advantage.

The last fifty years have produced no rival to him in his own kingdom. Rubinstein maintained that Chopin was the last of the great original composers, but in Mendelssohn, Brahms, Grieg, and Wagner, we have masters who each in his special department have been as supreme as the older men. The delightfully unconventional American critic Finck, in a most stimulating and sympathetic essay, declares that Chopin is as superior to all other piano composers as Wagner is to all other writers of dramatic music, and warns us against what he calls " æsthetic Jumboism," or worship of mere size as constituting superiority in art. If only one work of Chopin's were left to us, such as the first book of Études, or the Preludes, his fame would be immortal. If Chopin ranks below Bach, Beethoven, and Wagner, it is not because he wrote only for the piano, and for the most part small works, but because intrinsically he was a man of lesser mental calibre. But the fact remains that as a composer of works for the piano that are matchless for originality, sheer beauty and felicity of expression, works which, to quote Finck, revealed for the first time the infinite possibilities of varied and beautiful tone-colour inherent in the piano, Chopin is the supreme master.

Chopin's chief superiority lies in this genius for tone-colour. He was the first composer who thoroughly realised the subtleties of which the piano is capable in the hands of an artist who understands the real use of the *sostenuto* and *una corda* pedals. The evil habit of describing these as the loud and soft pedals is responsible for much misunderstanding on the part of the average amateur. Chopin in one of his letters said contemptuously of Thalberg, that he played "*forte* and *piano* with the pedals, not with his hands." The pedals should of course only be employed with a view to the quality and not the quantity of tone desired. Chopin was fully aware of his own limitations. When he was pressed by the Comte de Perthuis to write an opera, he said, "Ah, Count, let me compose nothing but music for the pianoforte, I am not learned enough to compose operas !"

Sir Hubert Parry in his summary of musical history says of Chopin : " He uttered his thought with complete certainty only through the medium of the pianoforte. He never became master of orchestration even sufficiently to write the accompaniment to his Concertos with due effect. But his work for the pianoforte is so marvellously perfect in its adaptation to the idiosyncrasies of the instrument, that it becomes historically important on that ground alone. His work is not often great in conception, or noteworthy in design, but it is the spontaneous expression of a poetical, refined, and sensitive temperament."

Hueffer points out that this very oneness of theme, which in a lesser man would have led to monotony, resulted in Chopin in concentration of the highest order. "Excepting Heine, and it may be Sappho, Chopin is the most perfect embodiment of lyrical power, properly so called, that the history of art or poetry can show."

Hadow at the end of his very delightful and sympathetic essay on Chopin says: "To sum up, Chopin can claim no place among the few greatest masters of the world. He lacks the dignity, the breadth, the high seriousness of Palestrina and Bach and Beethoven ; he no more ranks beside them than Shelley beside Shakespeare, or Andrea beside Michael Angelo. But to say this is not to disparage the value of the work that he has done. . . . In structure he is a child, playing with a few simple types, and almost helpless as soon as he advances beyond them ; in phraseology he is a master, whose felicitous perfection of style is one of the abiding treasures of the art. There have been higher ideals in music, but not one that has been more clearly seen or more consistently followed. There have been nobler messages, but none delivered with a sweeter or more persuasive eloquence."

III.—CHOPIN'S LIFE AND WORK.

CHOPIN was the only son of Nicholas Chopin and his wife Justina Krzyanowska ; he was born in 1810 at Zelazowa Wola, a village near Warsaw. This date has been the subject of much dispute, but is now finally settled. Chopin's father kept a private school, and Frederic received a good education there and later at the Warsaw Lyceum.

At a very early age he displayed great musical ability as a pianist and composer. When he was nine years old he appeared with success at a charity concert. At twelve he was already a composer, and a polonaise is extant to which the date 1822 is attached. His Opus 1, a Rondo in C minor, was published in 1825, and his Opus 2 appeared in 1828. This latter was the set of variations on "Là ci darem," which attracted the attention and earned the warm praise of Schumann.

During his boyhood Chopin's holidays were passed in the country, where he absorbed the national song and dance forms in which he heard the peasants indulging, for the Poles as a nation are almost as naturally musical as the Hungarians. Two mazurkas bear the date of 1825, Chopin's fifteenth year, and about this time he wrote a set of variations on a popular German air, and two polonaises. In all probability he wrote a great many more pieces than have survived, for he was always a severe critic of his own work. His musical education was carried on first by one Zywny, and then by Joseph Elsner, a composer of some repute. Both his teachers seem to have recognised that they had to deal with a boy of strikingly original genius, and under Elsner Chopin was allowed to develop his own musical individuality practically uncontrolled.

Young Frederic had had the advantage of associating with the children of the Polish nobility who attended his father's school, and amongst his intimate friends were the well-known family of the Radziwills. To these aristocratic surroundings and associations Chopin owed the delicate refinement for which he was distinguished all his life.

His first long journey was a trip to Berlin in 1828, and in July 1829 he visited Vienna, where he gave two concerts with conspicuous success. Chopin was an impressionable youth ; he had a boyish affection for a Miss Blahetka, but his first serious love affair was his devotion to a beautiful young opera singer, Constantia Gladkowska, whom he met in Vienna. Nothing is known of the unfortunate attachment, nor why it terminated, but on Chopin's side it was a very pure and genuine devotion, and undoubtedly had its influence in deepening the emotional side of his character.

He was again in Vienna in 1830, and this time he remained there for eight months, till July 1831. At his concerts he had relied chiefly on the compositions he had written to show off his powers as a virtuoso. These were the " Là ci darem " variations, his two concertos, the Krakowiak, and a fantaisie on Polish national airs. He went out a great deal into society, and perhaps owing to this, the uncertainty of his plans, and his unfortunate attachment to the beautiful Gladkowska, he composed very little. After prolonged hesitation he finally set out for Paris, where he arrived early in October 1831.

He already enjoyed a considerable reputation as a virtuoso with a particularly refined and individual style, and although he modestly intended to take lessons of Kalkbrenner, he decided after his first interview not to do so. In a short time his position was assured, and he became one of the most admired pianists and fashionable teachers of the day.

In December 1832 he published his first book of mazurkas, Opus 6, and from that time till failing health put an end to his creative powers in 1847, he wrote 122 separate works, large and small, or every year an average of eight compositions, of which it is not too much to say that each is a masterpiece. The only exceptions to this high level are a few pieces composed about 1833, which seem to reflect in their light and essentially French style, the shallowness of the Parisian society life into which Chopin at first plunged *con amore*. These pieces include the Boléro, the variations on an air of Halévy's, the third Rondo, and a Duo on airs from Robert le Diable. It seems as if his facile salon triumphs had for a brief time lowered his ideals, and perhaps his want of success as a performer before large audiences at public concerts was the blessing in disguise that drove him back upon himself, and led to the composition of his finer and more elevated work which may be said to begin anew with the B minor Scherzo and the first Ballade. Chopin was never so much at his ease before a large audience as he was when playing to a select few in a drawing-room. The knowledge that he was not doing himself justice led him to withdraw increasingly from what he called " the intimidation of the crowd." It was probably in the winter of 1831 that he heard of the marriage of his " ideal," Constantia Gladkowska, to a wealthy merchant of Warsaw. We are told nothing of the way the news affected him, but it is undeniable that from this time onward his music shows a deeper note of feeling.

Chopin usually spent his annual holiday in travelling. In 1835 he visited Dresden, and there fell in love with Marie Wodzinska, the pretty daughter of a wealthy Polish count. This was the Mdlle. Marie, to whom he dedicated one of the smaller valses. In 1836 he proposed, but the family did not approve of the engagement, and her refusal does not seem to have caused Chopin very serious unhappiness.

At Leipsic about this time he met Schumann, Clara Wieck, and Mendelssohn, who used to call Chopin with affectionate playfulness " Chopinetto." Schumann's enthusiastic admiration of Chopin's playing, and his affection for the composer, was as great as that he had already displayed for his music, but Chopin hardly seemed to reciprocate this appreciation. When he received a copy of Schumann's " Carnival," he put it down after looking at the title-page only, and all he said was : " How nicely they get up this style of thing in Germany."

It was in 1837 that Chopin first met George Sand. His friendship with the celebrated authoress lasted for eight years and is the most discussed episode of his life. No two authorities agree either on the extent or quality of the friendship, or as to the character of George Sand, some presenting her as a dissolute heart-less monster, and others as a charming woman, a good

mother, and a faithful friend.   Even Niecks, although
no admirer of the authoress, whom he thinks incapable
of telling the exact truth, is bound to admit that no one
can pronounce authoritatively on the moral aspect of
this extraordinary friendship.   Hadow accepts George
Sand's version that it was purely platonic, and on her
side exclusively a maternal affection ; but whatever the
truth, there is no doubt as to the result.   Chopin
certainly suffered cruelly towards the end, although at
first and for long intervals he enjoyed a happiness and
a sense of completion in his life that had till now been
lacking ; and this in spite of the first serious break-
down in his health, which occurred in the winter of
1838–9 after an attack of influenza.   This winter he
spent at Majorca with George Sand and her children
Maurice and Solange.   As usual, when people go
abroad for their health, the winter climate proved
exceptional.   After a fortnight of lovely gardens,
orange groves, olive woods, and beautiful and romantic
scenery, it turned cold and began to rain, and went on
raining for months, till in February, at the first opportunity, they took ship for Marseilles, where Chopin
spent the spring in convalescence, nursed devotedly by
his loving friend.   After this he spent four months of
every summer at George Sand's château at Nohant,
and it was here that the bulk of his best work was
produced.   In 1847 came the rupture between the
friends, and the ensuing winter was one of illness,
inaction, and consequent financial embarrassment.
The revolution of 1848 broke out in Paris, and Chopin
came to England.   He stayed in London till the
summer, when he went for a tour in Scotland with
Mendelssohn.

It is a curious fact that they are the only musical
geniuses to have visited that country.   Poor Chopin was
very ill all this time.   When he played in London he
had always to be carried upstairs to the first floor,
and in Scotland he complains incessantly of the
weather, which he said was killing him.   He found

nothing to his taste and declared all Scotch women were ugly. Mendelssohn, however, said "he should like to become a Turk, and settle in Edinburgh."

During the whole of his stay in England his health became steadily worse. Towards the end, the self-control and reserve of the sick man began to give way. He writes from Dover Street to his friend Grzymala : " A day longer here and I shall go mad or die "; and again : " I have never cursed any one, but now I am so weary of life that I am near cursing Lucrezia (George Sand). But she suffers too, and suffers more because she grows daily older in wickedness." There is no doubt that the rupture with George Sand hastened and embittered his last days, and yet there are always two sides to a quarrel, and in a letter of about the same date, George Sand says : " I have exhausted all that the cup of life contains of tribulation. I hoped at least for the old age on which I was entering the recompense of great sacrifices, of much work, fatigue, and a whole life of devotion and abnegation. I asked for nothing but to render happy the objects of my affection. Well, I have been repaid with ingratitude, and evil has got the upper hand in a soul which I wished to make the sanctuary and the hearth of the beautiful and the good."

What is one to believe ? All her biographers seem to agree that the authoress had a marvellous capacity for self-deception, and sympathy with Chopin leads one to think the stinging epigram of Alfred de Musset was not too severe on her : " If I no longer believe in tears, it is because I have seen her weep."

The anonymous generosity of Miss Stirling, his Scotch pupil and hostess, saved Chopin from actual want and discomfort, for, of course, with the inability to teach, compose, or play, his income had almost entirely ceased. He resigned himself to the prospect of death with a noble courage, and was tenderly nursed by his sister and his faithful friends Gutmann and Franchomme. To the latter he murmured towards the end : "She always said I should die in no other arms than hers." When he was almost *in extremis*, George Sand came to the landing outside his door, but Gutmann, fearing to agitate the dying man, refused her entrance.

The anecdote of the Countess Delphine Potocka singing to the composer is undoubtedly true, but there is the most extraordinary discrepancy in the accounts of those who were actually present as to what she sang.

Sentiment and cheap romance, however, have made the most of its opportunity. An anonymous writer in an extinct periodical says : "There is still quite an eager demand for a very bad engraving with the Countess sweetly singing and Chopin sweetly dying. Indeed, many people would seem to believe that Chopin spent his life dying, with the composition of his own funeral march by way of recreation. At his best they conceive him as an adorable invalid, an anæmic sentimentalist. Therefore, it is always a Chopin Nocturne that the mooney women of second-rate fiction dream over at black pianos in great dim rooms with French windows."

Chopin's funeral with its service at the Madeleine and the procession to Père-la-chaise was one of the important events of Parisian life in 1849. His funeral march was arranged for orchestra for the occasion, and Lefebure Wély played two of the Preludes on the organ : those in E minor and B minor from the twenty-four which make up Opus 28.

IV.—CHOPIN AS A VIRTUOSO.

WHEN Chopin told Mendelssohn that he had been to see Kalkbrenner with the idea of taking lessons from him, Mendelssohn said impulsively : "You play better than Kalkbrenner," and it is on record that he wrote to a friend : " How happy I am once again hearing a real musician, not one of those half-classical virtuosi who would so much like to combine the honours of virtue with the pleasures of vice in music."

From his earliest youth Chopin was a distinguished performer on the pianoforte. His first master Zywny taught him up to the age of twelve, when his progress was so extraordinary that they decided to allow him to follow the dictates of his instinctive genius. Like Schumann, he endeavoured to increase the flexibility of his hands by a mechanical device, but fortunately it was not attended in his case with the dire results that befell Schumann, whose attempt in this direction ended in a permanent crippling of his fingers, and stopped his career as a virtuoso. Chopin positively created a new school of technique, and developed pianoforte playing to a remarkable extent. The contemporary criticisms on his playing when he gave concerts in Vienna all go to prove that he was an artist of great individuality and of fine artistic conscience. One of the leading critics of the day wrote : " He is a young man who goes his own way, although his style of playing differs greatly from that of other virtuosi ; and indeed chiefly in this that the desire to make good music predominates noticeably in his case over the desire to please."

Moscheles has left us in his letters an interesting critique of Chopin. He says : " He played to me, and then for the first time I really understood his music and saw an explanation of the ladies' enthusiasm. The *ad libitum*, which with his interpreters degenerates into bad time, is, when he himself performs, the most charming originality of execution ; the harsh and dilettante-like modulations, which I could never get over when playing his compositions, ceased to offend when his delicate, fairy-like fingers glided over them ; his *piano* is so delicate that no very strong *forte* is required to give the desired contrast. Thus we do not miss the orchestral effects which the German school demands from a pianist, but feel ourselves carried away as by a singer who, paying little heed to the accompaniment, abandons himself to his feelings. He is quite unique in the pianistic world."

Chopin, too, had a delightful disposition, free from the pettiness and jealousy that so often mar artistic natures. When he and Moscheles played to Louis Philippe at St. Cloud, the latter wrote : " Chopin and I revelled like brothers in the triumph achieved by the individual talent of each ; there was no tinge of jealousy on either side."

Heine, who was one of Chopin's intimate circle in Paris, said that genius in the full acceptation of the term must be allowed to Chopin. " He is not a virtuoso only, he is also a poet ; he can make us apprehend the poetry which lives in his heart ; he is a ' tone-poet,' and no enjoyment is equal to that which he bestows upon us when he sits down at the piano and improvises."

The veteran Kühé heard Chopin play at the house of Mrs. Sartoris in Eaton Place ; he tells us he paid a guinea for his ticket, and that Chopin's performance was "the most perfect example of poetry in sound which ever greeted my ears. Were Chopin alive now, every seat would sell for five guineas within two hours of the announcement of a recital by him."

Sir Charles Hallé, who knew Chopin well in Paris, has left in his autobiography an enthusiastic record of his admiration of the composer as pianist.

" The same evening I heard him play, and was fascinated beyond expression. I sat entranced, filled with wonderment, and if the room had suddenly been peopled with fairies I should not have been astonished. The marvellous charm, the poetry and originality, the perfect freedom and absolute lucidity of Chopin's play-ing at that time cannot be described. It was perfection in every sense. . . . In listening to him you lost all power of analysis ; you did not for a moment think how perfect was his execution of this or that difficulty ;

you listened, as it were, to the improvisation of a poem and were under the charm as long as it lasted. . . . Chopin carried you with him into a dreamland, in which you would have liked to dwell for ever."

Von Lenz, who often heard Chopin play, writes : " That which particularly characterised Chopin's playing was his *rubato*, whereby the rhythm and time throughout the whole remained accurate. ' That left hand,' I often heard him say, ' is the conductor ; it must not waver, or lose ground, do with the right hand what you can and will.' In the fluctuation of the *tempo* Chopin was ravishing ; every note stood on the highest degree of taste, in the noblest sense of the term. When he embellished—which he very rarely did—it was always a species of miracle of good taste."

About Chopin's *rubato* playing, Berlioz said in his autobiography : " Chopin could never bear the restraint of time, and, I think, carried his independence too far ; he simply *could not* play in time. He was the delicate, refined virtuoso of small gatherings of groups of intimate friends ; but Liszt was at his very best with two thousand hearers to conquer."

With regard to this point Chopin said to Liszt : " I am not at all fit for giving concerts, the crowd intimidates me, its breath suffocates me, unknown faces make me dumb. But you are destined for it, for when you do not win your public you have the power to overwhelm it."

These few quotations will serve to illustrate the universally favourable opinion of Chopin as a player. A whole book of appreciations might be culled from the writings of those who were fortunate enough to have heard the poet-composer play his own compositions.

To conclude, we will take the evidence of an anonymous writer who heard Chopin play during his last visit to London :

" Over himself his art exercised a great charm. I have seen him look fifty when he took his place, and twenty-five when he quitted it ; sit down a meagre, worn, livid, panting man (his face, as some one described it, seamed with pain and anxiety), and as he proceeded, shadow after shadow gradually dissolve, and fold after fold soften, and the flush of health come back into the cheek, and the dim, glassy eyes brighten with a cheerful and living intelligence."

V.—CHOPIN AS A TEACHER.

CHOPIN increased the income he made from his compositions and his rare appearances in public by teaching. His fee for giving a lesson to pupils, of whom he, as a rule, had as many as he wanted, was twenty francs, but he never taught more than five hours a day, and every year he spent several months in the country. Although at one time he made quite a good income, he was generous and unbusinesslike, and consequently never saved money. It has been urged against his merits as a teacher that none of his pupils ever attained to the first rank amongst *virtuosi*. This, however, can easily be accounted for by the fact that a large majority of his pupils were amateurs. Two of his most promising professional pupils died young, Charles Filtsch and Paul Gunsberg. The former was a prodigy of marvellous musical organisation, and, indeed, by contemporary accounts he was as a pianist what the boy, Von Vecsey, is as a violinist. Amongst his most prominent pupils were George Mathias, professor of the piano at the Paris Conservatoire ; Tellefsen, a Norwegian ; and Adolph Gutmann, the master's favourite pupil *par excellence* as Niecks terms him. Chopin also taught Brinley Richards and Lindsay Sloper. He was always kind to his pupils, but occasionally very irritable ; and a pupil tells us that he used, when teaching amateurs, to break up pencils as a method of venting his annoyance. His pupils simply idolised him.   Smoothness of execution, beauty of tone, and intelligent phrasing were the points on which he most insisted.

In furtherance of the last two details, he always urged his pupils to hear good singing, and even to take singing lessons themselves, in order that they might develop a true and expressive method of *cantabile* playing.

VI—CHOPIN'S TASTE IN MUSIC.

" IN the great models and masterworks of art Chopin sought only what corresponded with his nature. What resembled it pleased him, what differed from it hardly received justice from him."

This was Liszt's *dictum* upon Chopin's preference in the musical art ; and bearing this undeniably true statement in mind, it is interesting and instructive to gather from various sources which were the composers whom Chopin greatly admired, and which again were antipathetic to him.

Chopin esteemed Mozart above all other composers. Liszt explains this by saying "that it was because Mozart condescended more rarely than any other composer to cross the steps which separate refinement from vulgarity." Niecks amplifies this explanation : "But what no doubt more especially stirred sympathetic chords in the heart of Chopin, and inspired him with that loving admiration for the earlier Master, was the sweetness, the grace, and the harmoniousness which in Mozart's works reign supreme and undisturbed." It is said that Chopin never travelled without the score of Don Giovanni or the Requiem, and Liszt tells us that even in Don Giovanni, Chopin discovered passages the presence of which he regretted.   It is curious that he adored Bach while seemingly neglecting Beethoven. When he wished to prepare himself for one of his

concerts, it was not his own music that he played, but
that of the great organist, whilst he always grounded
his pupils on the Preludes and Fugues, and adjured
them always to study Bach.

Hallé narrates how he played Chopin "at his
request, in his own room, Beethoven's Sonata in E flat,
Op. 30, No. 3, and after the finale he said that it was the
first time he had liked it, that it had always appeared
to him very vulgar."

Probably it was want of familiarity with the works
of Beethoven which was at the root of Chopin's in-
difference.   Von Lenz says : "He did not take a very
serious interest in Beethoven, he knew only his
principal compositions, the last works not at all.   This
was in the Paris air ! People knew the symphonies,
the quartets of the middle period but little, the last
ones not at all."

Of his contemporaries he played chiefly the compositions of Hummel, Field, and Moscheles.   The former
had been an admiration of his youth, and the concertos
particularly show that Hummel exercised a formative
influence on Chopin.   From Field, too, he adopted the
form of the Nocturne, although he infused into it a
warmth, a distinction, that are absent from even the
best work of the Englishman.   He was especially fond
of playing the duets of Moscheles, and certain pieces
of Schubert also found favour with him.

Of Weber he apparently did not entertain a high
opinion, and notwithstanding Schumann's extravagant
admiration and sincere affection for him, Chopin never
displayed the least admiration for the work of his
great romantic contemporary.

Chopin hated virtuoso music, and with the exception of a few pieces of Liszt's none of the efforts of
this school were ever to be found on his music desk.

VII.—EDITIONS OF CHOPIN'S WORKS.

THERE are a very great many editions of Chopin's works from amongst which the amateur or student may take his choice. To avoid confusion it will be advisable not to give a complete list of these, but to say at once that the three best are those published by Bote and Bock, edited by Karl Klindworth ; Schlesinger (Robert Lienau), edited by Theodor Kullak; and Breitkopf and Hartel of Leipzic.

The last is the most complete ; it has several editors, viz., Bargiel, Brahms, Franchomme, Liszt, Reinecke, and Rudorff. It contains the orchestral parts to the six pieces with orchestra, the works for stringed instruments and the songs, besides more posthumous works than any other edition.

Klindworth's is a purely pianoforte edition, and is generally considered the best from an editorial point of view, i.e., in the correctness of the text and the choice in variants, when such exist. Kullak's edition has the advantage of many notes and much interesting comment on the works. It contains the songs but not the trio and 'cello duets. Chopin, although he wrote and re-wrote his pieces with the utmost pains until he was satisfied with them, prepared his manuscript very negligently for his publishers. He often did not see the proofs, which were sometimes corrected for him by his friends. The consequence is that the original editions are often full of mistakes and misprints.

Schumann, for instance, in reviewing the Tarantella, said that " the first comprehension of this piece is unfortunately rendered very difficult by the misprints with which it is really swarming." The consequence is, that there exist several important differences between the various editions, and the editors, many of whom were pupils of Chopin's, have disputed right royally over the different readings. The first complete edition of the works was issued in 1864 by Gebethner and

Wolff of Warsaw, edited by Kleczynski. Amongst the other editions are those edited by Tellefsen, Scholtz, Mikuli, Richter, Jadassohn, Mertke, Köhler, and Bohn.

Breitkopf and Hartel have also issued a most complete thematic catalogue of the works, with several interesting lists and classifications.

BIBLIOGRAPHY.

NIECKS, Professor Frederick. "Frederick Chopin as a Man and Musician." Two Vols. Published by Novello & Co. London and New York.

THIS thorough and painstaking book is the standard authority on Chopin's life and works. There is a leisurely completeness about it, but the material is well arranged and it is never diffuse. The professor not only examined every scrap of documentary evidence in existence, but he had the advantage of personally interviewing the friends and pupils of Chopin who were alive at the time he began his researches. As far as dates and the facts of Chopin's life go, no other biography of the composer is worth reading ; Professor Niecks' book not only embraces everything of value in the works published before his, but all succeeding biographers have had perforce to follow in his footsteps, and their books are but a rearrangement of his material.

The chief sources from which Professor Niecks drew were Liszt's and Karasowski's biographies, and other works then extant were a short life by Joseph Bennett and a brief essay by Hueffer.

But apart from biographical details, it is always interesting to read what a musician of critical insight has to say about Chopin's position and capacities as a composer, and here the essays of Hadow and Finck, and the more elaborate works of Huneker, show their value ; whilst of variety of opinion in regard to the actual works, there is naturally no end. Finck, for instance, resenting Niecks' epithet of "decidedly commonplace," applied to some of Chopin's songs, is stung into remarking that "Niecks' two volumes are full of such preposterous opinions," and adds : "It is indeed a calamity that the task of writing the most elaborate work on the life and compositions of Chopin should have fallen into such hands."

Apart from the musical opinions, the fact remains that the professor's work is monumental and a model of what a musical biography should be, concise but full, appreciative, but free from the undiscriminating hero-worship and exaggeration that, as a rule, disfigure this class of work.

LISZT, Franz. "Life of Chopin," translated by John Broadhouse. Published by Wm. Reeves. London.

Shortly after Chopin's death, Liszt published a memoir of his friend of curiously unequal merit. As far as regards facts and dates it is most inaccurate and misleading, but as a sympathetic, critical appreciation of his work and position as a composer it is invaluable. It is the work of a great artist, and as full of insight, delicate discrimination, and justifiable enthusiasm as are Liszt's writings on Wagner.

George Sand described it as " *un peu exubérant en style, mais rempli de bonnes choses et de tres belles pages.*"

Certain chapters, particularly those describing the Mazurka and the Polonaise, are worse than exuberant in style, they are positively grotesque and nauseating in their sentimental extravagance. The researches of Mr. Ashton Ellis have made it quite clear that it is to the flowery pen of the Princess Carolyne Wittgenstein that these blemishes are attributable. Liszt allowed her to embellish his work at her own sweet will, with the result that the book, at any rate, for English readers, is quite spoilt. It cannot, however, be overlooked by the Chopin student, for the personal reminiscences of one of the greatest composers by one of the greatest executive artists of the world must be invaluable.

SCHUMANN, Robert. "Music and Musicians," translated by Fanny Raymond Ritter. Two Vols. Published by Wm. Reeves. London.

Scattered throughout the collected criticisms that Schumann published in the musical papers which he edited, are very many references to Chopin and his various compositions. These will be found incorporated in their natural connection in the body of this book. Amongst those who have written about Chopin's music, Schumann has the unchallenged right to the first place. Himself a genius of the highest rank, he discerned even in the earliest work of Chopin a kindred spirit. His admiration never wavered, he greeted every new composition of Chopin's with sympathetic appreciation, and his critical remarks are not only interesting from the point of view of musical history, but they are of real value to the student of Chopin's works. They are to be found in their translated form in the two volumes mentioned above.

HUNEKER, James. "Chopin, the Man and his Music." Published by Wm. Reeves. London. 1901.

Of works on Chopin published since Niecks' life, this is by far the most important. From a biographical point of view, like all who come after Niecks, Huneker can have nothing new to say ; but his comments on the works are fresh, varied, and stimulating. The chief faults of the book are a want of method in the arrangement, rendering quick reference very difficult and a tendency to exaggeration in style.

HUNEKER, James. "Mezzotints in Modern Music." Published by Wm. Reeves. London.

The third essay in this book, a series of studies on modern musicians, is devoted to a study of the Polish composer, entitled "The Greater Chopin." This is a sympathetic essay, and discriminates between the greater and smaller works of Chopin with nice critical insight. The book is interesting throughout, and has the gift of enthusiasm.

KARASOWSKI, Moritz. "Frederic Chopin, His Life, Letters, and Works," translated from the German by Emily Hill. Published by Wm. Reeves. London. 1879.

This was the first serious attempt at a biography of Chopin, and the letters that the author obtained from the composer's relatives give it value. In the Polish edition published in 1882 are some till then unpublished letters from Chopin to Fontana. Niecks criticises Karasowski's "unchecked partiality and boundless admiration for his hero, his uncritical acceptance and fanciful embellishments of anecdotes and hearsays, and the extreme paucity of his information concerning the period of Chopin's life which begins with his settlement in Paris." Karasowski's comments on the music are meagre and unsatisfactory.

FINCK, Henry T. "Chopin and other Musical Essays." Published by Charles Scribner's Sons. New York. 1899.

This essay on Chopin, which gives its title to the book, is a most brilliant bit of work. The writer is a daring and unconventional critic, never hesitating to give utterance to his most original ideas, whatever the weight of authority against him, and, as a consequence, he is always worth reading. Here in a short space he has put together more of value and interest than in many long works on the subject.

FINCK, Henry T. "Songs and Song-Writers." Published by John Murray. London. 1901.

In this fascinating book, covering a field in which hardly anything has been accomplished in a similar line, the student will find an admirably written chapter on Chopin's songs.

BENNETT, Joseph. "Frederic Chopin." Published by Novello & Co. London and New York.

This is a brief biography, in Novello's series of Primers of Musical Biography, which can be commended to those who have not the time to read Niecks' substantial volumes.

HUEFFER, Francis. "Musical Studies." Published by Adam and Charles Black. Edinburgh. 1880.

The second essay in this book on Chopin appeared originally in the *Fortnightly Magazine* in September 1877. It is brief, and has been quite superseded by other and more important works.

WILLEBY, Charles. "Frederic Francois Chopin." Published by Sampson Low, Marston & Co. 1892.

This is a curiously unsatisfactory book. The biographical part is merely a re-arrangement of Niecks', and the description of the music is introduced arbitrarily at intervals. The criticisms are strangely unappreciative; they strike one as the work of a very young man, who, while knowing certain pieces intimately, had very little knowledge of the composer's work as a whole.

HADDEN, J. Cuthbert. "Chopin." Published by J. M. Dent & Co., London; and E. P. Dutton & Co., New York.

This is a superfluous volume, one of the series known as "The Master Musicians," a set of musical biographies of very varying merit. It is a mere boiling down of Niecks', and if it was necessary to fill a gap in the series, the work should have been entrusted to the professor, if he would have undertaken it.

HADOW, W. H. "Studies in Modern Music." Second series. Published by Seeley & Co. London. 1901.

The second study in this book on Frederic Chopin is the most sympathetic, discriminating, and truly critical essay that has appeared in England. It has personality and distinction, and makes one wish that the writer could see his way to a larger work on the subject.

KLECZYNSKI, Jean. "The works of Frederic Chopin, and their proper interpretation." Published by Wm. Reeves. London.

This book consists of three valuable lectures, containing many interesting hints on "How to play Chopin."

KLECZYNSKI, Jean. "Chopin's Greater Works," translated by Janotha. Published by Wm. Reeves, London; Charles Scribners' Sons, New York.

These three further lectures deal with the Preludes, Ballades, Nocturnes, Polonaises, and Mazurkas. It is difficult to see why the Études, Scherzi, and Sonatas should be omitted in dealing with the "greater works," but these lectures, though wanting in method, contain much valuable instruction, and are by no means the least interesting of the many works on Chopin.

AUDLEY, Madame A. " Frederic Chopin, sa vie et ses
    Œuvres." Published by Plon and Cie. Paris.

This is a brief and readable life of the composer
founded on the work of Karasowski, but now of little
value.

WODZINSKI, Count. "Les trois Romans de Frederic
    Chopin." Calmann Lévy. Paris. 1886.

This book which, as Niecks says, is more of the nature
of a novel than of a biography, deals primarily with
Chopin's attachment to Constantia Gladkowska, Marie
Wodzinska, and George Sand, but has also a wider scope,
and cannot be altogether ignored.

BARBEDETTE, H. " F. Chopin. Essai de critique
    musicale."

This brochure was published in Paris shortly after
Chopin's death. It is interesting as containing a detailed
contemporary criticism of the whole of the works by one
who had the advantage of often hearing Chopin perform.

EHLERT, Louis. " Letters on Music to a Lady," trans-
    lated by Fanny Raymond Ritter. Published by Wm.
    Reeves. London. 1877.

In this book will be found a rhapsody on Chopin's
Mazurkas.

EHLERT, Louis. "Aus der Tonwelt." Two vols. B.
    Behr's verlag (E. Bock). Berlin. 1898.

The concluding essay on Chopin is a valuable contribution to the literature of the subject.

SCHUCHT, Dr. J. " Frederic Chopin und seine werke."
    Leipzig. L. F. Kahnt.

This short volume contains many interesting comments
on the music.

VON BÜLOW, Hans.

This celebrated virtuoso edited an edition of the Études
and Impromptus in which there is much valuable instruction as to performance, and some interesting critical
opinions.

KULLAK, Theodore.

This well-known teacher edited an edition of Chopin, published by Schlesinger. The professor's notes are valuable not only to the student of the piano, but from the point of view of artistic and critical interest.

RUBINSTEIN, Anton. " Conversations on Music," translated by Mrs. J. P. Morgan. Published by Charles F. Tretbar, New York.

This little book contains Rubinstein's opinions on many composers ; naturally he had a very high opinion of Chopin and expressed it very vigorously.

Of writers on musical history who have naturally said more or less interesting things about Chopin, it will be sufficient to mention the names of Sir Hubert Parry, who sums up Chopin with his usual felicity of diction and unerring insight in his invaluable work, " The Evolution of the Art of Music " ; Oscar Bie, who has a good deal to say about Chopin in his " History of the Pianoforte and Pianoforte Players " ; and H. H. Statham, in his " My Thoughts on Music and Musicians."

Sir Charles Hallé, Berlioz, Mendelssohn, Henselt, Moscheles, Scholtz, Heine, Kuhé, and other contemporaries of Chopin have frequent references to the composer and his works scattered throughout their autobiographies and letters.

Niecks has transmitted to us the personal reminiscences of Stephen Heller, Ferdinand Hiller, Ernst, and other friends of Chopin, and also tells us of Chopin's pupils and their remembrances of their beloved teacher. Prominent amongst these are Mathias and Gutmann. Contemporary critics have left on record their appreciation or depreciation of the great master. Our own critics, Davison and Chorley, who wielded such power in the forties, admired the Polish composer, but Rellstab, the German critic of the Berlin *Iris*, earned for himself unenviable fame by the retrograde and unappreciative nature of his criticism, which rivalled in violence the diatribes to which Hanslick and his school treated Wagner.

Von Lenz, a German, who made a cult of piano *virtuosi*,

has left us a very full account of Chopin's genius as a pianist.

Amongst critics who have incidentally said much that is interesting about Chopin, one must mention J. A. Fuller Maitland (especially with reference to Chopin's Sonatas), Arthur Hervey, and J. F. Runciman ; whilst in America, in addition to Huneker and Finck, H. E. Krebhiel, W. F. Apthorp, and W. J. Henderson must be remembered.

Amongst German and Polish writers whose contributions to Chopin literature are of little value, may be mentioned Niggli, La Mara, Sowinski, Tarnowski, &c. &c.

Of works dealing with George Sand, the most useful are that lady's own memoirs, "Histoire de ma vie," and her six volumes of correspondence. Henry James has an interesting article on her in his "French Poets and Novelists," and Bertha Thomas has written a life of this extraordinary woman.

Other works are extant by Brault, Stefanie Pol, and Wladimir Karénine. Charles Wood's "Letters from Majorca" contain well-written descriptions of Valdemosa and Palma.

The thematic catalogue published by Breitkopf and Härtel is a model compilation, and is invaluable to the earnest student.

TABLE OF THE WORKS OF FREDERIC CHOPIN

Opus No.	Name of Piece and Key	Composed	Published	Dedication
1	First Rondo in C minor	1828	1825	Mme. de Linde
2	Variations on "Là ci darem," with orchestral accompaniment. B flat major	1829	March 1830	Titus Woyciechowski
3	Introduction et Polonaise brillante, for piano and violoncello. C major		1833	Joseph Merk
4	Sonata in C minor	1828	Posth. 1851	Joseph Elsner
5	Rondo à la Mazurka. F major		1827	Mlle. la Comtesse Alexandrine de Moriolles
6 (1st Set)	Four Mazurkas No. 1. F sharp minor No. 2. C sharp minor No. 3. E major No. 4. E flat minor		1832	Mlle. la Comtesse Pauline Plater
7 (2nd Set)	Five Mazurkas No. 1. B flat major (5) No. 2. A minor (6) No. 3. F minor (7) No. 4. A flat major (8) No. 5. C major (9)		Dec. 1832	Mr. Johns
8	Trio for Piano, Violin, and Violoncello. G minor	1828	1833	M. le Prince Antoine Radziwill
9	Three Nocturnes No. 1. B flat minor (Larghetto) No. 2. E flat major (Andante) No. 3. B major (Allegretto)	Probably 1832	Jan. 1833	Mme. Camille Pleyel

TABLE OF THE WORKS OF FREDERICK CHOPIN—(continued)

Opus No.	Name of Piece and Key	Composed	Published	Dedicated
10	Twelve Grandes Études No. 1. C major (Arpeggios) No. 2. A minor (Chromatic scale) No. 3. E. major (Melody) No. 4. C sharp minor (Presto) No. 5. G flat major (Black keys) No. 6. E flat minor (Andante) No. 7. C major (Toccata) No. 8. F major (Allegro) No. 9. F minor (Molto agitato) No.10. A flat major (Rhythm and accent) No. 11. E flat major (Extended chords) No. 12. C minor (Revolutionary Étude)	1829–1831	1833	"À son ami," Franz Liszt
11	Grand Concerto. E minor, for piano and orchestra	1830	Sept. 1833	Fr. Kalkbrenner
12	Variations on an air from the Opera of "Ludovic," by Hérold. ("Je vends des Scapulaires.") B flat major		1833	
13	Grande Fantaisie on Polish Airs with orchestral accompaniment. A major	1828	1834	Mr. J. P. Pixis
14	Krakowiak. Grand Concert Rondo for Piano, with Orchestra. F major	1828	1834	Madame la Princesse Adam Czartoryska
15	Three Nocturnes No 1. F major (Andante cantabile) No. 2. F sharp major (Larghetto)	1833	Jan. 1834	Ferd. Hiller

16	No. 3. G minor (Lento) Rondo. E flat major		1834	Mlle. Caroline Hartmann
17 (3rd Set)	Four Mazurkas No. 1. B flat major (10) No. 2. E minor (11) No. 3. A flat major (12) No. 4. A minor (13)		1834	Mlle. Lina Freppa
18	Grand Valse. E flat major		July 1834	Mlle. Laura Horsford
19	Boléro. C major		Oct. 1834	Mlle. la Comtesse E. de Flahault
20	First Scherzo. E minor	1829	1835	Mr. T. Albrecht
21	Second Concerto. F minor. For piano and orchestra		April 1836	Madame la Comtesse Potocka
22	Grande Polonaise brillante. E flat major. (Précédé d'un Andante spianato.) For piano and orchestra	1830	1836	Madame la Baronne d'Est
23	Ballade. G minor		1836	M. le Baron de Stockhausen
24 (4th Set)	Four Mazurkas No. 1. G minor (14) No. 2. C major (15) No. 3. A flat (16) No. 4. B flat major (17)		1835	M. le Comte de Perthuis
25	Twelve Etudes No. 1. A flat major (The Shepherd Boy) No. 2. F minor (Presto) No. 3. F major (Allegro) No. 4. A minor (Syncopations) No. 5. E minor (Scherzo) No. 6. G sharp minor (Double notes)	1830-1834	1837	Madame la Comtesse d'Agoult

TABLE OF THE WORKS OF FREDERIC CHOPIN—*(continued)*

Opus No.	Name of Piece and Key	Composed	Published	Dedication
25	Études—*(continued)* No. 7. C sharp minor (Duo) No. 8. D flat (Rhythm) No. 9. G flat (Butterfly's Wings) No. 10. B minor (Octaves) No. 11. A minor (Winter Wind) No. 12. C minor (Arpeggios)			
26	Two Polonaises No. 1. C sharp minor No. 2. E flat minor		1836	Mr. J. Dessauer
27	Two Nocturnes No. 1. C sharp minor (Larghetto) No. 2. D flat (Lento sostenuto)		May 1836	Madame la Comtesse d'Appony
28	Twenty-four Preludes No. 1. C major (Agitato) No. 2. A minor (Lento) No. 3. G major (Vivace) No. 4. E minor (Largo) No. 5. D major (Allegro molto) No. 6. B minor (Lento assai) No. 7. A major (Andantino) No. 8. F sharp minor (Molto agitato) No. 9. E major (Largo) No. 10. C sharp minor (Allegro molto) No. 11. B major (Vivace) No. 12. G sharp minor (Presto)		Sept. 1839	"À son ami Pleyel," and Mr. J. C. Kessler, in the German edition

	Work	Date	Dedication
	No. 13. F sharp (Lento) No. 14. E flat minor (Allegro) No. 15. D flat (Sostenuto) No. 16. B flat minor (Presto con fuoco) No. 17. A flat (Allegretto) No. 18. F minor (Allegro molto) No. 19. E fla: (Vivace) No. 20. C minor (Largo) No. 21. B flat (Cantabile) No. 22. G minor (Molto agitato) No. 23. F major (Moderato) No. 24. D minor (Allegro appassionato)		
29	Impromptu. A flat major	1838	Mlle. la Comtesse de Lobau
30 (5th Set)	Four Mazurkas No. 1. C minor (18) No. 2. B minor (19) No. 3. D flat major (20) No. 4. C sharp minor (21)	1838	Madame la Princesse de Wurtemberg, née Princess Czartory-ska
31	Second Scherzo. B flat minor	1837	Mlle. la Comtesse Adèle de Fürstenstein
32	Two Nocturnes No. 1. B major (Andante sostenuto) No. 2. A flat major (Lento)	1837	Mme. la Baronne de Billing
33 (6th Set)	Four Mazurkas No. 1. C sharp minor (22) No. 2. D major (23) No. 3. C major (24) No. 4. B minor (25)	1838	Mlle. la Comtesse Mostowska

TABLE OF THE WORKS OF FREDERIC CHOPIN—(continued)

Opus No.	Name of Piece and Key	Composed	Published	Dedication
34	Trois Valses brillantes No. 1. A flat (Vivace) No. 2. A minor (Lento) No. 3. F (Vivace). (The Cat Valse)		1838	Mlle. de Thun-Hohenstein
35	Sonata. B flat minor	1838	1840.	
36	Second Impromptu. F sharp minor	1838	1840	
37	Two Nocturnes No. 1. G minor (Andante sostenuto) No. 2. G major (Andantino)	1838–1839	1840	
38	Second Ballade. F major	1838	1840	Mr. R. Schumann
39	Third Scherzo. C sharp minor	1838–1839	1840	Mr. A. Gutmann
40	Two Polonaises	1838	1840	Mr. J. Fontana
41 (7th Set)	Trois Mazurkas No. 1. C sharp minor (26) No. 2. E minor (27) No. 3. A flat (28)	1838–1839	1840	Mr. E. Witwicki
42	Valse. A flat major		1840	
43	Tarantelle. A flat major		1841	
44	Polonaise. F sharp minor		1841	Madame la Princesse Charles de Beauvau
45	Prelude. C sharp minor		Nov. 1841	Mlle. la Princesse Elisabeth Czernicheff
46	Allegro de Concert. A major	1841	Jan. 1842	Mlle. F. Müller
47	Third Ballade. A flat major	1841	Jan. 1842	Mlle. P. de Noailles

	Work			Dedication
48	Two Nocturnes No. 1. C minor No. 2. F sharp minor	1841	Jan. 1842	Mlle. L. Duperré
49	Fantaisie. F minor	1841	Jan. 1842	Madame la Princesse L. de Souzzo
50 (8th Set)	Three Mazurkas No. 1. C major (30) No. 2. A flat major (31) No. 3. C sharp minor (32)	1841	1842	M. Léon Szmitkowski
51	Third Impromptu (Allegro vivace) G flat major	1842	1843	Mlle. la Comtesse Esterházy
52	Fourth Ballade. F minor	1842	1843	Madame la Baronne C. de Rothschild
53	Polonaise. A flat major		1843	Mr. A. Leo
54	Scherzo No. 4. E major		1843	Mlle. J. de Caraman
55	Two Nocturnes No. 1. F minor No. 2. E flat major		1844	Mlle. J. W. Stirling
56 (9th Set)	Three Mazurkas No. 1. B major (33) No. 2. C major (34) No. 3. C minor (35)	1844	1844	Mlle. C. Maberly
57	Berceuse. D flat major	1844	1845	Mlle. Elise Gavard
58	Sonata. B minor	1844	June 1845	Madame la Comtesse de Perthuis
59 (10th Set)	Three Mazurkas No. 1. A minor (36) No. 2. A flat major (37) No. 3. F sharp minor (38)		Jan. 1846	
60	Barcarolle. F sharp major		1846	Madame la Baronne de Stockhausen
61	Polonaise Fantaisie. A flat		1846	Mme. A. Veyret

TABLE OF THE WORKS OF FREDERIC CHOPIN—(*continued*)

Opus No.	Name of Piece and Key	Composed	Published	Dedication
62	Two Nocturnes No. 1. B major (Andante) No. 2. E major (Lento)		1846	Mlle. R. de Könneritz
63 (11th Set)	Three Mazurkas No. 1. B major (39) No. 2. F minor (40) No. 3. C sharp minor (41)		1847	Madame la Comtesse L. de Czosnowska
64	Three Valses No. 1. D flat major No. 2. C sharp minor No. 3. A flat		1847	Mme. la Comtesse Potocka Mme. la Baronne de Rothschild Mme. la Baronne Bronicka
65	Sonato for Piano and Violoncello. G minor		Oct. 1847	Mr. C. Franchomme

WORKS PUBLISHED POSTHUMOUSLY WITH OPUS NUMBERS

Opus No.	Name of Piece and Key	Composed	Published	Dedication
66	Fantaisie Impromptu. C sharp minor	1834	1855	
67 (12th Set)	Four Mazurkas No. 1. G major (42)	1835	1855	

68 (13th Set)	Four Mazurkas		
	No. 2. G minor (43)	1849	
	No. 3. C major (44)	1835	
	No. 4. A minor (45)	1846	1855
	Four Mazurkas		
	No. 1. C major (46)	1830	
	No. 2. A minor (47)	1827	
	No. 3. F major (48)	1830	
	No. 4. F minor (49)	1849	1855
69	Two Valses		
	No. 1. F minor	1835	
	No. 2. B minor	1829	
70	Three Valses		
	No. 1. G flat major	1835	
	No. 2. F minor	1843	
	No. 3. D flat major	1829	
71	Three Polonaises		
	No. 1. D minor	1827	
	No. 2. B flat major	1828	
	No. 3. F minor	1829	
72	Nocturne. E. minor	1827	1855
	Marche Funèbre	1829	1855
	Three Ecossaises	1830	1855
73	Rondo for two Pianos. C major	1828	1855
74	Seventeen Polish Songs	1829-1847	1855

WORKS WITHOUT OPUS NUMBERS PUBLISHED AFTER THE COMPOSER'S DEATH

Name of Piece and Key	Composed	Published
Variations. E major. On a German Air	1824 ?	1851
Mazurka. G major	1825	
Mazurka. B flat major	1825	
Mazurka. D major	1829-1830	
Mazurka. D major. A remodelling of the preceding Mazurka	1832	
Mazurka. C. major	1833	
Mazurka. A minor. Dédiée à son ami mile Gaillard		
Valse. E minor		1868
Polonaise. G sharp minor. Dédiée à Mme. Dupont	1822	1864
Polonaise. G flat major. Of doubtful authenticity		1872
Polonaise. B flat minor. Adieu! an Wilhelm Kolberg	1826	
Valse. E major	1829	

WORKS WITHOUT OPUS NUMBERS PUBLISHED DURING THE COMPOSER'S LIFETIME

Name of Piece and Key	Composed	Published
Grand Duo concertant. E major. For piano and violoncello, on themes from " Robert le Diable "	1829, with A. Franch- omme	1833
Trois nouvelles Études. F minor, A flat major, D flat major		1840
Variation VI. E major (Largo). From the " Hexameron "		1841
Mazurka. A minor ("Notre temps ")		1842

CHRONOLOGICAL LIST OF CHOPIN'S WORKS
IN THE APPROXIMATE ORDER OF
THEIR COMPOSITION

Composed	Name of Piece and Key	Opus No.
1822	Polonaise. G sharp minor	
1824	Variations on a German Air	
1825	Mazurka. G major	
	Mazurka. B flat major	
	Rondo. C minor	1
1826	Polonaise. B flat minor. Dedicated to W. Kolberg	
1827	Mazurka. A minor	68. No. 2
	Polonaise. D minor	71. No. 1
	Nocturne. E minor	72. No. 1
	Rondo à la Mazur	5
1828	Polonaise. B flat major	71. No. 2
	Rondo for two Pianos	73
	Variations on " Là ci darem "	2
	Sonata. C minor	4
	Trio for Piano, Violin, and 'Cello	8
	Fantaisie on Polish Airs	15
	Krakowiak	14
1829	Valse. B minor	69. No. 2
	Valse. D flat major	70. No. 3
	Valse. E major	
	Polonaise. F minor	71. No. 3
	March Funèbre	72. No. 2
	Mazurka. D major (remodelled 1822)	
	Polonaise for Piano and 'Cello	3
	Second Concerto. F minor	21
1829-1831	Twelve Études	10
1829-1847	Seventeen Polish Songs	74
1830	Mazurka. C major	68
	Mazurka. F major	68. No. 3
	Trois Écossaises	72. No. 3
	Concerto. E minor	11
	Grande Polonaise brillante	22
1830-1834	Twelve Études	25
1832	Four Mazurkas	6
	Five Mazurkas	7
	Three Nocturnes	9
1833	Variations on an Air by Halévy	12
	Three Nocturnes	15

Composed	Name of Piece and Key	Opus No.
1833	Mazurka. C major	
	Grand Duo for Piano and 'Cello	
1834	Fantaisie Impromptu	66
	Rondo. E flat	16
	Four Mazurkas	17
	Valse. E flat major	18
	Boléro	19
1835	First Scherzo. B minor	20
	Mazurka. G major	67. No. 1
	Mazurka. C major	67. No. 3
	Valse. G flat major	70. No. 1
	Valse. F minor	69. No. 1
1836	Two Polonaises	26
	Two Nocturnes	27
1837	Second Scherzo. B flat minor	31
	Two Nocturnes	32
1838	First Impromptu. A flat	29
	Four Mazurkas	30
	Four Mazurkas	33
	Sonata. B flat minor	35
	Second Impromptu	36
	Two Nocturnes	37
	Second Ballade	38
	Two Polonaises	40
1838-1839	Third Scherzo	39
	Three Mazurkas	41
	Twenty-four Preludes	28
1840	Valse. A flat	42
1841	Tarantelle	43
	Polonaise. F sharp minor	44
	Prelude. C sharp minor	45
	Allegro de Concert	46
	Third Prelude	47
	Two Nocturnes	48
	Fantaisie. F minor	49
	Three Mazurkas	50
	Hexameron Variations	
1842	Third Impromptu	51
	Fourth Ballade	52
	Mazurka. A minor (" Notre temps ")	
1843	Polonaise. A flat	53
	Valse. F minor	70. No. 2
	Fourth Scherzo. E major	54
1844	Two Nocturnes	55
	Three Mazurkas	56
	Berceuse	57

Composed	Name of Piece and Key	Opus No.
1844	Sonata. B minor	58
1846	Mazurka. A minor	67. No. 4
	Three Mazurkas	59
	Barcarolle	60
	Polonaise Fantaisie	61
	Two Nocturnes	62
1847	Three Mazurkas	63
	Three Valses	64
	Sonato for Piano and 'Cello	65
1849	Mazurka. G minor	67. No. 2
	Mazurka. F minor	68. No. 4
No date obtainable	Mazurka. A minor. Dedicated to E. Gaillard. Probably about 1829	
	Valse. E minor. Probably about 1829	
	Trois nouvelles Études. Probably 1835-1840	

OPUS I.—First Rondo.   C minor.

Dedicated to Mme. de Linde.   Published 1825.

THE Opus 1 of any well-known composer has always a
special interest of its own.   Schumann who had in
1831 reviewed Chopin's Opus 2 (the variations on Mozart's
air " Là ci darem ") with lyric fervour, evidently inquired
for and obtained his Opus 1, for early in the next year he
wrote to Wieck (the father of Clara Wieck, who subsequently became Madame Schumann): " Chopin's first work
(I firmly believe that it is his tenth) is in my hands ; a lady
would say that it was very pretty, very piquant, almost
Moschelesque.   But I believe you will make Clara study
it, for there is plenty of *Geist* in it and few difficulties.
But I humbly venture to assert that there are between
this composition and Opus 2 two years and twenty
works."

We know of two compositions that were composed
before 1825, the year in which this was presumably
written.   These are the Polonaise in G sharp minor, to
which the date 1822 is assigned, and the Variations on a
German national air "Der Schweizerbub," dated in the
Breitkopf and Härtel edition, 1824.

There are also two Mazurkas of the same year, 1825, but
doubtless there were several other early efforts that
Chopin destroyed.

The publication of this Rondo was for Chopin *the* event
of this year, " Only he who has experienced the delicious
sensation of seeing himself for the first time in print can
realise what our young author felt on this occasion." *

Madame de Linde, to whom the piece was dedicated,
was the wife of his father's friend, the rector, and Chopin
often used to play duets with her.

* Niecks.

A

The group of works to which this piece naturally belongs consists of five Rondos, of which it is the first and simplest. The other four are Opus 5—Rondo a la Mazur, Opus 16—Rondo in E flat, Opus 14—Rondo or Krakowiak, and Opus 73—Rondo for two pianos.

The latter piece was composed in 1828, so that the whole group belongs to Chopin's earlier work. Although quite a boy when he wrote his first Rondo (he was only fifteen), there is immense promise shown in the inventive power and in the technical ability displayed in the writing ; the leading subjects are well contrasted, and we see at once that it is the work of one who thoroughly understands the instrument for which he is writing.

Niecks says of these earlier works : " They have a natural air which is alike free from affected profundity and insipid childishness. They can hold their ground without difficulty and honourably among the better class of light drawing-room pieces." He points out the want of cohesiveness as a weak point, " the different subjects are too loosely strung together."

Although not strikingly original, it cannot be said that Chopin in this Rondo showed himself the imitator of any particular master. There are traces of the influence of Weber, and perhaps even more of Hummel, whom we know Chopin admired immensely.

Karasowski thinks this Rondo Chopin's weakest work. " His individuality was not at that time fully developed and Hummel's influence was unmistakable. It is no disparagement of his talent to say this, for every young pianist of that period made Hummel his model, and, moreover, every genius, however independent, begins by unconsciously imitating his favourite composers and artists. As an instance of this, we need only mention Beethoven."

Hadow says : " This Rondo is a singular example of Chopin's strength and weakness in composition. No doubt a concert rondo should not be criticised with the same severity as the rondo movement of a sonata ; yet even with all laxity of concession we can find passages and even pages through which Elsner ought to have drawn his pencil."

" We cannot help liking the C minor Rondo. There is

lightness, joy in creation, which contrast with the heavy dour quality of the C minor Sonata, Opus 4. Loosely constructed, in a formal sense, and too exuberant for his strict confines, this Opus 1 is remarkable, much more remarkable than Schumann's Abegg Variations." (Huneker).

OPUS. 2.—Variations on : " Là ci darem sa mano." With orchestral accompaniment. B flat major.

Dedicated to Titus Woyciechowski.
Composed 1828. Published March 1830,

PERHAPS the chief interest attaching to these variations is that their mastery, grace, and novelty roused in Schumann so great an admiration that they caused him to write his celebrated critical essay entitled "An Opus 2." This, he subsequently reprinted at the commencement of his collected writings, and by this immediate recognition of the work of an original genius he proved himself gifted with an insight that can almost be termed prophetic. He saw at once that here was something entirely removed from the mere mechanical trills and arpeggios of Kalkbrenner, Herz, and their school.

Chopin undoubtedly wrote these variations in order to show off his own powers as a virtuoso, but his genius shone through the mere technical aim, and the various sections of the work are instinct with true grace and poetical intention. In the concluding sentence of Schumann's criticism lies its true value, " I bend before Chopin's spontaneous genius, his lofty aim, his mastership."

It would not do to compare these variations with such work as Brahms' superb studies on an air of Paganini's, nor even with Schumann's own " Études Symphoniques."

We should see immediately that we are dealing with the work of Chopin's earliest youth ; the want of depth and emotional power would be at once felt. Chopin unfortunately never attempted this form when he had fully developed his powers. If he had, there is but little doubt that he would have given us a supreme example of

the style. The orchestral accompaniment, according to
Niecks, " shows an inaptitude in writing for any other
instrument than the piano that is quite surprising considering the great musical endowments of Chopin in other
respects." The orchestral accompaniments are, however,
not necessary to a complete enjoyment of the work. It
begins with a long introduction, a free improvisation on
the air. Schumann speaks of it admiringly as " so self-
concentrated." Then follows the theme, treated simply,
though " Zerlina's answer has a sufficently enamoured
character."

Between each variation an orchestral tutti intervenes
with great effect in a kind of ritornello.

The first variation, according to Schumann, " expresses
a kind of coquettish courteousness—the Spanish grandee
flirts amiably with the peasant girl in it."

The second variation is a wild rush of demi-semiquavers.
" It is comic, confidential, disputatious, as though two
lovers were chasing each other, and laughing more than
usual about it." *

In the third variation all is changed. The demi-semiquavers are now in the bass only, in passages in which
Schumann sees Masetto at a distance, swearing audibly
without making any effect on Don Juan. The movement
is filled with " moonshine and fairy magic."

The fourth variation is of a brilliant bravura character.
" How boldly, how wantonly it springs forward to meet
the man."

The fifth is the adagio. " It is in B flat minor, as it
should be, for in its commencement it presents a moral
warning to Don Juan. It is at once mischievous and
beautiful that Leporello listens behind the hedge, laughing
and jesting, that oboes and clarionettes enchantingly
allure, and that the B flat major in full bloom correctly
designates the first kiss of love."

In the finale the beautiful air is turned into a brilliant
polacca.
" It is the whole of Mozart's finale, popping champagne
corks, ringing glasses ! Leporello's voice between, the
grasping, torturing demons, the fleeing Don Juan—and
then the end that beautifully soothes and closes all."

* This variation is omitted in the existing pianola rolls.

OPUS 3.—Introduction et 'Polonaise Brillante for Piano and Violoncello. C major.

Dedicated to Joseph Merk.
Composed 1829. Published 1833.

IN a letter from Warsaw, dated November 14, 1829, Chopin says to his dear friend, Titus Woyciechowski, "I wrote an 'Alla Polacca' with 'cello accompaniment during my visit to Prince Radziwill. It is nothing more than a brilliant drawing-room piece suitable for the ladies. I should like Princess Wanda to practise it. I am supposed to have given her lessons. She is a beautiful girl of seventeen, and it was charming to direct her delicate fingers."

This extract shows us that we need not look for any special merit in this work. "The leaning towards Hummel is still evident ; the motives are easily comprehensible, harmonious, clear, and simple in their development." (Karasowski.)

It is dedicated to Joseph Merk, of whom we read in one of Chopin's letters : "On Thursday there was a soirée at Fuchs's, when Limmer introduced some of his own compositions for four violoncellos. Merk as usual made them more beautiful than they really were by his playing, which is so full of soul. He is the only violoncellist I really respect."

"On the whole we may accept Chopin's criticism as correct. The Polonaise is nothing but a brilliant *salon* piece. Indeed, there is very little in this composition, one or two pianoforte passages and a *finesse* here and there excepted—that distinguishes it as Chopin's. The opening theme verges even dangerously to the commonplace. More of the Chopinesque than in the Polonaise may be discovered in the introduction, which was less of a *pièce d'occasion*. What subdued the composer's individuality was no doubt the violoncello, which, however, is well provided with grateful *cantilene*." (Niecks.)

"Chopin himself pronounced this a brilliant *salon* piece. It is now not even that, for it sounds antiquated and threadbare. The passage work at times smacks of Chopin and Weber (a hint of the Mouvement Perpetuel), and the 'cello has the better of the bargain, evidently written for my lady's chamber." (Huneker.)

" The only portion worthy of Chopin is the counter theme for the 'cello in F major, this with its brilliant piano accompaniment is the only redeeming feature of the piece." (Willeby.)

OPUS 4.—Sonata in C minor.

Dedicated to Mr. Joseph Elsner.
Composed 1828.   Published posthumously 1851.

THIS Sonata, written at the age of eighteen, may be classed with the Trio Opus 8, and the Rondo for two pianos, Op. 73, as an example of the works Chopin wrote as a student.   He himself says of it : " As a pupil of his, I dedicated it to Elsner."   Between the master and his pupil there existed a warm affection and respect.   Chopin learnt more from Elsner than he did from his other teacher Zywny, although he had a good opinion of both his masters.

" From Messrs. Zywny and Elsner even the greatest ass must learn something," he is reported to have said to some Viennese gentleman who told him that people were astonished at his having learnt all he knew at Warsaw. Liszt wrote of the master, " Joseph Elsner taught Chopin those things that are most difficult to learn and most rarely known : to be exacting to oneself, and to value the advantages that are only obtained by dint of patience and labour."

Of this Sonata Niecks says : "It is indeed a pupil's work, an exercise, and not a very successful one.   The exigences of the form overburdened the composer and crushed all individuality out of him.   Nowhere is Chopin so little himself, we may even say so unlike himself.   The distribution of keys and the character of the themes show that the importance of contrast in the construction of larger works was still unsuspected by him.   The two middle movements, a *Minuetto* and *Larghetto*, although in

the latter the self-imposed fetters of the $\frac{5}{4}$ time prevent
the composer feeling quite at his ease, are more attractive
than the rest.   In them are discernible an approach to
freedom and something like a breath of life, whereas in
the first and in the last movement there is almost nothing
but painful labour and dull monotony.   The most curious
thing, however, about this work is the lumbering passage
writing of our graceful, light-winged Chopin."

In Karasowski's opinion this Sonata "shows a striving
after classic forms, but does not give us the idea that the
composer was working from inspiration, his wishes and
capacities do not seem always to correspond, and the
work altogether awakens no lasting interest.   The third
movement is most worthy of notice, but this does not
satisfy us completely ; it sounds rather forced and
laboured, probably on account of the unusual $\frac{5}{4}$ measure."

Barbedette considers the final movement the most
brilliant.   " Chopin never wrote but one piano Sonata
that has a classical complexion, in C minor, Opus 4," writes
Huneker.   " It demonstrates without a possibility of
doubt that the composer has no sympathy with the form.
Little of Chopin's precious essence is to be tasted in
the first Sonata.   The first movement is wheezing and all
but lifeless . . . and it is technically difficult.   The
Minuetto is excellent, its trio being a faint approach to
Beethoven in colour.   The unaccustomed rhythm of the
slow movement is irritating."

He does not agree with Niecks that the finale is but
barren waste.   " There is the breath of a stirring spirit,
an imitative attempt that is more diverting than the other
movements.   Above all, there is movement, and the close
is vigorous though banal.   The Sonata is the dullest
music penned by Chopin, but as a whole it hangs together
better than its two successors.   So much for an attempt at
strict devotion to scholastic form."

Chopin deliberately designed this Sonata for publication, and sent it to Haslinger in Vienna together with the
" *La ci darem* " variations, Opus 2.   With one excuse or
another Haslinger deferred publishing it, and it was not
till Chopin's death had given it a fictitious value that it
was at length brought out in 1851.

The first movement, *Allegro maestoso* can unhesitatingly

be described as the only really *dull* composition in the whole range of Chopin's works. A few early pieces may legitimately be termed weak, but they are always brilliant. This Allegro, however, is tedious, and the criticism showered on it with regard to lack of contrast in key and thematic material is amply justified.

With the Minuetto things improve. It is derivative but well written, and not uninteresting. The experiment in the always difficult and risky $\frac{5}{4}$ time of the Larghetto is a failure. There is no rhythmic beat in it, such as makes the barbaric second movement of Tschaikowsky's "Pathetic" Symphony so fascinating. It has simply the effect of having no backbone, no structure, and the chief thing to be thankful for is that Chopin evidently felt this too, and brought the movement to a rapid conclusion that cannot be considered untimely.

Barbedette and Huneker are more right about the last movement, and the brilliant passages in the bass do not deserve Niecks' epithet of lumbering. Nevertheless we have much to be thankful for to Elsner. " Leave him in peace," he said of his gifted pupil, " his is an uncommon way because his gifts are uncommon. He does not strictly adhere to the customary method, but he has one of his own, and he will reveal in his works an originality such as has not been found in any one."

Chopin made no more experiments in piano sonatas in strict classical form, for his two masterpieces, Opus 35 and Opus 58, are of such different calibre that it would serve no good purpose to group them arbitrarily with this youthful effort and the last published Sonata in G minor for piano and 'cello, simply because they are all called Sonatas.

OPUS 5.—Rondo a la Mazur.   F major.

Dedicated to Mlle. la Comtesse Alexandrine de Moriolles. Published in 1827.

THIS is the second of the group of five Rondos (for particulars of which see page 2). Both this and the first Rondo first saw the light at Warsaw, but they did not become known outside Poland till they were published in Germany in 1836. Schumann, reviewing it then, thought it probable that it was the work of Chopin's eighteenth year. " The extreme youth of the composer is only to be guessed at in certain involved passages, from which he has found it difficult to extricate himself at once ; but the Rondo is, notwithstanding, Chopin-like throughout, lovely, enthusiastic, full of grace. He who does not yet know Chopin had best begin the acquaintance with this piece."

The advance Chopin made in this Rondo, compared with his Opus 1, is very marked. It is the only one of the Rondos not written in the traditional $\frac{2}{4}$ time. It is, as the title implies, a Mazurka in Rondo form, and as such it naturally has a touch of that national feeling which was from now on to become so striking a characteristic of much of Chopin's music. After his fourteenth year Chopin passed his summer holidays in the country round Warsaw, and there, listening to the peasants singing and dancing their mazurkas, his sensitive musical intelligence absorbed those national elements of the music of the countryside which, passing through the alembic of his own personality, issued in a refined and idealised form in the Mazurkas and Polonaises. It is the work of a poetical and impressionable youth, as opposed to the first Rondo, which is that of a light-hearted boy. It has not the same mastery of effect nor the brilliant virtuosity of the Krakowiak, but it is superior in feeling to the Rondo in E flat major which belongs to that short period of Chopin's life during the early years of his residence in Paris, when a kind of blight seemed to fall on the poetry and idealism of his compositions.

The first subject has the rustic tang of a true mazurka redolent of the countryside, while the secondary theme is of refined and graceful beauty. It is highly individual, there is no hint of imitation of any other composer, and more than an indication of one of Chopin's most marked characteristics—widespread chords and skips.

The Comte de Moriolles, to whose daughter this Rondo is dedicated, was tutor to the adopted son of the Grand Duke Constantine, then governor of Warsaw. Chopin frequently visited at the palace, his talents and charming

manners rendering him always a welcome guest amongst
the most wealthy and cultivated people in the capital.
This environment acting on his innate refinement gave
him the aristocratic tastes and nature that he exhibited
throughout his life in so marked a degree.

Kleczynski, who is never tired of combating the idea
that Chopin's music is all melancholy, draws attention to
the " brilliant passages, cascades of pearly notes, and bold
leaps which we find in this Rondo.

" Is this the sadness and the despair of which we hear
spoken ?   Is it not rather youth exuberant with intensity
and life ; is it not happiness, gaiety, love for the world and
men."

" Who could fail in this Rondo to recognise Chopin in
the peculiar, sweet, and persuasive flows of sound, and the
serpent-like winding of the melodic outline, the widespread chords, the chromatic progressions, the dissolving
of the harmonies, and the linking of their constituent parts.
The harmonies are often novel and the matter is more
homogeneous and better welded into oneness."   (Niecks.)

" This Rondo is a further advance. It is sprightly,
Polish in feeling and rhythmic life, and a glance at any of
its pages gives us the familiar Chopin impression—florid
passage work, chords in extensions and chromatic progressions."   (Huneker.)

THE MAZURKAS.

T HE Mazurka in its native home, the district of Mazovia,
   was sometimes sung and sometimes danced. " In the
minor key, laughs and cries, dances and mourns, the Slav,"
says a German writer, and doubtless when Chopin spent
his summer holidays in the country he often heard the
villagers expressing their primitive emotions in their
characteristic fashion.   In ballrooms the Mazurka became
more animated and graceful, and although it has never
been much in vogue in England it is much affected in
St. Petersburg, where its votaries display an amazing
grace and dexterity.   In its essence, however, it is the
dance of the people, as opposed to the Valse, the dance of

Society. In Chopin's hands, however, the Mazurka ceased to be an actual dance tune, and became a tone poem, a mirror of moods, an epitome of human emotions, joy and sadness, love and hate, tenderness and defiance, coquetry and passion.

"There is in them," says Finck, "an inexhaustible variety of ideas, making each of them unique nothwithstanding their strong family likeness. They are like fantastic orchids, or like the countless variety of hummingbirds, 'those winged poems of the air,' of which no two are alike, while all resemble one another."

Of all the works perhaps they are the least well known, and least played, and yet they are full of exquisite melodic, rhythmic, and harmonic details of intense interest, novelty and beauty. In them Chopin has concentrated, as Huneker points out, "the sorrow and tribal wrath of a down-trodden nation, and the Mazurkas have for that reason an ethnic value." Some of the earlier ones are quite short and simple, but in the later numbers Chopin elaborated the form considerably, and both in emotional content and musical interest they become very valuable. They lend themselves in the most extraordinary way to the mood of the moment. In most of Chopin's compositions the work evokes the mood, but with a Mazurka you may play it one day merrily and lightly, and the next you may find it harmonising with your most depressed spirits, which, however, it will not fail to soothe and comfort. We read that Chopin never played them twice alike. In all of them, nevertheless, there is that undercurrent of melancholy which caused it to be said of him, "his mind is gay, but his heart is sad." Many of them contain intervals and scales of Eastern origin which give them a curious foreign fragrance that is occasionally taken for mannerism. Mendelssohn, for instance, said of a book of the Mazurkas that they "are so mannered that they are hard to understand."

It is on record that Chopin, who, especially in his younger days, was full of fun and jokes, would occasionally play one of his Mazurkas in strict metronomic time, to the great amusement of those who had heard him play them properly.

Liszt said that "to do justice to the Mazurkas one would

have to harness a new pianist of the first rank to each one of them.   The latent and unknown poetry in the original Polish Mazurkas was only indicated, and was by Chopin divined, developed, and brought to the light of day. Whilst he preserved the rhythm of the dance, he ennobled its melody and enlarged its proportions, weaving into its tissues harmonic lights and shades which were as new in themselves as the themes to which he adapted them."

In Liszt's book on Chopin will be found a most elaborate, flowery and fanciful description of the Mazurka and how it was danced in Poland.   No Englishman can read this extravagant, unrestrained and almost indecent rhetoric without feeling sick.   But it is comforting to know that it is not to Wagner's noble-minded friend, not to the great creative artist, that we owe these highly-coloured pages. The researches of Mr. Ashton Ellis have brought to light the fact that the whole section was written by Princess Carolyne Wittgenstein, whom Liszt with foolish fondness constantly allowed to mutilate and disfigure his work.

Finck says : " It seems strange at first sight that the Mazurkas, those exquisite love-poems, should be so much less popular than the Valses, for they are quite as melodious and much easier.   Perhaps the cause of their comparative neglect is that they are so thoroughly Polish in spirit ; unless they are played with an exotic rubato their fragrance vanishes."

They are of all Chopin's works the least known.   Even though they are mostly within the technical grasp of the average amateur they are neglected.   Possibly their very number, and the fact that they are so difficult to identify by opus number and key, is partly responsible.

There are in all fifty-six Mazurkas by Chopin.   Only forty-one were published during his lifetime, in eleven different sets of three, four, or five each.   Eight were published by Fontana posthumously as Opus 67 and Opus 68.   One appeared in a musical magazine without Opus number during Chopin's life, and six others, mostly of early dates, were discovered at various times.

OPUS 6.—Four Mazurkas.

1st Set.—No. 1 in F sharp minor ; No. 2 in C sharp
minor ; No. 3 in E major ; No. 4 in E flat minor.

Dedicated to Mlle. la Comtesse Pauline Plater.
Published December 1832.

MANY writers have said felicitous things about Chopin's
Mazurkas, some of which have been already quoted
in the introductory chapter.   In surveying the four very
characteristic specimens of the type composing the first
set, one is reminded of what Oscar Bie has said : " The
Mazurkas are bourgeois little joys, half bathed in sorrow,
half crushing their pain in the jubilation of the rhythm in
an unparalleled series of intellectual inspiration."   They
are the first published work of Chopin's in which the
individual characteristics of his genius shone forth clearly
and unmistakably ; the first-fruits of Chopin as a poet.
The five preceding works have shown him to us as the
boy, the youth, the virtuoso, the *salon* composer, and the
student.

The national dance form was always a favourite of
Chopin's.   Some of his earliest efforts were Mazurkas,
which may be found amongst the posthumous compositions, and a Mazurka was the last thing he wrote during
his final illness when he was too feeble even to try it on
the piano.   This set is dedicated to Countess Plater, and
Karasowski tells us of an occasion at her house when
Liszt, Heller, and Chopin were present, and a lively
discussion arose on national music.   Chopin maintained
that no one who had not been in Poland and inhaled the
perfume of its meadows could have any true sympathy
with the folk-songs.   As a test of this, it was proposed to
play the well-known Mazurka, " Poland is not lost yet."
Liszt, Heller, and other pianists performed, but those
present acknowledged that Chopin surpassed them all in
comprehending the true spirit of the Mazurka.

Karasowski wishes to combat the idea that the Mazurkas
are too sad, too much in the minor.   As a matter of fact,
an analysis shows that of the total of fifty-six, exactly

half are in the major keys and half in the minor. He
says : The propensity to melancholy, to musing, is not in
itself a weakness ; a delicate nature is not necessarily a
feeble nature. Chopin, a Pole, could not avoid that
which is characteristic of our nation, Our peasants like
dances in minor keys ; they return often, and sometimes
persistently, to that somewhat monotonous tone which,
nevertheless, with them indicates so well the loving and
generous depth of their being."

Elsewhere in a lecture on the Mazurkas, Kleczynski
becomes dithyrambic in their praise. " The book of
Mazurkas is an inexhaustible well of poetry. Nearly every
one of these works is a masterpiece, In these first Mazurkas
at once appears that national life from which, as from an
inexhaustible treasury, Chopin drew his inspirations."

The contemporary critic J. W. Davidson wrote, " If
Chopin had done no more than reveal to us through his
Mazurkas the national musical feeling of the country—a
country at once so wedded to misfortune and so politically
interesting as Poland—he would have achieved enough to
entitle him to unanimous sympathy."

Chorley, the critic of the *Athæneum*, who heard Chopin
play some Mazurkas in London, said : " They lose half their
meaning if played without a certain freedom and licence,
impossible to imitate, but irresistible if the player at all feels
the music."

Hadow says that the Mazurkas, in short, bear somewhat
the same relation to the tunes of the peasantry as the
songs of Robert Burns to those of the forerunners whom
he superseded.

Huneker speaks of the Mazurkas as " impish, morbid,
gay, sour, sweet little dances. They are a sealed book to
most pianists, and if you have not the savour of the Slav
in you, you should not touch them. Yet Chopin has done
some good things in this form."

Krebhiel lays stress on the fact that national colour
comes out more clearly in Chopin's Mazurkas than in any
of his other compositions. " Unlike the Polonaise this
was the dance of the common people, and even as conven-
tionalised and poetically refined by Chopin, there is still
in the Mazurka some of the rude vigour which lies in its
propulsive rhythm."

No. 1 in F sharp minor.

This first Mazurka is very characteristic of the type. It begins with a triplet figure in the first beat of the bar, which Kleczynski tells us is a detail which has since been copied in all the Mazurkas of other composers. " It is to be observed that this must not be played too quickly or it will thereby lose its characteristic. It is almost invariably used in expressing feelings and exhibiting different shades. Simple and natural in the opening of the Mazurka, it bends, immediately from the fifth bar, into various effective shapes, permitting a free execution. Later on, as if fatigued by so much repetition, it begins again slowly. At the end of the first part, again, it smiles pleasingly, passing quietly by, and resting with a country-like air of stupidity on the last note. At the ninth bar of the second part it recurs with a passionate and fiery character, and how many characters does it not take in the following Mazurkas."

Huneker, who writes of this set, " They are perfect of their kind," says : " This Mazurka first in publication is melodious, slightly mournful, but of a delightful freshness. The third section with the *appoggiaturas* realises a vivid vision of country couples dancing determinedly."

Hadow quotes it as an instance of the right use of a single phrase repeated in similar shapes, which is a characteristic of Polish national music, often, however, carried to excess in their songs. The third section, marked *Scherzando*, forms a delightful contrast to the rather melancholy tone of the Mazurka as a whole.

No. 2 in C sharp minor.

Here we are introduced to another characteristic device much used by Chopin, especially in the earlier Mazurkas, a drone bass which gives a very rustic tone to the dances in which it is used. The trio marked *gajo* expresses real light-hearted country gaiety.

Kleczynsky instances this Mazurka and the following one as exemplifying how Chopin discovered inexhaustible treasures where no one before him had ever thought of them. He calls it " equally picturesque and peasant-like, yet each in quite a different style. In the first you hear at the commencement the bass murmur in lovely strains, while the violinist, preserving a firm tone on the second chord, purrs quietly to himself, and wavers somewhat roughly in the rhythm of the melody. Then follows a song so sad, heartfelt, naïve, diversified and caressing, and so wonderfully constructed upon the two contrasts of *piano* and *forte*, that one cannot listen long enough to it, after which the middle is so gay and village-like that it sets one's feet moving as though to a dance. Then the former bass passages return, and the first motive follows them with the wonderful change (marked *rubato*), in which one sees the real ideal peasant with his rather intoxicated fantasy and an eagerness to expand the impulses of his soul."

Huneker quotes it as "having the native wood note wild," and speaks of its "slight twang, and its sweet —sad melody. There is hearty delight in the major, and how natural it seems."

No. 3 in E major.

Here again we have a drone bass to commence with, accompanied with a quaint irregular accent. This Mazurka should be played quicker and with less *rubato* than the others of the set.

Huneker says : " We are still on the village green, and the boys and girls are romping in the dance. The harmonisation is rich, the rhythmic life vital."

Kleczynski sees in it the approach from a distance of a wedding festival. " The music comes steadily nearer, and the whole cavalcade hurries on the scene in leaps and noisy movement. How true this is to life, how natural, yet how largely endowed with musical riches even if we refer only to the harmony of the third part (marked *risvegliato*). This with its chromatic harmony is so characteristic that it becomes a real model, followed inevitably by all Chopin's imitators from sheer necessity."

No. 4 in E flat minor.

This Mazurka, which is very short and without any definite end, is very plaintive and in the nature of a sketch. It is a tone-picture of the kind of mood when one cannot get one's thought away from some trouble that is besetting the mind.

Huneker says : " The harmonies are closer and there is sorrow abroad. The incessant circling around one idea, as if obsessed by fixed grief, is used here for the first, but not for the last time by the composer."

OPUS 7.—Five Mazurkas.

No. 1 in B flat major ; No. 2 in A minor ; No. 3 in F minor ; No. 4 in A flat major ; No. 5 in C major.

Dedicated to Mr. Johns.
Published December 1832.

THE Mr. Johns to whom this set of Mazurkas was dedicated, was an American whom Chopin introduced to Heller as " a distinguished amateur from New Orleans." We may wonder now what the distinguished amateur thought when he read some of the current criticisms on the music Chopin dedicated to him. It was of this set that Rellstab, the critic of the Berlin musical paper, *Iris*, wrote : " In the dances before us the author satisfies the passion (of writing affectedly and unnaturally) to a loathsome excess. He is indefatigable, and I might say inexhaustible in his search for ear-splitting discords, forced transitions, harsh modulations, ugly distortions of melody and rhythm. Everything it is possible to think of is raked up to produce the effect of odd originality, but especially strange keys, the most unnatural position of chords, the most perverse combinations with regard to fingering. . . . If Mr. Chopin had shown this composition to a master, the latter would, it is to be hoped, have torn it and thrown it at his feet, which we hereby do symbolically."

B

This style of criticism sounds very strange and ridiculous to us now, for these very modulations and transitions are what constitute the chief charm of the Mazurkas to modern ears. As Finck says, modulation is an even deeper source of emotional expression than melody, and in every one of these Mazurkas there are some bars that are exquisite to linger over and play again and again to oneself with different tone-colouring, rolling them on one's tongue as it were to get the exquisite flavour of them.

Von Lenz said that the Mazurkas of Chopin were a literature in themselves, and a systematic study of them as a whole makes one realise the truth of this saying. This set, though containing nothing of the importance of the later opus numbers, is a microcosm of the series, containing pictures of every mood, from the gay bonhomie of the opening one, through the wild sadness of the second, the rugged strength of the third, the exquisite cheerfulness of the fourth, to the dainty vagueness of the coda-like fifth.

As Huneker says : " The Mazurkas are dancing preludes, and often tiny single poems of great poetic intensity and passionate plaint."

No. 1 in B flat major (5).

This is perhaps the best known of all the Mazurkas ; for this popularity it is indebted to its technical simplicity and straightforward cheerful mood.

" There is an expansive swing, a *laissez-aller* to this piece, with its air of elegance, that are very alluring. The *rubato* flourishes and at the close we hear the footing of the peasant. A jolly, reckless composition that makes one happy to be alive and dancing." (Huneker.)

" An exquisite Mazurka, buoyant and full of elegance. What movement, what grace, and noble charm in the later short notes. In the third part we have the popular note again, in a characteristically monotonous bass and with it the never-to-be-ignored *rubato*, which, whatever else it may be, is purely Polish-Slavonic and entirely peasant-like. In these wavering strains one recognises the whole soul of a Slav, with its free impulses and its expansion under emotion." (Kleczynski.)

No. 2 in A minor (6).

Karasowski considers this one of the best of the Mazurkas. Huneker says that "it is as if one danced upon one's grave ; a change to major does not deceive, it is too heavy-hearted."

The trio (marked *dolce*) in a major with its *scherzando* closing bars is beautiful, and notwithstanding Huneker's remark, forms a sufficient contrast to the very sad strains of the opening.

No. 3 in F minor (7).

Kleczynski and Karasowski unite in admiration of this very beautiful Mazurka, " where to a sort of sad theme of violins the bass supports the rhythm so cheerfully, and where the middle part is so original and full of energetic fantasy."

" Guitar-like is the bass in its snapping resolution. The section that begins on the dominant of D flat is full of vigour and imagination ; the left hand is given a solo. This Mazurka has the true ring." (Huneker.)

No. 4 in A flat major (8).

" What is besides inexpressibly interesting, is the variety of ideas. One Mazurka laughs, another weeps, one is thoughtful, another dances." Thus Kleczynski, and what he says of all is true of this particular Mazurka. It is a veritable kaleidoscope of moods, and the trio is a priceless treasure, with its characteristic Polish repetition of a single phrase and then the sudden change to A major, in which there is, as Huneker says, " much to ponder." It is one of those episodes to which one recurs again and again with ever increasing pleasure.

No. 5 in C major (9).

This is a sketch, a kind of coda to the set. It is a little masterpiece with a single idea, but not so exquisitely delicate and gem-like as the seventh prelude, which it somewhat resembles. Huneker calls it a silhouette with a marked profile, and says it is full of the echoes of lusty happiness. It has not any definite end and it is difficult to leave off playing it. Kullak suggests closing on the first note of the twelfth bar, but the effect is vastly greater and more poetical if the melody is allowed to die away inaudibly on the dominant *senza fine* as indicated by Klindworth.

OPUS 8.—Trio for Piano, Violin, and Violoncello. G minor.

Dedicated to M. le Prince Antoine Radziwill.
Composed 1828.   Published 1833.

THIS is one of the four works of Chopin in which the violoncello is concerned and the unique instance in which he composed for the violin.

Niecks classes it with the early works of Chopin's eighteenth year that he wrote as a student, and it seems to be generally considered his most successful essay in the classical form, although Hadow says that "the first movement is as badly drawn as some of the later Correggios."

In a letter of Chopin's to Titus Woyciechowski, dated September 1828, we read: "As to new compositions I have nothing besides the still unfinished trio which I began after your departure. The first Allegro I have already tried with accompaniments."

In August 1830 he wrote: "Last Saturday I tried the Trio, and, perhaps because I had not heard it for so long, was satisfied with myself. 'Happy man,' you will say, won't you? It then struck me that it would be better to use the viola instead of the violin, as the first string predominates in the violin, and in my trio is hardly used at all. The viola would, I think, accord better with the 'cello."

This is one of the rare instances in which Chopin discusses a technical musical question in his letters.

The Trio was not published till five years after its composition, and Schumann, in reviewing it, says: "In regard to the Trio by Chopin, I may remind my readers that it appeared a few years ago and is already known to many. Let no one take it amiss in Florestan that he prides himself on having first introduced a youth from an unknown world, to publicity, unfortunately in a very somniferous spot.* And how finely Chopin has realised his prophecy, how triumphantly he has issued from the fight with the ignoramuses and Philistines, how nobly he still strives onward, ever more simply and artistically ! Even this Trio belongs to Chopin's earlier works, when he still gave the preference to the virtuoso. But who could have well foreseen the development of such an anomalous originality, such an energetic nature, that would rather wear itself out than submit to the laws of others ? Chopin has already left several periods of development behind him ; the difficult has become so easy to him that he throws it aside, and like all thorough artists, turns with preference to the simple. What can I say of this Trio, that every one who understands it has not already said to himself ? Is it not as noble as possible, more enthusiastic than the song of any poet, original in detail as in the whole, every note life and music ? Wretched Berlinese reviewer, who couldest not comprehend anything of all this, and never willst. How I despise, yet pity thee, miserable man ! " †

Willeby, who is not often moved to enthusiasm, regards this Trio as " One of the most perfect and, unfortunately, most neglected of Chopin's works. It is in sonata form, and has the four movements, Allegro, Scherzo, Adagio, and Finale."

The prevalence of the tonic key seems to him the only blot marring the first movement. "The Scherzo is delightful and the movement so flowing and full of life that it carries us along irresistibly, while it is difficult in the domain of chamber-music to name a more beautiful movement than the Adagio."

Finck, always original and interesting, thinks it "admirably adapted to the instruments for which it is written," and tells us how in an amateur Trio club, to which he belonged, it was the universal favourite of the members, and that with it they always closed their evening's entertainments.

"Twelve years after it was written, one of Chopin's pupils, Mme. Streicher, tells us that when studying the Trio with him he drew her attention to some passages

* *The Allgemeine Musikalische Zeitung.* Cf. **Op. 2.**
† **Rellstab, the Berlin critic of the** *Iris.*

which displeased him, saying that he would write them differently now."

Huneker seems to think that the Sonata form cramped Chopin's individuality and imagination, and also notices the sameness of key complained of by Willeby. However he says : "The Trio opens with fire, the Scherzo is fanciful, and the Adagio charming, while the Finale is cheerful to liveliness. Its classicism you may dispute, nevertheless it contains lovely music."

Barbedette does not consider it equal to the masterpieces of Beethoven and Schubert, but declares that it contains such beautiful melodies, such happy modulations, and effects so unexpected and arresting, that one cannot help playing it with pleasure ; while Niecks thinks " it has enough of nobility, enthusiasm, originality, music, and life to deserve more attention than it has hitherto obtained."

THE NOCTURNES.

THE Nocturnes are the form of composition with which perhaps Chopin's name is most indelibly associated. He did not, however, invent either the name or the form. The term " nocturn " actually occurs in the preface to the Prayer Book as a service of the Church intended originally to be celebrated at night.   John Field, the burly Englishman, who lived chiefly in Paris and Russia, had already popularised the name and form, but, as Ehlert said : " After Chopin even noble John Field's nectar tastes to us but as excellent sugar and water."

There is in these Nocturnes of Chopin infinite variety : some are reveries instinct only with the stillness and solemnity of the night and the glamour of moonlight ; others are dramatic with a sense of the emotions that sway the soul in the hours of darkness ; they are introspective like the one in which Chopin originally wrote "after a performance of Hamlet " ; or again, they are sensuous and luxuriant, heavy with the scent of exotic flowers, and only to be compared with the stanzas in Keats' " Ode to the Nightingale " about the "embalméd darkness," the " verdurous glooms and winding mossy ways."

Although Chopin's gift of melody is nowhere more lavishly exhibited than in these Nocturnes, it is not only in melody that they excel, but in exquisite grace and beauty of detail, in subtleties of harmony and modulation that are even a deeper source of emotional expression than melody. So original and daring are these harmonic flights that Schumann said of the G minor Nocturne, " he saw in it a terrible declaration of war against a whole musical past." It is probable that many of the accusations of being morbid and unintelligible are based on a theoretical study of these recondite modulations, whereas when they are brought to hearing in the way in which Chopin played them, they become at once not only clear in meaning but beautiful in expression.

There are eighteen Nocturnes that were published during Chopin's lifetime in eight Opus numbers. The first two books contain three each, and the other six two each. Besides these one in E minor was published by Fontana as No. 1 of Opus 72. In 1895 a Nocturne in C sharp minor, a work of Chopin's earliest youth, was discovered and published, but it is in none of the editions of the collected works. The Berceuse and the Barcarolle can almost be looked upon as belonging to the same class of pieces as the Nocturnes, with which they have considerable affinity.

The earliest of the Nocturnes is the posthumous one in E minor which was written in 1827. The three of Opus 9 can be approximately attributed to the year 1832, after which the year of composition probably agrees very closely with the year of publication.

" Among Chopin's Nocturnes some of his most popular works are to be found. Nay, the most widely prevailing idea of his character as a man and musician seems to have been derived from them. But the idea thus formed is an erroneous one ; these dulcet, effeminate compositions illustrate only one side of the master's character, and by no means the best or most interesting. Notwithstanding such precious pearls as the two Nocturnes Opus 37 and a few others, Chopin shows himself greater, both as a man and a musician, in every other class of pieces he has originated and cultivated, more especially in his polonaises, ballads, and studies." (Niecks.)

" Chopin, seldom exuberantly cheerful, is morbidly sad and complaining in many of the Nocturnes. The most admired of his compositions, with the exception of the valses, they are in several instances his weakest. Yet he ennobled the form originated by Field, giving it dramatic breadth, passion, and even grandeur. Set against Field's naïve and idyllic specimens, Chopin's efforts are often too bejewelled for true simplicity, too lugubrious, too tropical —Asiatic is a better word—and they have the exotic savour of the heated conservatory and not the fresh scent of the flowers reared in the open by the less poetic Irishman. And then Chopin is so desperately sentimental in some of these compositions. They are not altogether to the taste of this generation ; they seem to be suffering from anæmia. However, there are a few noble Nocturnes, and methods of performance may have much to answer for the sentimentalising of some others. More vigour, a quickening of the time-pulse, and a less languishing touch will rescue them from lush sentiment. Chopin loved the night and its soft mysteries as much as did Robert Louis Stevenson, and his Nocturnes are true night pieces, some with agitated, remorseful countenances, others seen in profile only, while many are whisperings at dusk. Most of them are called feminine, a term psychologically false. The poetic side of men of genius is feminine, and in Chopin the feminine note was over-emphasised—at times it was almost hysterical—particularly in these Nocturnes." (Huneker.)

OPUS 9.—Three Nocturnes.

No. 1 in B flat minor (Larghetto) ; No. 2 in E flat major (Andante) ; No. 3 in B major (Allegretto).

Dedicated to Mme. Camille Pleyel.
Probably composed 1832. Published January 1833.

No. 1 in B flat Minor.

IT was only natural that Chopin's first published essay in the form already popularised by Field should have been extensively compared with the older composer's works. Sikorski, one of the best and most conscientious Polish critics says : " On comparing Field's Nocturnes with those of Chopin, it must be candidly confessed that the former do not surpass the latter ; although it is not to be denied that in spite of some striking Chopin traits, Opus 9 somewhat resembles Field's works in depth of feeling and particular turns of expression. These differences may be thus described : Field's Nocturnes represent a cheerful blooming landscape, bathed in sunshine, while Chopin's depict a romantic mountainous region, with a dark background and lowering clouds flashing forth lightning."

Contemporary reviewers were rather inclined to put their heads together and say " he has stolen it from Field." They even went so far as to assert that Chopin was a pupil of that composer, who was then living in St. Petersburg.

Chopin, however, wrote : " I have the *cognoscenti* and the poetic natures on my side."

Karasowski says : "Field was satisfied with writing tender, poetical, and rather melancholy pieces ; while Chopin not only introduced the dramatic element, but displayed, in a striking manner, a marvellous enrichment of harmony and of the resources of pianoforte composition."

Of Opus 9 he writes : " The three Nocturnes are true Petrarchian sonnets, overflowing with grace, fairy-like charm, and captivating sweetness ; they seem like whisperings in a still summer night, under the balcony of the beloved one."

Niecks says of this Nocturne that it is pervaded by a voluptuous dreaminess and cloying sweetness : it suggests twilight, the stillness of night, and thoughts engendered thereby, while Kleczynski is of opinion that it exhibits a musical form unknown until that time ; a thrilling sadness, together with a novel elegance of construction. In the middle part, which should not be played too fast, the melody drags along in heavy octaves as though the soul were sinking beneath the weight of thought and the heat of a summer's night.

" One of the most elegiac of his Nocturnes is the first in B flat minor. Of far more significance than its two companions, it is for some reason neglected. While I am far from agreeing with those who hold that in the early

Chopin all his genius was completely revealed, yet this Nocturne is as striking as the last, for it is at once sensuous and dramatic, melancholy and lively. Emphatically a mood, it is best heard on a grey day of the soul, when the times are out of joint ; its silken tones will bring a triste content as they pour out upon one's hearing. The second section in octaves is of exceeding charm. As a melody it has all the lurking voluptuousness and mystic crooning of its composer. There is flux and reflux throughout, passion peeping out in the Coda." (Huneker.)

" When Chopin took ' the Nocturne ' in hand he invested it with an elegance and depth of meaning which had never been given to it before. The No. 1 in B flat minor is especially remarkable for this, and is by turns voluptuous and dramatic ; it was certainly not in the cold nature of Field to pen such bars as the sixteenth and seventeenth of this work. A couple of bars later there occurs a phrase, which we look upon as one of the most purely 'Chopinesque' that the master ever wrote. As an example of pure, unaffected, and beautiful music, he has never surpassed this phrase. Notice in the next bar how the sadness is intensified by the enharmonic change. Again, what could be more *triste* than the phrase in D flat, which occurs some thirty-four bars later, marked *legatissimo?* After a return to the initial theme, he brings the work to a close with the chord of the tonic major." (Willeby.)

Kullak points out that this Nocturne is written in " four larger divisions, which are related to each other, not like chief and secondary subjects, but rather like the strophes of a poem." The structure is very characteristic of Chopin's Nocturnes. The accompaniment figure in the bass is unchanged throughout. The first stanza is decidedly melancholy, but the second subject in octaves is beautiful and full of truth and expression. It brings before one the atmosphere of a summer's night and reminds one of Matthew Arnold's lovely lines :

> " Roses that down the alleys shine afar,
>   And open, jasmine muffled lattices
>   And groups under the dreamy garden trees,
>   And the full moon, and the white evening star."

The third strophe (bar 52) is more cheerful, and when the fourth section is reached the original theme returns, but with less sadness and more resignation. There is a burst of passionate energy in the coda, and it ends with soft, sweet chords in the major.

Madame Camille Pleyel, *née* Marie Moke, to whom these Nocturnes are dedicated, was a brilliant young pianist with whom the composer, Ferdinand Heller, was violently in love. She, however, did not reciprocate his affection, and became engaged to Hector Berlioz. During his absence in Rome Mlle. Moke, at the instigation of her mother, married Pleyel. Berlioz in his memoirs tells us how he started for Paris with a disguise, loaded pistols, and bottles of poison, bent on murdering the faithless Marie and her mother, and intending to commit suicide. The luggage containing the disguise went astray, and during the consequent delay his rage flickered out, and instead of wreaking condign vengeance he spent an enjoyable holiday on the Riviera.

No. 2.—Nocturne in E flat (Andante).

This is probably the best known and most celebrated, not only of the Nocturnes but of all Chopin's works. It certainly did more for his popularity in Paris than anything he had published up to that time. It is this particular piece that sketchy amateurs generally mean when they ask one to play " Chopin's Nocturne."

It approximates more closely than any other to the form of Field's Nocturnes, but this very fact only throws into greater relief the superiority of Chopin's work. As a curiosity of criticism it is interesting to read what Rellstab, a well-known German critic of the thirties, said at the time :

" Where Field smiles, Chopin makes a grinning grimace ; where Field sighs, Chopin groans ; where Field shrugs his shoulders, Chopin twists his whole body ; where Field puts some seasoning into the food, Chopin empties a handful of Cayenne pepper. In short, if one holds Field's charming romances before a distorting concave mirror, so that every delicate expression becomes a coarse one, one gets Chopin's work. We implore Mr. Chopin to return to nature."

, Most of the critics are a little hard on this Nocturne. Willeby says : " It is æsthetically and psychologically inferior to its companions, and savours somewhat of affection." Niecks seems to think that because fashionable *salon* composers have copied its tone and phraseology that its tone must be one of sentimentality and not true natural feeling. He allows, however, that it has eloquence, grace, and genuine refinement. Huneker finds it graceful, shallow of content, but adds that "if it is played with purity of touch and freedom from sentimentality it is not nearly so banal as it usually seems. It is Field-like, therefore play it as did Rubinstein in a Field-like fashion."

All agree that it can easily be spoilt in the rendering ; that it should be played with simplicity and naturalness ; the time not too slow.

" It has become essentially a domain of the younger feminine world ; they do well in selecting it for making their *début* in the sphere of the finest salon music and free delivery ; only let them beware of distorting it by immoderate *rubatos* and hyper-sentimentality. The feelings which underlie the contents of this Nocturne are too true and natural to require rouge." (Kullak.)

It is one of the shortest of the Nocturnes, written in a simple two-part song form, with a fascinating coda. It reminds one critic, of Keats' " Ode to a Nightingale," but it has not the depth and variety of that immortal lyric ; it is a poem of tender and devoted love, and reminds one of the lines from Tennyson's " Gardener's Daughter," when :

" Every daisy slept, and Love's white star
   Beamed through the thicken'd cedar in the dusk.
       *   *   *   *
   Love at first sight, first born, and heir to all
   Made the night thus."

No. 3.—Nocturne in B major (Allegretto).

This Nocturne has come in for remarkably little mention by any of the critics, and yet it is by no means the least interesting.

Niecks calls it " exquisite salon music. Little is said, but that ·little very prettily. Although the atmosphere is close, impregnated with musk and other perfumes, there is here no affectation. The concluding Cadenza, that twirling line, reads plainly Frederic Chopin."

Barbedette finds the style of it a little precious. (*Un peu cherché*).

Gracious, even coquettish, is the first part ; well knit, " the passionate intermezzo has the true dramatic Chopin ring. It should be taken *alla breve*. The ending is quite effective." (Huneker.)

This Nocturne is the first of a type of which there are several examples. There is a first subject which opens brightly in the major and is contrasted in the middle section with an agitated and dramatic theme in the minor. The chief subject is then resumed, and the whole closes with one of those codas which, in Chopin's works, are so often separate inspirations of extraordinary beauty and charm.

The chief subject is divided into three strophes, which, as Kullak points out, are different, but not essentially unlike in point of contents, and they constantly alternate with each other.

The middle section is march-like in treatment and must be played strictly in time. Its modulatory changes and frequent dynamic nuances are very interesting.

The coda begins with an arresting change of harmony, and the concluding cadenza is even more elaborate and interesting than that of the E flat minor Nocturne.

OPUS 10.—12 Grandes Études.

No. 1, C major (Arpeggios) ; No. 2, A minor (Chromatic scale) ; No. 3, E major (Melody) ; No. 4, C sharp minor (Presto) ; No. 5, G flat major (Black keys) ; No. 6, E flat minor (Andante) ; No. 7, C major (Toccata) ; No. 8, F major (Allegro) ; No. 9, F minor (Molto agitato) ; No. 10, A flat major (Rhythm and accent) ; No. 11, E flat major (Extended chords) ; No. 12, C minor (Revolutionary Étude).

Dedicated "A son ami," Franz Liszt.
Composed 1829–1831. Published in 1833.

AS early as October 1829 we read in one of Chopin's letters to his friend, Titus Woyciechowski : "I have composed a study in my own manner." The last three

words are pregnant with meaning ; "his own manner"
meant that his nature, matured by experience of life and
stimulated by emotion, had obtained spontaneous self-
expression in a series of works in a form untrammelled
by tradition, in which, despite their obvious technical
purpose, all the poetry and charm of his nature revealed
itself fully for the first time.   Of these Études there are in
all twenty-seven, twelve in Opus 10, published in 1833,
another twelve in Opus 25, published in 1837, and three
more which appeared in the " Méthode des Méthodes "
for the piano, by Moscheles and Fétis in 1840, and which
were subsequently republished separately as " Trois
Nouvelles Études " without opus number.   Again, in a
letter of November 1829, Chopin wrote : " I have written
some studies, in your presence I would play them well."
It seems well established that No. 12 of Opus 10, " The
Revolutionary Étude," was written under the stress of
emotion caused by the news of the taking of Warsaw
by the Russians, which took place in September 1831, but
with this exception it is impossible to ascertain the exact
date of the composition of any of these studies.   It seems
probable that they were all written between 1829 and
1834, and that they are therefore the work of Chopin's
nineteenth to his twenty-fourth years.   Sowinski tells us
that Chopin brought the first book of his Études with him
to Paris in 1831, and a Polish musician heard Chopin play
the studies contained in Opus 25 in 1834.
Schumann in reviewing this later set, and evidently
writing with authoritative knowledge, tells us that most of
them were written about the same time as those of Opus
10, and that only the first and last were of later date.
It would be a great mistake if we were misled by
the title Studies into thinking that the perfecting of
technique is their sole aim.   Each of them certainly has
its own special technical problem, but they are just as
much studies in melody, harmony, rhythm, and emotional
expression as of pure technique, and indeed Finck
suggests that Chopin, finding them generally misunderstood when he played them, gave them the title of
Studies with ironic intention.   From whatever point of
view they are looked at, the Studies are likely to remain
the supreme examples of their kind.

Liszt remarks on the unassuming nature of the titles of Chopin's " Studies and Preludes," and says : " Yet the compositions which are thus modestly named are none the less types of perfection in a mode which he himself erected and stamped as he did all his other works with the deep impress of his poetic genius. Written when his career was only just beginning, they are marked by a youthful vigour not found in some of his later works, even when they are more elaborate and finished and richer in combinations."

Schumann in an article on Pianoforte Études said that amongst the younger men of his day Chopin was the first to command public attention : " His Études, nearly all giving proof of a remarkable mind, soon resounded throughout Germany, where they will long resound, since they are far in advance of general cultivation, and even if they were not so, they possess the real geniality that has value at all times. With Chopin difficulty is only a means to an end, and when he makes the greatest use of it, it is only because the desired effect requires it. Great means, great meaning, great effect—in Chopin we nearly always find them united."

Huneker has devoted perhaps more attention to the Études than to any other of the works. He calls them Titanic experiments, and thinks they will live for ever. He says : " They are enormously misunderstood and mis-read. Studies in moods, as well as in mechanism, they are harnessed with the dull, unimaginative creatures of the conservatory curriculum, and so in the concert room we miss the flavour, the heroic freedom of the form. When will these series of palpitating music-pictures be played with all their range of emotional dynamics ? "

Later on he speaks of the Études as " that delightful region where the technic-worn student discerns from afar the glorious colours, the strangely plumaged birds, the exquisite sparkle of falling waters, the odours so graceful to nostrils forced to inhale Czerny, Clementi, and Cramer."

Niecks says : " Whether looked at from the æsthetical or technical point of view, Chopin's Studies will be seen to be second to those of no composer. Were it not wrong to speak of anything as absolutely best, their excellences would induce one to call them unequalled. A striking

feature in them compared ‚with Chopin's other works is
their healthy freshness and vigour.   Even the slow,
dreamy, and elegiac ones have none of the faintness and
sickliness to be found in not a few of the composer's
pieces, especially in several of the Nocturnes.   The diver-
sity of character exhibited by these Studies is very great.
In some of them the æsthetical, in others the technical
purpose predominates ; in a few the two are evenly
balanced ; in none is either of them absent.   They give a
summary of Chopin's ways and means, of his pianoforte
language ; chords in extended position, widespread arpeggios, chromatic progressions (simple, in thirds, and
in octaves), simultaneous combinations of contrasting
rhythms, &c.—nothing is wanting."

Kullak commences his edition of Chopin's works with
the Études, "for the very reason that in them Chopin
displays in concentrated form almost the entire range of
his technique."

He says : " The name of Frederic Chopin marks a new
epoch in the history of the Étude ; for not only does he
offer us genuine pianoforte technique of surprising boldness of invention, but in this form also—although originally
designed chiefly for an external end—he pours forth the
entire fulness of his transporting poesy.   But then the
specific peculiarity of his genius lay in his ability to give
contents of incomparable significance precisely in the
smaller musical forms.   Hence, whenever we speak of the
ideal of an Étude the name of Chopin almost involun-
tarily falls from our lips, and this without any disposition
to detract from the great merits of others ; as, for instance,
Cramer, Clementi, Moscheles, Liszt, &c.—not to forget
either, on any account, those of old John Sebastian Bach."

These first twelve Studies are dedicated by Chopin " to
his friend Franz Liszt," and it has been asserted by Lina
Ramann, Liszt's biographer, that their style was influenced
by the great virtuoso.   Dates, however, are against this
theory, and the influence indeed was the other way.   The
works of the new school of romantic composers for the
piano demanded a new and increased range of technique.
It is no wonder, therefore, that at first both performers and
critics cried out against the difficulties of these Études.
Moscheles complained that his fingers were constantly

stumbling over hard, inartistic, and to him incomprehensible modulations ; whilst Rellstab characteristically remarks : " Those who have distorted fingers may put them right by practising these Studies; but those who have not, should not play them, at least, not without having a surgeon at hand."

There are numerous editions of the Études, but the three best are Klindworth's, Kullak's, and Von Bülow's. There exist all sorts of perversions and transcriptions of the Études, which are only of interest to students of technique, and all allusions to these are therefore omitted from this book. From an artistic point of view they are to be deplored, although there is no denying the cleverness of some of them ; for instance, Godowsky's version of the Black Key study and the G flat (" Butterflies' Wings ") combined together. Even Brahms has made a version of the F minor, Op. 25, No. 2, and as Huneker says, " has broken it on the wheel of double sixths and thirds."

No. 1.—Étude in C major.

This study is intensely characteristic of Chopin's piano technique ; it is perhaps more technical and of less emotional value than any of the others.

Barbedette thinks it the least happy of any, and says that it is difficult without being beautiful. It is formed entirely of arpeggios on extended chords for the right hand, whilst the left plays a melody in octaves.

Von Bülow says that these octaves should be struck fully and with weight, but without hardness, and therefore must be played by raising the tight-stretched hand.

The metronome sign is 176 for a crotchet, but Kullak thinks that 152 is quite fast enough ; the faster time is very proper for the highest bravura, but it impairs the majestic grandeur of the character of the piece. He says: " Above a ground bass, proudly and boldly striding along, flow mighty waves of sound. The Étude is to be played on a basis of *forte* throughout ; with strongly dissonant harmonies; the *forte* is to be increased to *fortissimo*, diminishing again with consonant ones."

Huneker considers the study heroic. He says : " Extended chords had been sparingly used by Hummel and

C

Clementi, but to take a dispersed harmony and transform it into an epical study, to raise the chord of the tenth to heroic stature—that could have been accomplished by Chopin only. The irregular, black, ascending and descending staircases of notes strike the neophyte with terror. Like Piranesi's marvellous aerial architectural dreams, these dizzy acclivities and descents of Chopin exercise a charm, hypnotic if you will, for eye as well as ear. Here is the new technique in all its nakedness, new in the sense of figure, design, pattern, web, new in a harmonic way. The old order was horrified at the modulatory harshness, the young sprigs of the new, fascinated and a little frightened. A man who could explode a mine that assailed the stars must be reckoned with. The nub of modern piano music is in the study, the most formally reckless Chopin ever penned. . . . This study suggests that its composer wished to begin the exposition of his wonderful technical system with a skeletonised statement. It is the tree stripped of its bark, the flower of its leaves, yet, austere as is the result, there is compensating power, dignity, and unswerving logic."

No. 2.—Étude in A minor.

The purpose of this Study is severely technical, but for pianists a complete mastery of it is essential; without facility in the fingering it employs it is impossible to render appropriately some of Chopin's most important compositions. The chromatic scale has to be played with the third, fourth, and fifth fingers, whilst the thumb and first finger play perfectly distinctly and yet transiently, (with strict observance of their value as semiquavers only as Von Bülow directs), the harmonies underneath the scale on each beat of the bar. As Huneker says : " The entire composition, with its murmuring, meandering, chromatic character, is a forerunner to the whispering, weaving, moonlit effects in some of his later studies."

In spite of its technical difficulties, it is when properly rendered, as delicate as a silver-point drawing, as rounded and finished as a lyric of Heine. The treble ripples up and down over the lightly accentuated harmonies, and the concluding scale drops as delicately as a bird alighting on a swaying branch.

No. 3.—Étude in E major.

Von Bülow considers that this Étude in its essential importance is a study of expression, and in his invaluable critical edition of the studies couples it with No. 6 in E flat minor. He gives most minute and elaborate instructions as to the rendering of each particular section, more especially in regard to the *rubato* to be employed.

Kullak calls it a " wondrously beautiful tone-poem, more of a Nocturne than an Étude, and as regards architecture and contents, comparable to the Nocturne in F sharp major " (Opus 15, No. 2). .

Gutmann has left us an interesting anecdote that Chopin declared to him that he had never in his life written another such a beautiful melody, and on one occasion, when Gutmann was studying it, the master lifted up his arms with his hands clasped and exclaimed, " Oh, my fatherland ! "

Niecks thinks that this composition may be reckoned as among Chopin's loveliest ; he also, like Von Bülow, ranks it with the sixth number of the same opus, and says that these two studies combine classical chasteness of contour with the fragrance of romanticism.

Huneker says, that in this study "the more intimately known Chopin reveals himself. This one in E is among the ᵗᵉˢᵗ flowering of the composer's choice garden. It is simpler, less morbid, sultry, and languorous, therefore saner, than the much bepraised study in C sharp minor, No. 7, Opus 25."

Regarding Von Bülow's remarks about the *tempo* licence to be indulged in, he says : " It is a case which innate taste and feeling must guide. You can no more teach a real Chopin *rubato*—not the mawkish imitation—than you can make a donkey comprehend Kant."

" If we might single out any particular Étude as being more beautiful than its companions, it would be this one ; it is one long chain of entrancing melody and harmony throughout." (Willeby.)

No. 4.—Étude in C sharp minor.

Kullak calls this a bravura study of velocity and light-ness in both hands, and says the accentuation should be fiery. Von Bülow considers.that the interest it inspires may easily become a stumbling-block in attempting to conquer its technical difficulties, and gives minute instruc-tions as to the way it should be practised ; he calls it "a purely classical and model piece of music."

This Étude, if phrased properly, rushes along with magnificent swing, culminating in the seventieth bar with a glorious crashing climax, *fff*.

Huneker calls it "a joy." "How well Chopin knew the value of contrast in tonality and sentiment ! A veritable classic is this piece, which, despite its dark key colour, C sharp minor, as a foil to the preceding one in E, bubbles with life and spurts flame. . . . One wonders why this study does not figure more frequently on programmes of piano recitals. It is a fine, healthy, technical test, it is brilliant, and the coda is very dramatic. . . . A veritable lance of tone is this study, if justly poised."

No. 5.—Etude in G flat. (Black key study.)

Chopin, in a letter that he wrote whilst at Marseilles on his return from Majorca, said : "Did Miss Wieck play my Étude well ? Could she not select something better than just this Étude, the least interesting for those who do not know that it is written for the black keys ? It would have been far better to do nothing at all."

Von Bülow seems to share Chopin's rather depreciatory idea of this study, for he calls it a "Damensalon Étude, which, even in its very pleasingness is ensnaring and illusory."

Kullak says it is an "exceedingly piquant composition bubbling over with vivacity and humour, now audacious and anon softly insinuating, restlessly hurrying ever, tarrying never, its execution must be at once coquettish and graceful and full of Polish elegance."

This Étude is, perhaps, owing to what Barbedette calls its bizarre combination (the right hand playing on the black keys only), the best known of all the Études ; it is used as a show piece, performers vying with one another to see how fast they can play it, but when used thus, merely as a vehicle for display, it becomes rather an empty thing. It has perhaps less depth of emotion than any of the others.

Huneker says : " It is certainly graceful, delicately witty, a trifle naughty, arch and roguish, and it is delightfully invented. Technically, it requires smooth, velvet-tipped fingers and a supple wrist." But even if the main theme is a little commonplace, the concluding section entirely redeems it ; the melody falls over, as it were, in a miniature silver waterfall (bar 65), and spreads out into little pools of harmony in the left hand (bars 67 to 72).

No. 6.—Étude in E flat minor.

This Étude approximates in its form to that of a Nocturne, but leaves more the impression of a dark, cloudy day, although relieved here and there by an occasional gleam of watery sunshine. The gloom lightens a little where the key changes to E major (bar 21), but speaking generally, it appears throughout, as one commentator has said, as if it were written in a sort of double minor, as much sadder than ordinary minor is sadder than major.

Hadow speaks of Chopin's skill in keeping the recurrent shape of the accompaniment unchanged throughout, preserving its unity without allowing it to become wearisome or monotonous.

Both Niecks and Von Bülow couple this as a study in expression, with No. 3 of Opus 10, and Huneker says : " It is beautiful, if music so sad may be called beautiful, and the melody is full of stifled sorrow. In the E major section, the piece broadens to dramatic vigour. Chopin was not yet the slave of his mood. There must be a psychical programme to this study, some record of a youthful disillusion, but the expression of it is kept well within chaste lines. The Sarmatian composer had not yet unlearned the value of reserve. A luscious touch, and a sympathetic soul is needed for this nocturne study."

In the fifth bar from the end, there is a change to the major, which is like a transient gleam of not over warm sunshine, but the clouds gather again only to be dispelled in the last bar by a change, as unexpected as it is beautiful.

No. 7.—Étude in C major.

This bright and fascinating study is a striking contrast to the preceding one, and perhaps the most beautiful of all. It is not as emotional as the Revolutionary Étude (No. 12), nor has it the grand rush of the A minor study, known as the " Winter Wind " (No. 11), but it has a freshness, a delicacy, and a bewitching charm, the sense of sunshine and fresh air, it suggests beauty, health, and lightheartedness, and all the time, from the point of view of technique, it is an invaluable study of the value of double notes and in learning how to change the fingers on one key.

Huneker calls it a genuine toccata with moments of tender twilight, and thinks it as healthy as the toccata by Robert Schumann. " Were ever Beauty and Duty so mated in double harness ? " At the seventeenth bar (marked *delicato*) there is a delicious passage in the bass, " Puck-like rustlings in a mysterious forest," as Huneker imaginatively calls it.

Kullak says : " The Étude is to be executed with elegance, the spirited *tempo* demands great lightness of hand."

No. 8.—Étude in F major.

This, again, is one of the lighter of the studies from the point of view of emotion. Von Bülow calls it " a bravura study par excellence " for cultivating fluency of the right hand. Kullak warns modern virtuosi against playing it too fast ; " since English mechanism has supplanted the German, the pianoforte tone has become nobler, more sonorous, and greater both in volume and its capacity in nuances. In my individual opinion, pianoforte passages, even in the most fiery *tempo*, must yield some of that former quick-fingeredness, which so easily degenerated into expressive trifling and be executed with greater breadth of style."

One can never play Chopin beautifully enough, therefore never play his music too fast.

Huneker says : " There can be no doubt as to the wisdom of a broader treatment of this charming display piece. How it makes the piano sound—what a rich, brilliant sweep it secures ! It elbows the treble to its last euphonious point, glitters and crests itself, only to fall away as if the sea were melodic and could shatter and tumble into tuneful foam ! The emotional content is not marked. The piece is for the fashionable salon or the concert-hall. One catches at its close the overtones of bustling plaudits and the clapping of gloved palms. Ductility and aristocratic ease, a delicate touch and fluent technique will carry off the study with good effect. Technically it is useful ; one must speak of the usefulness of Chopin, even in these imprisoned, iridescent soap bubbles of his."

No. 9.—Étude in F minor.

In this study we enter again into the realm of emotion ; it is on record that Chopin wrote it especially for Moscheles. The very beautiful, agitated, complaining melody in the treble is supported by an unchanging wide-stretched figure in the bass, which seems to anticipate its more marked and dramatic figure in the D minor prelude No. 24. The end dies away like a sigh. Huneker finds its mood more petulant than tempestuous. The melody is morbid, almost irritating, and yet not without certain accents of grandeur. There is a persistency in repetition that foreshadows the Chopin of the later, sadder years.

No. 10.—Étude in A flat.

Von Bülow considers this study the most typical piece of the entire set. " He who can play this study in a real finished manner may congratulate himself on having climbed to the highest point of the pianist's Parnassus. The whole repertoire of pianoforte music does not contain a study of perpetual motion so full of genius and fancy as this particular one is universally acknowledged to be, except perhaps Liszt's ' Feux Follets.' "

Kullak calls it "an exceedingly piquant composition, possessing for the hearer a wondrous fantastic charm ; if played with the proper insight the *tempo* is spirited, but force finds less scope here than pleasantness and grace."

Almost above any, this Étude needs careful phrasing, its chief characteristic is the delicious contrasting play of light and shade caused by the alternations of phrasing in doublets and triplets. Huneker says of it : "The study is one of the most charming of the composer. There is more depth in it than in the G flat and F major studies, and its effectiveness in the virtuoso sense is unquestionable. A savour of the salon hovers over its perfumed measures, but there is grace, spontaneity and happiness. Chopin must have been as happy as his sensitive nature would allow when he conceived this vivacious caprice."

No. 11.—Étude in E flat major.

Huneker considers that in the whole list of the Nocturnes there is no such picture painted as this study. "A Corot, if ever there was one. Its novel design, delicate arabesques—as if the guitar had been dowered with a soul—and the richness and originality of its harmonic scheme gives us pause to ask if Chopin's invention is not almost boundless. The melody itself is plaintive ; a plaintive grace informs the entire piece. The harmonisation is far more wonderful, but to us the chord of the tenth and more remote intervals, seems no longer daring ; yet there are harmonies in the last page of this study that still excite wonder. The fifteenth bar from the end is one that Richard Wagner might have made. From that bar to the close every group is a masterpiece."

Later on he speaks of the aerial effect, the swaying of the tendrils of tone, intended by Chopin, which is exactly the kind of effect which should be aimed at in performance.

It is marked *allegretto*, and must certainly not be played faster than seventy-six to the crotchet. "The colour scheme is celestial and the ending a sigh, not unmixed with happiness."

No. 12.—Étude in C minor. Known as " The Revolutionary Étude."

This is not only one of the finest of the Études but one
of the most interesting of Chopin's works. We have it on
good authority that it was the direct musical expression of
the emotions aroused in the composer on hearing of the
taking of Warsaw by the Russians in 1831. In these
latter days, living in a generation in scorn of whom
Rossetti wrote that scathing sonnet " On the Refusal of
Aid Between Nations," we can hardly realise the wave of
indignation and sympathy that ran through England when
the free kingdom of Poland sank beneath the triple
onslaught of Russia, Austria, and Germany. But we can
well imagine the tornado of emotion that overwhelmed
the sensitive and patriotic composer. In this great tone-
poem he uttered the feelings of every Pole who, hearing of
the fall of the capital, realised that it was the death-knell
of their independent national life.

The music begins with a crash of passionate surprise,
followed by a downward swirl of indignation and despair
(bars 1–9), and then the melody rises proud, defiant, and
majestic (bar 10). When the key changes to G minor
(bar 29), we realise how modern Chopin is in the sense
that all great art is modern. For just as in Bach, we say
every now and then " How like Wagner ", here in Chopin
we get chords and progressions that would be in place in
Tristan and Isolde, and that are of the essence of all
modern emotional melody. When the return comes to the
first theme (bar 50) its force is broken, it stammers in its
utterance, the rage dies out of it, only the pathos is left,
and it ends with a questioning phrase like a broken sob as
modern and as human as Siegmund's questioning of
Brunhilde (bar 75). Then with a dying effort it gathers
itself up and rushes with a defiant shout on the guns and
bayonets of the enemy (bars 80–84).

Von Bülow says : " This C minor study must be considered as a finished work of art in an even higher degree
than the study in C sharp minor (see page 36). Among
Chopin's contemporaries and successors, Franz Liszt alone
has shown an equal pre-eminence in his great studies No. 5
in B flat major and No. 10 in F. minor. The chromatic

meandering in bars 17 and 18 (amplified in bar 73 and following bars) was first introduced into pianoforte music by Beethoven in the first movement of the fifth Concerto Op. 73, but intermingled there with diatonic intervals, and it has since then been commonly employed by many modern pianoforte composers.

From the technical point of view Kullak considers it " A bravura study of the very highest order for the left hand."

In Karasowski's " Life of Chopin " we read : " Grief, anxiety, and despair over the fate of his relatives and his dearly beloved father filled the measure of his sufferings. Under the influence of this mood he wrote this C minor Étude ; out of the mad and tempestuous storm of passages for the left hand, the melody rises aloft, now passionate and anon proudly majestic, until thrills of awe stream over the listener, and the image is evoked of Zeus hurling thunderbolts at the world."

" How superbly grand ! The composer seems to be fuming with rage ; the left hand rushes impetuously along, and the right hand strikes in with passionate ejaculations." (Niecks.)

" Four pages suffice for a background upon which the composer has flung with overwhelming fury the darkest, the most demoniac expressions of his nature. Here is no veiled surmise, no smothered rage, but all sweeps along in tornadic passion—it is one of the greatest dramatic outbursts in piano literature. Great in outline, pride, force, and velocity, it never relaxes its grim grip from the first shrill dissonance to the overwhelming chord at close. This end rings out like the crack of creation. It is elemental." (Huneker).

OPUS 11.—Grand Concerto. In E minor. For piano and orchestra.

Allegro maestoso, E minor; Romance, Larghetto, E major; Rondo vivace, E major.

Dedicated to Fr. Kalkbrenner.
Composed 1830. Published September 1833.

CHOPIN wrote two concertos, and their chronology has been the cause of much misunderstanding. The second in order of publication, Opus 21, in F minor, which appeared in 1836, was composed the year before this one, in 1829. Karasowski is responsible by a careless mistranslation for the muddle into which some commentators have fallen. The matter is of some importance, as in the slow movement of each we have two of the rare instances in which Chopin has left on record the poetic ideas which inspired him. He says of the first, " The Adagio in E major is conceived in a romantic, quiet, half melancholy spirit. It is to give the impression of the eye resting on some much-loved landscape which awakens pleasant recollections, such as a lovely spring moonlight night."

And in a letter of October 3, 1829, we read : "I have— perhaps to my misfortune—already found my ideal, whom I worship faithfully and sincerely. Six months have elapsed, and I have not yet exchanged a syllable with her of whom I dream every night. Whilst my thoughts were with her I composed the Adagio of my concerto." (The " second " in F. minor.)

Both the movements are marked Larghetto, but Chopin uses the term Adagio generically to indicate the slow movement.

The " Ideal " was a young opera singer Constantia Gladkowska.

Willeby's comments, founded as they are on the misunderstanding, are perhaps all the more interesting. He says of the first : " When we remember the circumstances under which he wrote, and the ' Ideal ' who inspired it, we wonder that there is so little of real inspiration in the Larghetto, for it cannot be compared to the corresponding portion in the companion concerto in F minor. It exhales a sickly sweetness, which causes us to long for a purer atmosphere."

Whilst of the second he says : " It is far and away the most spiritual piece of work Chopin has given us in any of his compositions for piano and orchestra." This says something for the Gladkowska as a source of inspiration, and incidentally is a credit to Willeby's intuition.

Schumann reviewed both the Concertos, but for once what " Florestan " says is not much to the point.

A reviewer (probably Rellstab again) had said that Chopin's compositions were fit for nothing but to tear in pieces, and this upsets Schumann so much that he rather neglects his subject. After a long tirade he says : " But shall I remember these things to-day just as I have fallen in with Chopin's F minor concerto. Heaven forbid ! Milk *versus* poison cool blue milk ! What is a whole yard of music paper compared to a Chopin Concerto ? What is a magister's anger compared to poetic rage ? What are ten editorial crowns compared to an Adagio in the second concerto ? "

Elsewhere he says : " Were a genius like Mozart to arise in our day, he would rather write Chopin concertos than Mozartian ones."

But Liszt thought that, though beautiful, the concertos reveal "more effort than inspiration." " His creative genius was imperious, fantastic, impulsive, and the beauties of his work were only fully manifested in absolute freedom. We cannot help thinking that he did violence to the peculiar nature of his genius when he endeavoured to subject it to rules, to classifications, and to regulations not of his own making, and which he could not bind into harmony with the requirements of his own mind."

There is a general consensus of opinion that Chopin's orchestration is weak, and it is almost conclusive evidence of this that Klindworth has published a version of the F minor and Tausig one of the E minor concerto.

Huneker in his " Mezzotints in Modern Music " devotes a section of his monograph on the Greater Chopin to a masterly analysis of these different versions, and quotes Krebhiel (another of the brilliant band of New York critics) as saying : "It is more than anything else a question of taste that is involved in this matter, and, as so often happens, individual likings, rather than artistic principles, will carry the day."

No less an authority on instrumentation than Berlioz says in his autobiography : "In Chopin's compositions all the interest centres in the piano ; his orchestral concerto accompaniments are cold and practically useless."

Both the concertos are modelled not only in form but in general style on Hummel. Chopin was still a very young man when he wrote them ; they were the work of his nineteenth and twentieth years, and it is only natural that we should be able to trace the influence of the master for whom he had a declared admiration.

Chopin frequently played these compositions at his concerts, and it is a curious comment on the advance of musical taste that in those days it was not at all unusual for vocal solos to be sandwiched in between the parts of a concerto.

Not that there was any lack of appreciation of these works when they were produced. They invariably met with applause and sympathetic criticism. In Vienna one critic said : "The execution of his newest concerto in E minor, a serious composition, gives no cause to revoke our former judgment. One who is so upright in his dealings with genuine art is deserving our genuine esteem."

The E minor concerto opens with a vigorous orchestral introduction which rehearses at full length the first and second subjects, which are subsequently repeated as piano solos. This is universally considered a mistake, and even when the original orchestration is used, this introduction of 138 bars is usually curtailed. The piano enters most effectively ; both the first and second themes are beautiful and characteristically pianistic. There is an episode in semiquavers (twenty-four bars after the first theme), marked *tranquillo*, which is peculiarly Chopinesque. But as Huneker says : "It is true the first movement is too long, too much in one set of keys, and the working out section too much in the nature of a technical study."

Von Lenz, who admired this first movement very much, describes the second as a "tiresome Nocturne." A Nocturne it undoubtedly is, but it is very ungrateful, not to

say untrue, to speak of it as tiresome. A little too unchanging in its sweetness it may be, but throughout this
and the brilliant lilting rondo, with its infectious gaiety,
one must say with Niecks : " Such is the charm, loveliness, delicacy, elegance, and brilliance of the details that
one again and again forgives and forgets their shortcomings as wholes."

Friederich Kalkbrenner, to whom this concerto is
dedicated, was a celebrated virtuoso to whom Chopin
went to play on his arrival in Paris. Kalkbrenner was
horrified at Chopin's unorthodox and novel fingering,
and wanted him to study under him for three years.
Mendelssohn on hearing this said, " Why, you play *better*
than Kalkbrenner," and Chopin finally decided not to go
to him, " as he did not want to play like him," and started
to give lessons himself.

OPUS 12.—Variations on an air from the Opera of
    " Ludovic," by Hérold, "Je vends des scapulaires."
    B flat major.

Dedicated to Mdlle. Emma Horsford.
Published in 1833.

THIS is by general consent one of the weakest of
    Chopin's compositions. It is undeniably graceful,
not to say elegant, but belongs to the small group of pieces
composed about this time, which show a distinct falling
off from the force and poetry of the Études (see Opus 16).

The only critic who has a good word to say for them is
Barbedette, who finds them simple, sober, and elegant,
and prefers them to the decidedly superior variations on
" Là ci darem." Schumann was kind, but discriminating.
He said : " They belong altogether to the drawing-room
or concert-hall, and with the exception of the last, are far
removed from any poetic sphere. For even in this style
we must award the prize to Chopin. Like that great
actor who, though he merely crossed the stage carrying
laths, was recognised with delight by the public, he cannot
conceal or deny his lofty mind in any position ; what he is

surrounded by takes its colour from him and accommo-
dates itself, be it ever so coy, to his master hand. Still it
must be confessed that these variations ought not to be
compared to his original works."

Hadow finds in them only " graceful embroideries of an
exceedingly poor texture."

Niecks is analytical and crushing. "If ever Chopin is
not Chopin in his music, it is in these variations." Did
we not know that he must have composed the work about
the middle of 1833, we should be tempted to class it with
the works which came into existence when his individuality was as yet little developed. But knowing what we
do, we can only wonder at the strange phenomenon. It
is as if Chopin had here thrown overboard the Polish part
of his natal inheritance, and given himself up unre-
strainedly and voluptuously to the French part. Besides
various diatonic runs of an inessential and purely orna-
mental character, there is in the *finale* actually a plain and
full-toned C flat major scale. What other work of the
composer could be pointed out exhibiting the like feature ?
There can be nothing more amusing than the contemporary critical opinions regarding this work, nothing more
amusing than to see the, at other times, censorious Philistines unwrinkle their brows, relax generally the sternness
of their features, and welcome, as it were, the return of
the prodigal son. We wiser critics of to-day, who, of
course, think very differently about this matter, can
nevertheless enjoy and heartily applaud the prettiness
and elegance of the simple first variation, the playful
tripping second, the *schwärmerische*, melodious third, the
merry, swinging fourth, and the brilliant *finale*."

Huneker is very decided. " This rondo in B flat is the
weakest of Chopin's muse. It is Chopin and water, and
Gallic *eau sucrée* at that. The piece is written tastefully,
is not difficult, but woefully artificial."

Kullak, with the outlook of a teacher, says : " Although
these variations by no means belong to Chopin's most
important creations, still they are constructed with so
much taste and elegance that the teacher will gladly
employ them for the formation of a graceful delivery."

Granted that these variations are Chopin's weakest
work, if everything by other composers inferior to them

had to be burnt there would be a vast bonfire.   The air itself is very taking and by no means trivial.

OPUS 13.—Grande Fantaisie on Polish airs with orchestral accompaniment.   In A major.

Dedicated to Mr. J. P. Pixis.
Composed 1828.   Published 1834.

" WHEN I had led the ladies from the stage I played my Fantasia on National airs.   This time I understood myself, the orchestra understood me, and the public understood us both.   The Mazovian air at the end made a great sensation.   I was so rapturously applauded that I had to appear four times to bow my thanks." Thus, Chopin in a letter after a concert at Warsaw in 1830.   This was one of the works he wrote to show off his powers as a virtuoso, and it was for years a favourite piece in his *repertoire*.   It is one of the six pieces with orchestral accompaniment, which Willeby says fulfils its object here better than in the other works.   Barbedette also thought the instrumentation remarkable, but Niecks says " it shows an inaptitude in writing for any other instrument than the piano that is quite surprising considering the great musical endowment of Chopin in other respects."   It is, however, never heard now at concerts, and when Mlle. Janotha played it some years ago it was not received very encouragingly.   From a pianist's point of view it is interesting and grateful to play.   After an introduction, a simple, plaintive national Polish air is introduced, and two brilliant variations ensue.   A characteristic rustic air *allegro* ushers in a theme by Charles Kurpinski which, according to Kleczynski, " moves and saddens us ; but the composer does not give time for this impression to become durable ; he suspends it by means of a long trill, and then suddenly, by a few chords and with a brilliant prelude, he leads us to a popular dance (the Kujawiak), which makes us wish to mingle with the peasant couples of Mazovia.   Does the finale in F minor indicate by its minor key the gaiety of a man devoid of hope, as the Germans tell us ?   It may perhaps be true that the minor key in which the greater number of our national dances are written may be accounted for by our proverb, 'a fig for misery.' But this circumstance gives to these airs a character of elevated beauty, not of sepulchral gaiety."

Huneker says : " It is Chopin brilliant. Its orchestral background does not count for much, but the energy, the colour, and Polish character of the piece endeared it to the composer."

Niecks says that this and the Krakowiak are the most overtly Polish of all Chopin's works. " After this he never incorporates national airs and imitates so closely national dances. Chopin remains a true Pole to the end of his days, and his love of, and attachment to, everything Polish increases with the time of absence from his native country. But as the composer grows in maturity he subjects the raw material to a more and more thorough process of refinement and development, before he considers it fit for artistic purposes. The popular dances are spiritualised, the national characteristics and their corresponding musical idioms are subtilised and individualised."

Criticising this Fantasia he accounts for its present neglect thus : " It is not altogether satisfactory in the matter of form and appears somewhat patchy. The connection of parts is anything but masterly. Here the arabesque element predominates again quite unduly. The best part is the exceedingly spirited Kujawiak."

OPUS 14.—Krakowiak. Grand Concert Rondo for piano with orchestra. F major.

Dedicated to Mme. la Princesse Adam Czartoryska. Composed 1828. Published July 1834.

THIS is the third (in order of opus numbers) of the group of five Rondos.* It is one of the six works for which Chopin wrote orchestral accompaniments, and, according to Hadow, it is the most carefully scored of all

* See p. 2.

his orchestral compositions. Huneker, however, considers it thin, although he admires the bold and merry spirit, and the very Slavic feeling of the composition generally. We know from one of Chopin's letters to his friend, Titus Woyciechowski, that it was completed by December 27, 1828. " The score of my Rondo Cracovienne is ready, the introduction is almost as funny as I am in my great coat." (A very long winter overcoat in which his friends said he cut a very comical figure.)

It was one of the compositions that Chopin wrote to show off his powers as a virtuoso, and it was always a favourite piece of his earlier concerts in Vienna and Warsaw. In another letter we read : " The Cracovienne produced a tremendous sensation ; there were four rounds of applause."

The piece takes its name from a dance indigenous to the district of Cracovia. Casimir Brodzinski, the Polish poet and critic, describes the Krakowiak " as a simplified Polonaise ; it represents, compared with the latter, a less advanced social state."

Sowinski, the Polish musician, says : " The Cracovians dance it in a very agitated and expressive manner, singing at the same time words made for the occasion, of which they multiply the stanzas and which they often improvise." It is a lively dance in $\frac{2}{4}$ time, and with the accent on a usually unaccented part of the bar, especially at the end of a phrase. Paderewski has a rather fascinating specimen in his " Humoresques de Concert."

Chopin was only once inspired by its lilting rhythm, and Niecks terms the result the most overtly Polish of his works. " In no other compositions of the Master do the national elements show themselves in the same degree of crudity ; indeed, after this, he never incorporates national airs and imitates so closely national dances. The un-restrained merriment of the Krakowiak justifies, or, if it does not justify, disposes us to forgive much. Indeed, the Rondo may be said to overflow with joyousness ; now the notes run at random hither and thither, now tumble about head over heels, now surge in bold arpeggios, now skip from octave to octave, now trip along in chromatics, now vent their gamesomeness in the most extravagant capers."

Although never heard in our concert-rooms the neglect

of this brilliant Rondo is undeserved.   Barbedette speaks of it as *une œuvre grande et magistrale*.   Without going quite as far as this, one can certainly say that it only requires to be known to be popular.   While demanding for its adequate rendition the highest degree of virtuosity, it is, as music, infinitely better than the many bravoura pieces of Liszt that meet with enthusiastic, if somewhat indiscriminating, applause.

When Chopin first wanted to play the piece at one of his Vienna concerts, he was obliged to abandon the idea because the band parts were so badly written that the players could not read them.   Chopin had to substitute an improvisation.   At a second concert, however, it was given with great success.   In the *Wiener Zeitschrift* a contemporary critic wrote : "Chopin performed a new Rondo for pianoforte and orchestra of his own composition.   This piece is written throughout in the chromatic style, rarely rises to geniality, but has passages which are distinguished by depth and thoughtful working out."

On page 230 of Klindworth's edition, lines 2 and 3, there is a passage that bears a curiously distinct likeness to the climax of the C sharp minor, Étude Op. 10, No. 4.

OPUS 15.—Three Nocturnes.

No 1, F major (Andante cantabile) ; No. 2, F sharp major (Larghetto) ; No. 3, G minor (Lento).

Dedicated to Ferdinand Hiller.
Probably composed 1833.   Published January 1834.

THIS set of three Nocturnes shows a distinct advance in Chopin's art when compared with the three of Opus 9.   Niecks finds in them " a higher degree of independence and poetic power."

In depth of feeling, melodic beauty and craftsmanship, they are undoubtedly superior.   They show us the real Chopin as opposed to the virtuoso and *salon* favourite as we see him in a group of his other works, composed during the same year.*

* See p. 55, Opus 16.

In the first in F major, we have a specimen of the type of Opus 9, No. 3. A serene and tender Andante is followed by a stormy theme marked *con fuoco*, which, after waves of emotion, dies down into the opening theme, and on this occasion is brought to a close without a *coda*, by two tender arpeggioed chords.

Barbedette sees in it a calm and beautiful lake, ruffled by a sudden storm and becoming calm again. Certainly this Nocturne does not express night. There is sunlight in it, and the middle section is storm, but not darkness.

Kullak quotes from Ossian, and says it is "like the dream of the hunter on the hill of heath; he sleeps in the mild beams of the sun; he awakes amidst a storm; the red lightning flies around; trees shake their heads to the wind! He looks back with joy on the day of the sun, and the pleasant dreams of his rest."

Ehlert speaks of "the ornament in triplets with which Chopin brushes the theme as with the gentle wings of a butterfly"; and Kullak says they should be played "as if breathed out."

The opening theme should be played simply without much pedal and with but little *rubato*, whilst the middle section can be given with a restless fire. The contrast between the two sections is particularly marked and of peculiar emotional power.

No. 2.—Nocturne in F sharp major (Larghetto).

This is certainly one of the most beautiful of the Nocturnes. All the commentators speak warmly of it: Karasowski considers it "one of the best," and Willeby classes it as one of the most important. Barbedette declares it to be full of details of ravishing beauty, and Kleczynski sees in it a revelation of Chopin's love of mankind, tracing its inspiration to the poems of the Polish poet Mieckiewicz. In it Chopin seems to say: "All that I have is yours." It certainly has a generous warmth of colour, that gives it almost an Oriental atmosphere.

An anonymous writer in an extinct magazine, *The Dome*, calls it "quite Persian in style; it paints the palm and the cypress, the rose thicket, and the great stars burning low in the Southern sky."

With the exception of some of the Etudes of Opus 10,
· this is the first of Chopin's works which is equal to his
best efforts.   It is a flawless gem, a true poem, in that it
satisfies Milton's definition of poetry as " simple, sensuous,
and passionate."

The chief subject is a melody of heavenly beauty, tender
and full of fervour, and yet most reposeful, contrasting
effectively with the second section which is taken at
double the pace.   This suddenly increased movement,
coupled with a highly novel and original figure in
quintuplets beginning *sotto voce* with both pedals, and
climaxing with a brief but powerful *crescendo*, pictures
the clashing of unfamiliar but soul-stirring emotions.   It
moves rapidly and incessantly through a chromatic series
of the most daring modulations, dies away as if exhausted,
and is followed by a recurrence of the first theme, the
calm of which, Kullak says, "touches one like a benediction."

The *fiorituri* with which this melody is so lavishly
bejewelled are not merely ornaments, they are an integral
part of the melody, enriching it and strengthening its
emotional power to a wonderful extent.   The *coda* is one
of Chopin's happiest inspirations ; it is a sigh of absolute
contentment.

Kleczynski devotes ten pages of his book "Chopin's
Greater Works " to a detailed and most instructive
description of how this masterpiece should be played.
" The performer," he says, " has an opportunity for the
display of his intelligence in the way in which he takes the
first note of the composition.   Chopin here enters
suddenly into the middle of his theme, and the note
requires a certain accent, a certain pressure of the fingers,
to show that it is the commencement of an expressive
thought."

Niecks says of this Nocturne : " The brightness and
warmth of the world without have penetrated into the
world within.   The *fiorituri* flit about us lightly as
gossamer threads.   The sweetly-sad longing of the first
section becomes more disquieting in the *doppio movimento*,
but the beneficial influence of the sun never quite loses its
power, and after a little there is a relapse into the calmer
mood, with a close like the hazy distance on a summer
day.

No. 3.—Nocturne in G minor (Lento.)
Published January 1834.

On the manuscript of this Nocturne Chopin wrote originally "After a performance of Hamlet," but on consideration he struck it out, saying : "No ! let them guess for themselves." This is interesting as showing that, sometimes at any rate, Chopin owed his inspiration to some definite poetic idea. It is a striking tribute to Shakespeare's overwhelming genius, that composers of every nation have found in his plays "the fundamental brain-stuff" round which some of their finest music crystallised itself. In the present instance, the profound philosophy and the subtle psychology of the great Shakespearean tragedy are clearly mirrored in Chopin's music, and this work marks a distinct step forward in his development. Schumann noted this unerringly. He saw that Chopin had now definitely laid aside his virtuosity, and he says of this Nocturne that in it " he read a declaration of war with the entire past" (*i.e.*, Chopin's musical past). We need not, of course, expect to find in the music an objective description of the chief event of the drama ; it is a picture of the subjective mental mood, into which a contemplation of the great tragedy threw the sensitive composer.

The first subject is marked *languido e rubato*. It might be a reflection of the mood in which Hamlet says :

> "O God, O God,
> How weary, stale, flat and unprofitable
> Seem to me all the uses of this world."

It halts and wavers ; in it there are sighs, sobs, and protests, but after a feverish climax the music dies down ; and then three soft, bell-like notes usher in a beautiful enharmonic change, and there supervenes with the second theme a mood of consolation and hope, of philosophy and resignation :

> " There's a divinity that shapes our ends
> Rough-hew them how we will."

There is no return to the first subject, there could not be, so true and deeply felt is the poetical emotion, that it would not be musically possible.

It is interesting to compare this masterpiece with the one that Grieg wrote and called " After a Performance of Macbeth." (" Lyrische Stücke," Book I.)

Huneker tells us that Rubinstein made much of this Nocturne. " In the fourth bar, and for three bars, there is a held note, F, and I heard the Russian virtuoso, by some miraculous means, keep this tone prolonged. The *tempo* is abnormally slow, and the tone is not in a position where the sustaining pedal can sensibly help it ; yet under Rubinstein's fingers it swelled and diminished, and went surging into D, as if the instrument were an organ. I suspected the inaudible changing of fingers on the note, or a sustaining pedal. It was wonderfully done."

Kullak speaks of the " unostentatious simplicity with which with but few strokes complete expression is given to highly poetic contents." He sees in this Nocturne a picture of grief for the loss of a beloved one lulled by the consolations of religion.

Niecks considers it the finest of the three forming Opus 15. " The words *languido e rubato* describe well the wavering pensiveness of the first portion of the Nocturne, which finds its expression in the indecision of the melodic progressions, harmonies, and modulations. The second section is marked *religioso*, and may be characterised as a trustful prayer, conducive to calm and comfort."

OPUS 16.—Rondo.   E flat major.

Dedicated to Mlle. Caroline Hartmann.
Published in 1834.

THIS is the last of the group of Rondos.* It is prefaced with an introduction that Niecks styles dramatic, but which is without any special depth of expression. The ensuing Rondo, though brilliant and containing some very graceful passage writing, is curiously shallow and lacks poetry. It is perhaps the least interesting of any of Chopin's works. It is difficult to fix the exact date of its composition, but by internal evidence it seems to belong

* See p. 2.

to the year preceding its publication, 1833. Chopin had
been settled in Paris for two years ; he was the idol of
fashionable *salons*, and much sought after at concerts and
parties.

The somewhat frivolous nature of his life in the capital
seems to be reflected in a group of his compositions about
this time. In the Boléro, the first Valse, the variations on
an air from Halévy's Ludovic, and the Duo on airs from
Robert le Diable, we seem to see a concession to the
shallow taste of the public, a falling off from the poetic
ideals he had apparently set before himself in the Études
and Nocturnes. Perhaps his want of success as a performer before large audiences was the blessing in disguise
that drove him back upon himself, and led to the composition of his finer and more elevated work, which may be
said to begin anew with the first Scherzo, the first Ballade,
and the C sharp minor Polonaise.

"Opus 16, a lightsome Rondeau, with a dramatic
introduction, is, like the Boléro, not without its beauties ;
but in spite of greater individuality, ranks, like it, low
among the Master's works, being patchy, unequal, and
little poetical." (Niecks.)

Huneker tells us that Richard Burmeister has supplied
an orchestral accompaniment to this piece which is in
great favour at the Conservatoires. He speaks of it as
" neat rather than poetical, although the introduction has
dramatic touches," and draws attention to its " Weber-ish
affinities."

OPUS 17.—Four Mazurkas.

No. 1 in B flat major ; No. 2 in E minor ; No. 3 in A flat
major ; No. 4 in A minor.

Dedicated to Mme. Lina Freppa.   Published 1834.

No. 1 in B flat major.

THIS is an important set amongst the Mazurkas. A
distinct advance is marked in emotional intensity, and
in structural development on the two earlier numbers,
Opus 6 and Opus 7. Karasowski thinks the first two are

amongst Chopin's best efforts in the form, and Niecks
selects this opus for special analysis, probably on account
of its representative character. Here we have the
contrast of moods between the different Mazurkas that
form one of the chief charms of these brief poems.
Chivalry, tenderness, pessimism, contemplative resignation, are some of the notes struck. In the first number we
meet, says Niecks, " with the marked chivalrous element
that distinguishes the Polish character. The three first
parts are bold and glittering, but not without regretful
backward glances ; in the last part the piquant melody
and the strongly-marked rhythm picture to us the graceful motions of the dancers, and suggest the clashing of the
spurs and the striking of heels against the ground."

Willeby draws attention to the sequences of chords of
the seventh as a noticeable technical detail (see bars
15 and 16.)

It is curious how the peasant note so prominent in the
earlier Mazurkas here gives way to a more aristocratic
tone.

No. 2 in E minor.

Niecks suggests " The Request" as a suitable title for
this Mazurka ; " all the arts of persuasion are tried, from
the pathetic to the playful, and a vein of longing, not
unmixed with sadness, runs through the whole, or rather
forms the basis of it." The G major section is charming,
and a wonderfully modulated passage marked *stretto*
takes us to the *coda*, wherein the first theme mounts, as
Huneker says, " with passion, but is never shrill."

Some Mazurkas can be made to express many different
emotions, but the trio of this one is emphatically an
expression of persuasiveness. At bars five to seven it
asks, with every shade of feeling, for the desired boon.
At bar thirteen it pleads. At bar fourteen it implores.
Disappointed, it returns at the *stretto* to its original
request, and ends unsatisfied with a vague longing.

No. 3 in A flat major.

Niecks has hit off the mood of this Mazurka very aptly
when he says "a helpless, questioning uncertainty and indecision characterise it."

Huneker calls it pessimistic, threatening, and irritable, and says that the trio, although in E major (usually such a cheerful key) " displays a relentless sort of humour. A dark page ! "

The second section exhibits a sudden burst of unavailing anger ; the whole piece is exactly as if one was horribly worried about something and could not make up one's mind what was the best thing to do. " Syncopations, suspensions, and chromatic notes form here the composer's chief stock-in-trade ; displacement of everything in melody, harmony, and rhythm is the rule. Nobody did anything like this before Chopin, and nobody has given to the world an equally minute and distinct representation of the same intimate emotional experiences." (Niecks.)

No. 4 in A minor.

So far this is the longest and most important of the Mazurkas. It is sometimes referred to as " The Little Jew." Szulc, a Polish writer, who collected, and, shall we say, possibly invented, anecdotes of Chopin, says that this Mazurka was known by this title before Chopin left Warsaw. If so it would make it one of his earliest works in the form ; but, if this is the case, internal evidence goes for nothing. It belongs emphatically to the period of Chopin's artistic development after he had got over his first excitement of life in Paris. Szulc's anecdote is silly, pointless, and not worth repeating. No definite programme could usefully be assigned to this Mazurka, of which the chief feature is its vague and elusive quality. Niecks finds it " bleak and joyless, till with the entrance of the A major a fairer prospect opens. But those jarring tones that strike in wake the dreamer pitilessly. The commencement as well as the close on the chord of the sixth, the chromatic glidings of the harmonies, the strange twists and skips, give a weird character to this piece."

Huneker finds it " full of hectic despair," whatever that may mean, " and its serpentining chromatics, and apparently suspended close, give an impression of morbid irresolution modulating into a sort of desperate gaiety. Its tonality accounts for the moods evoked, being indeterminate and restless."

It is impossible to exaggerate the fascination that this Mazurka possesses. The opening, with its characteristic triplet in the fourth bar, the appealing " helplessness " of bars 9–12, the exquisite grace of the bar marked "*delicatissimo*," and the subsequent bars similarly ornamented, are details one can linger over endlessly. In the A major trio the repetition of the D in the second and fourth bars may be noted ; and towards the end from where it is marked *sotto voce*, and the little grace notes are added, every bar is a fresh study, and a source of intimate delight.

THE VALSES.

CHOPIN left extant fifteen valses, eight of which only were published during his lifetime. These are :

(1) Opus 18.   Grande Valse.   E flat major.   Vivo.   1834.
    Opus 34.   Trois Valses brillantes.   1838.
(2)   No. 1, A flat major.   Vivace.
(3)   No. 2, A minor.   Lento.
(4)   No. 3, F major.   Vivace (the cat valse).
(5) Opus 42.   Valse, A flat major.   Vivace.   1840.
    Opus 64.   Trois Valses.   1847.
(6)   No. 1, D flat major.   Molto vivace (the dog valse).
(7)   No. 2, C sharp minor.   Tempo giusto.
(8)   No. 3, A flat major.   Moderato.

These eight divide themselves naturally into two classes : those that are really dances idealised, and those that are lyric poems in the form of a valse. In the first division will be found the first, second, fifth, and sixth ; and in the second, the third, fourth, seventh, and eighth.

As pure dance tunes they are far finer than anything of Strauss or Lanner ; at the same time the very fact that they are more poetical and more inspired would unfit them for general use in the ball-room. Schumann speaks of " Chopin's body and soul-inspiring valse," and says it must have been improvised in the ball-room ; and of the A flat (Opus 42) he says that, like his earlier one, it is a *salon* piece of the noblest kind, and that if it were played for dancers, half the ladies should be countesses at least. This extravagant declaration, however, exactly hits off the distinguished and elevated nature of these valses.

When Chopin was in Vienna, the publication of a new set of dances by Strauss was a musical event of the highest importance, and Chopin wrote in a letter to his parents : " I have acquired nothing of that which is specially Viennese by nature, and accordingly I am still unable to play valses."

The ordinary popular valse of the Viennese was indeed foreign to his nature; but he proved amply that though he was unable to play down to the common level of the ballroom he could write dance tunes, which, to be worthily danced, would require Schumann's symbolical countesses.

Of the masterpieces of the second group, one can only say that, within the limits of the form, they attain perfection.   In these lyric poems some sections lose their pure Valse rhythm and approach to that of the Mazurka.   In this we trace the influence of Chopin's nationality, and see the native strain of melancholy and swift contrast of moods that distinguish the Slav temperament.

In 1855 Fontana published posthumously two Valses as Opus 69, and three Valses, Opus 70.   In 1868 a Valse in E minor was published and later one in E major, dating from 1829.

If, as some contend, all Chopin's MSS. left unpublished at his death ought to have been destroyed, the musical world would have sustained a severe loss in these seven Valses.

Kullak says of them that they waver between the two groups, but they certainly have more of the nature of the lyric poem than the dance.   There are two of the year 1829, one of which Chopin tells us was inspired by " her," Constantia Gladkowska, the ideal of his nineteenth year. They are both very melancholy, and like the others, which are of various and later dates, are distinctly sketches. They all end abruptly, and are much slighter than those he selected for publication, but they are, without exception, beautiful, and they become intensely interesting, as in studying Chopin's development they fall into their places in line with his other work.

The following is a complete list of the Valses in the chronological order of their composition :

(1) 1829. Valse. E major (without opus number).
(2)   „   „   E minor   „   „   „
(3)   „   Op. 69. No. 2. B minor.
(4)   „   Op. 70. No. 3. D flat major (Constantia Gladkowska).
(5) 1834. Op. 18. E flat major.
(6) 1835. Op. 70. No. 1. G flat.
(7)   „   Op. 69. No. 1. F minor ("pour Mlle. Marie").
(8) 1838. Op. 34. No. 1. A flat.
(9)   „   Op. 34. No. 2. A minor.
(10) „   Op. 34. No. 3. F major.
(11) 1840. Op. 42. A flat major.
(12) 1843. Op. 70. No. 2. F minor.
(13) 1847. Op. 64. No. 1. D flat.
(14) „   Op. 64. No. 2. C sharp minor.
(15) „   Op. 64. No. 3. A flat major.

" Of the Chopin valses, it has been said that they are dances of the soul and not of the body. . . . They are the most objective of all Chopin's works, . . . less intimate in the psychic sense, but exquisite exemplars of social intimacy and aristocratic abandon. . . . It is going too far not to dance to some of this music, for it is putting Chopin away from the world he at times loved. Certain of the Valses may be danced, the fifth and sixth, and a few others. The dancing would be of necessity more picturesque and less conventional than required by the average valse, and there must be fluctuations of *tempo*, sudden surprises, and abrupt languors." (Huneker.)

" Chopin's valses, partly because they are least technically difficult, partly on account of the popularity of this dance form, have become most widely known. Musically considered, they offer less of interest and novelty than his other compositions. What they lose in the rhythm of the dance they gain in innate grace and outward brilliancy, such as no composer hitherto has been able to impart to this form. The most interesting are those which are pervaded by that peculiar melancholy, *schwärmerisch*

vein, which is one of the chief charms of Chopin's music."
(Karasowski.)

" Chopin's valses, the most popular of his compositions,
are not *poésie intime*, like the greater number of his works.
In them the composer mixes with the world ; looks
without him rather than within, and as a man of the
world conceals his sorrows and discontents under smiles
and graceful manners. The bright brilliancy and light
pleasantness of the earlier years of his artistic career,
which are almost entirely lost in the later years, rise to the
surface in the Valses. These Valses are *salon* music of the
most aristocratic kind." (Niecks.)

OPUS 18.—Grande Valse Brillante.   E flat major.

Dedicated to Mlle. Laura Horsford.
Published July 1834.

THIS Valse was the first of the eight that were published
during Chopin's lifetime. It is the most dance-like
of all the Valses, and is the one that Schumann called
" Chopin's body and soul-inspiring valse." He speaks of
it as " enveloping the dancer deeper and deeper in its
floods," but Niecks resents this " extravagant and
romantic " criticism, and says : " It is altogether out of
proportion with the thing spoken of. It differs from the
Master's best valses in being not a dance poem but simply
a dance, although it must be admitted that it is an
exceedingly spirited one, both as regards piquancy and
dash."

In 1834 Chopin had arranged to attend the Lower
Rhenish Music Festival at Aix-la-Chapelle with Hiller.
The Festival was postponed, and Chopin spent the money
he had put aside for the trip ; probably he had given it
away to some needy countryman, for he was always
exceedingly generous. Then news came that the Festival
was to take place after all. Hiller was the guest of the
Committee, but Chopin could not afford to go. Hiller
urged him to see if he could not raise the money somehow ;
and at last Chopin bethought himself of the manuscript

of this Valse. He took it to Pleyel and returned with 500 francs.

The music calls for no special description or comment. It dashes along with a fascinating *entrain*, an originality, brightness, and freshness, a gaiety and a swing that make it ideal dance music.

Huneker says of it : "It is a true ball-room picture, spirited and infectious in rhythms. The D flat section has a tang of the later Chopin. There is bustle, even chatter in this valse," but he considers it inferior to the one in A flat, Opus 34, No. 1. In his "Mezzotints in Modern Music," in a more depreciatory mood, the same critic speaks of it as mediocre, and asks : "Is it not actually vulgar ? "

OPUS 19.—Boléro. In C major.

Dedicated to Mlle. la Comtesse E. de Flahault.
Published in 1834.

THE actual date of this composition is conjectural. It may have been written as late as the year of publication, but Niecks thinks it dates from a good many years earlier, "for it has so much of Chopin's youthful style about it, and not only of his youthful style, but also of his youthful character—by which I mean that it is less intensely poetic." It is not impossible that Chopin was instigated to write it by hearing the Boléro in Auber's "La Muette de Portici " (Masaniello), which opera was first performed on February 28, 1828. The Boléro opens with an introduction developed in the style of a free fantasia. The leading theme is Spanish in character, but not especially so ; as Niecks says, it may be described as a *Boléro à la Polonaise*. It is livelier and lighter than Chopin's real Polonaises, but apart from the first theme, there is very little local colour about it. Chopin's individuality, and the influence of his nationality, were too strong to allow of his subordinating them to the imitative faculty necessary to the production of music with strong local colouring. The Boléro is a Spanish national dance, which in its original form was sung as well as danced, and to this it owes its lyric grace and passionate character.

The rhythm of the bass is identical with that of the Polonaise form.

Huneker falls out with Willeby about the key in which it is written. The introduction is in C major, but the Boléro proper begins in A minor, and the *coda* formed from the second subject ends in A major. He says: "There is but little Spanish in its ingredients. It is merely a memorandum of Chopin's early essays in dance forms."

The Boléro strikes one, on close acqaaintance, as too finished a work to be relegated to Chopin's earlier years. It seems to belong to the small group of pieces composed about 1833 to suit the taste of the fashionable Paris public (see Opus 16), in which there is a distinct falling off from the poetic ideal of the Études and later works.

From a letter of Chopin's of later date, we learn that he received 500 francs for the Boléro, which was published under the fanciful title of "Souvenir d'Andalousie." The Comtesse de Flahault, to whom it was dedicated, was one of Chopin's many aristocratic pupils.

THE SCHERZI.

UNDER the title of Scherzo Chopin has left us four of his most individual and characteristic works. In them he created a new type, and he must have experienced considerable difficulty in finding a generic name to describe these compositions.

The word Scherzo signifies a jest, but certainly these works are not jests, and one has to ask with Schumann, "how seriousness is to be clothed if jest is to go about in dark-hued veils?" Neither are they Capriccios, for that title would seem to imply something playful and light. Some new name seems to be wanted, some term which should include and comprehend scorn and irony, with a touch of defiance and humour of a rather sardonic kind. They are perhaps the works in which Chopin most expressed his own inner feelings. The melancholy, the protest in them are personal, not national as in the Polonaises.

Liszt considered that it was in the studies and Scherzos that Chopin gave freest rein to the darker moods of his usually placid nature. There are passages in them that seem like " breathings of stifled rage and of suppressed anger ; they picture a concentrated exasperation and despair which are at one time manifested in bitter irony, at another in intolerant pride. These gloomy apostrophes of his muse have not been so well understood or attracted so much attention as his more tenderly coloured poems, and the personal character of Chopin no doubt had much to do with this general misconception. Being kind, courteous, and affable, and of tranquil and almost joyful manners, he would not allow those secret convulsions which tormented him to be even suspected."

Karasowski says of the Scherzos : " They did not exist before Chopin, or at least not in the same measure of independence, daring boldness, and almost Shakesperean humour. To appreciate to the full Chopin's creative powers, his pianoforte pieces must be compared with those of his contemporaries, for the Scherzi still appear so modern that it might well be said they were thirty years in advance of their time. The rhythm of the Scherzi far more than of the Mazurkas expresses a certain spirited opposition, a fascinating arrogance ; they may be regarded as a wonderfully true expression of Chopin's courageous individuality, decisive both outwardly and inwardly, noble, amiable, and poetic."

In his essay on " the greater Chopin," Huneker treats the scherzo movements of the two Sonatas as part of the group, and says : " These six compositions are the finest evidences of Chopin's originality, variety, power, and delicacy." But the Scherzi of the Sonatas must be considered as integral parts of the compositions in which they appear : in form, character, and intention they differ from the isolated masterpieces of this group.

The Scherzo in the Sonata and symphony was practically developed by Beethoven from the Minuet and Trio, which, in the hands of Haydn and Mozart, was the usual form of the third movement. From being simply the lighter and shorter form of dance measure, it became the

E

vehicle of the robust and titanic humour of the great German. Mendelssohn used the term as synonymous with capriccio when it was a question of an individual instrumental piece, but his efforts in this form were of a light, graceful, and fanciful nature, and derived from the earlier Italian masters. Several of Schumann's pieces in the Kreisleriana, for instance, are more nearly akin to Chopin's type, but as Huneker says : " The Pole practically built up a new structure, boldly called it a Scherzo, and, as in the case of the Ballades, poured into its elastic mould most disturbing and incomparable music."

OPUS 20.—First Scherzo in B minor.

Dedicated to Mr. T. Albrecht.
Published 1835.

THE B minor Scherzo begins with two crashing dissonant chords that must have appeared audacious in the extreme to Chopin's contemporaries.

"Is this not like a shriek of despair?" asks Niecks ; " and what follows, bewildered efforts of a soul shut in by a wall of circumstances through which it strives in vain to break ? At last sinking down with fatigue, dreaming a dream of idyllic beauty ? But beginning the struggle again as soon as its strength is recruited ? "

The first section is a whirl of stormy emotion ; Chopin seems to rage, to protest, to demand explanations. Huneker points out here a spirited likeness to the principal figure in the C sharp minor Fantaisie Impromptu.

The second section of the first part, marked *agitato* contains some of those curious harmonies which sound quite wrong if played slowly and determinedly, and yet are wonderfully interesting and beautiful if skimmed over rapidly in the way they are intended to be played. This section and the first, divided by a very striking and original passage of chords and octaves, are repeated alternately till the slow movement is reached (*molto piu lento*). Of the last two lines Huneker writes : " The questioning chords at the close of the section are as imaginative as any Chopin ever wrote." And he instances the *appoggiaturas* as evidences of his originality in minor details.

The slow movement, with its wide-stretching bass figure, and its "lapping, lilting tenths, in the richly coloured, luscious key of B major is by consent one of Chopin's masterpieces."

It contrasts wonderfully with the feverish agitation of the first part ; the re-entry of the opening dissonant chord breaks in with dramatic effect on the dreamy contemplative mood of the trio, but the composer is so enrapt that the one interruption is insufficient to break the charm.

The interrupted figure continues for a bar, then the second chord strikes in inexorably. Still the mood lingers, and a passage of ineffable sadness, strangely akin to the mournful piping of the shepherd in "Tristan," is finally interrupted by the re-entry of the first theme, *molto con fuoco.*

This Scherzo is perhaps a little over long, and it is often shortened by *virtuosi* by omitting the repeat of the section marked *agitato*, and going straight to the *coda*, a miracle of passion and fury ending with a chromatic scale which Liszt used to play in interlocked octaves, an innovation which should only be followed when technique is faultless.

A noble virile work—perhaps a record of Chopin's protest against a body too weak to allow the greatness of his soul full play.

Ehlert, in his Letters on Music, says : " I once heard the B minor Scherzo played among such a company of common buffoons (that is, on a programme of trivial show pieces) that it seemed to me like a rose bound in a bunch of thistles. For you will not suppose that the same taste that has an instinctive sense of the poetry of a Chopin work, also perceives the vulgarity of a bad virtuoso piece ? "

" This Scherzo is a proof of that regard for forms which even the most intense passion never prevented Chopin from observing." (Kleczynski.)

Of the *coda* Huneker says : " The heavy accentuation on the first note of every bar must not blind one's rhythmical sense to the second beat in the left hand which is likewise accented. This produces a musical rhythm that greatly adds to the general murkiness and despair of the finale."

OPUS 21.—Second Concerto in F minor.   For piano and orchestra.

Dedicated to Mme. la Comtesse Delphine Potocka.
Composed 1829.   Published April 1836.

" THE first allegro of the F minor concerto (not intelligible to all) received indeed the reward of a 'Bravo,' but I believe this was given because the public wished to show that it understands and knows how to appreciate serious music.   There are people enough in all countries who like to assume the air of connoisseurs ! The Adagio and Rondo produced a very good effect." This is a characteristic extract from one of Chopin's letters, dated March 17, 1830, after one of his concerts at Warsaw. (For the chronology and general review of the concertos see Opus 11.)

    The first movement *maestoso* is more compact and direct than that of the E minor concerto.

    Huneker says that it "far transcends it in breadth, passion, and musical feeling, but it is short and there is no *coda*.   Richard Burmeister has supplied the latter deficiency in a capitally made cadenza which Paderewski plays.   It is a complete summing up of the movement." The Larghetto which Chopin wrote when "his thoughts were with his ideal" (see Opus 11) is very beautiful. Liszt says of it that it "is resplendent with rare dignity of style, and contains passages of wondrous interest and astonishing grandeur.   Chopin played it frequently, and showed for it a decided preference.   The principal phrase is of admirable breadth, and the accessory details are in his best style.   It alternates with a recitative in a minor key, which seems to be its antistrophe.   The whole movement is of an almost ideal perfection ; its expression is now radiant with light and anon full of tender pathos."

    Hermann Scholtz, another celebrated pianist, said : " It

is a piece full of poetic charm.   In it all the attributes of a perfect work of art appear in the happiest union : noble melody, choice harmonies, agreeable figures, and the perfection of form, while the thoroughly original ideas are finely contrasted."

Kleczynski calls this middle movement an exquisite idyll, and draws attention to the very beautiful ornamenting that the original form of the melody in bars 7 to 10 undergoes in bars 26 to 29, and again to the indescribable richness of detail when the theme recurs for the third time after the recitative.   These beautiful ornamentations, however, must not be too much dwelt upon ; and enlargement of the details or sentimentalism would entirely spoil them.

Huneker thinks the final movement (Allegro Vivace in ¾ time) "Mazurka-like, very graceful and full of pure sweet melody."   But Willeby finds it impossible to speak of it in terms of unqualified praise.   It is certainly not as good as the finale of the E minor, and so helps to redress the balance which, as far as regards the two first movements, is in favour of the former work.

It is a pity that Chopin never attempted to write a third concerto when his powers were more fully developed. It might have been a masterpiece as supreme amongst its kind as his piano works in the smaller forms.   But perhaps the genius knew his own limitations and was wise not to essay something which was a little beyond his powers.   The weakness of his orchestration, and his resentment of the constraint of classical form, probably prevented his ever attempting it, and although the supreme master when writing for the piano alone, Schumann, Tschaikowsky, and Grieg have each surpassed him in the concerto form.

The Countess Delphine Potocka was one of the very few people to whom Chopin dedicated more than one of his works.   Her name appears on number one of the three Valses, Opus 64.   She had a beautiful soprano voice, and sang to Chopin on his death-bed, having hurried from Nice to Paris on hearing of his fatal illness.   Kwiatkowski said that she took as much trouble and pride in giving choice musical entertainments as other people did in giving choice dinners.   She was a very talented amateur, and gave Mikuli considerable assistance in editing his edition of Chopin's works.

THE POLONAISES.

IF we include the Polonaise Fantaisie, Chopin published during his lifetime eight works in this form. To these must be added the three forming Opus 71, which were written in 1827, 1828, and 1829 respectively. There is also extant a Polonaise in G sharp minor, which was published in 1864 and to which the date 1822 is appended. Chopin was only twelve years old when this was written, if the date is correct, but Niecks thinks that it was probably composed a few years later. A fifth posthumous Polonaise, dedicated as an *adieu* to William Kolberg, is attributed to the year 1826. Opus 3, a Polonaise for piano and violoncello, has been treated in its place as one of the three works composed as duets for the two instruments.

A Polonaise in G flat major, published in 1872, is of more than doubtful authenticity. There are, therefore, thirteen of these characteristically national works to be considered.

They are wonderfully individual and distinct, and reflect in a curious manner the events in Chopin's life and the changes in his character.

In the works of 1822 and 1826 a boyish grace is the leading characteristic, whilst in the three forming Opus 71 we can trace the deepening poetical and emotional value which became so marked in the two Polonaises of Opus 26. Between these came Opus 22, probably written in Vienna just before Chopin came to Paris ; it is a very good example of the music Chopin wrote to show off his own powers as a virtuoso. In Opus 40 we have two works of Chopin's prime, and Opus 44 and Opus 53 are masterpieces, and two of his great achievements. In the Polonaise Fantaisie, which was written in 1846, the year before his health finally failed, we can read signs of his approaching end. Although it shows no falling off in inspiration and musical beauty it exhibits traces of a broken spirit.

Appended is a list of the Polonaises in the chronological order of their composition :

1822   G sharp minor.
1826   B flat minor. (Adieu to William Kolberg.)
1827   Opus 71.   No. 1, B minor.
1828   Opus 71.   No. 2, B flat major.
1829   Opus 71.   No. 3, F minor.
1830   Opus 22.   Grande Polonaise Brillante, E flat major.
               (Précédée d'un Andante spianato—For
               piano and orchestra.)
1836   Opus 26.   No. 1, C sharp minor.
1836   Opus 26.   No. 2, E flat minor. (" Siberian " or
               " Revolt.")
1838   Opus 40.   No. 1, A major.   (Poland's Greatness.)
1838   Opus 40.   No. 2, C minor.   (Poland's Downfall.)
1841   Opus 44.   F sharp minor.
1843   Opus 53.   A flat major. (Heroic.)
1846   Opus 61.   Polonaise Fantaisie, A flat major.

One of the most brilliant chapters of Liszt's book is
devoted to the description of the origin and nature of the
Polonaise. Its beginnings are lost in antiquity, but it is
popularly supposed to have first taken definite shape
when, after the election of Henry III. of France to the
throne of Poland, the Polish nobles and their wives
defiled before their new sovereign to stately and measured
music. From that it became first a ceremonial, then a
political dance. Polonaises were written with words, and
so it gradually grew into a national expression, not only
of the political feelings and aspirations of the people, but
a mirror of their characteristics, their love of fighting,
their chivalry, gallantry, and fondness for display. The
palmy days of the Polonaise as a dance were over before
Chopin's time, and the type of music had become conven-
tionalised when Weber suddenly revived its glories.
Chopin followed, and whilst eclipsing Weber in his rendering of the warlike and distinguished phases of the
dance, he succeeded in expressing not only the glories of
the past but the sorrows and wrath of the present, and
the melancholy foreboding of the future.

The distinguishing rhythm of the Polonaise is an imposing and majestic triple time that tends to emphasise the
second beat of the bar, frequently syncopating it and
accentuating the second half of the first beat.

OPUS 22.—Grand Polonaise Brillante, E flat major.
Précédée d'un Andante spianato. For piano and
orchestra.

Dedicated to Mme. la Baronne D'Est.
Composed 1830. Published 1836.

THIS Polonaise was probably written in Vienna shortly
before Chopin came to Paris. It is the sixth and last
composition for which he wrote orchestral accompaniments, and after this he evidently decided that he had
better confine his efforts to composing for the piano alone.
Chopin played this Polonaise in Paris with the orchestra
in 1835, but this is the only occasion on record when he
did so. It is preceded by an Andante spianato, an Italian
term signifying equalised. It is in G major and $\frac{6}{8}$ time.
Niecks says of it : " It makes one think of a lake on a calm
bright summer day. A boat glides over the pellucid,
unruffled surface of the water, by and by halts at a shady
spot by the shore, or by the side of some island ($\frac{3}{4}$ time),
then continues its course ($\frac{6}{8}$ time), and finally returns to its
moorings ($\frac{3}{4}$)."

Huneker also sees a lake in the Andante : " It is a
charming liquid-toned, nocturne-like composition, Chopin
in his most suave, his most placid mood : a barcarolle,
scarcely a ripple of emotion disturbs the mirrored calm of
this lake."

Karasowski describes this Andante as "marvellously
tender and imaginative." Its beauty must be left to speak
for itself. It requires no excessive pathos or exaggerated
expression.

A short orchestral introduction ushers in the Polonaise ;
Chopin evidently wrote it to provide himself with a showy
piece for the display of his powers as a virtuoso. Although
it is lacking in emotional depth it is a most brilliant piece
of work. Perhaps it is a little long and lacking in variety ;
but as Huneker says, every note tells, " the figuration is
rich and novel, the movement spirited and flowing. The
theme on each re-entrance is varied ornamentally, the
second theme in C minor has a Polish and poetic ring,
while the *coda* is effective."

Scharwenka has re-scored the orchestral accompaniments, but it is on record that the Polonaise did not sound as characteristic as when played as a solo.

Niecks speaks of the general airiness of the style, and his remarks are rather slighting ; but if we take it for what it is, and do not compare it with Chopin's maturer efforts, it stands out as a work of genius. As a specimen of Chopin's compositions at the age of twenty, writing for himself as a virtuoso, it is intensely characteristic and interesting.

THE BALLADES.

THE four Ballades of Chopin are amongst his greatest works. As in the Scherzos we here see in him the creator of a new type. It is generally believed that Chopin owed the inspiration of these works to the poems of the Polish poet Mickiecwicz.

There is not in them the same personal revelation that there is in the Scherzi, nor have they the exclusively national Polish feeling of the Polonaises ; these Ballades are more universal, more broadly human. The kernel of each is distinctly a legend ; there is a story, a narrative to be expressed, and more than one commentator has postulated as necessary that a performer must have a definite idea of the story he thinks the music conveys before he can give a clear and consistent rendering of it.

Rubinstein, who had a very definite story in mind which he found expressed in the Ballade in F major, was, however, careful to insist that a performer must not be fettered to any particular interpretation. He said : " I am for the to-be-divined, and to-be-imagined, not for the given programme of a composition ; I am convinced that every composer writes not merely notes in a given key, *tempo*, and rhythm, but, on the contrary, encloses a mood of the soul (that is a programme) in his composition, in the rational hope that the interpreter and hearer ‘ may apprehend it. Sometimes he gives his composition a general name as a guide, and more than this is not necessary, for an extended programme of emotion is not to be reproduced in words."

Karasowski tells us that contemporary critics were puzzled at the novelty of the form of the Ballades ; some of them regarded them as a variety of the Rondo, whilst others, with more accuracy, called them " poetical stories." They are all in triple ($\frac{6}{4}$ or $\frac{6}{8}$) time, which something in the nature of music seems to render inseparable from the idea of narration.

Ehlert says of them : " Each one differs entirely from the others, and they have but one thing in common, their romantic working out and the nobility of their motives. Chopin *relates* in them ; he does not speak like one who communicates something really experienced ; it is as though he told what never took place, but what has sprung up in his inmost soul, the anticipation of something longed for."

Oscar Bie thinks that Chopin found his true form in the Ballades and Scherzi ; "this is the extempore form, which even in the Impromptus has for so long not been so un-fettered.   The dividing lines of the sections are drawn from free invention and the thought is constrained by no scheme.   In these Ballades we reach again one of those solitary peaks of piano literature in which improvisatorial invention and artistic construction meet again in a higher unity."

Niecks thinks that "none of Chopin's compositions surpass in masterliness of form and beauty and poetry of content his Ballades.   In them he attains, I think, the acme of his power as an artist."

Kleczynski says that the Ballades are certainly Chopin's "most complete and finished works, the works which have the greatest musical value. . . . They are veritable dramatic recitations, always changing, and full of sur-prises."

Krebhiel considers the Ballades among Chopin's finest inspirations, and Huneker describes them as " not loosely-jointed, but compact structures glowing with genius and presenting definite unity of form and expression " ; in short, all the commentators are agreed that in these four Ballades we have the finest flower of Chopin's genius and a priceless artistic possession.

OPUS 23.—Ballade in G minor.

Dedicated to M. le Baron de Stockhausen.
Published 1836.

WHEN Schumann told Chopin that he liked this
Ballade the best of all his compositions, Chopin,
after a long, meditative pause, said, with great emphasis,
" I am glad of that, it is the one I too like best."

This anecdote is from a letter written by Schumann to
Capellmeister Heinrich Dorn, and is therefore absolutely
authentic. In the letter referring to the Ballade he writes :
" It seems to me the most pleasing, but not the cleverest of
his works." Elsewhere, when reviewing the second
Ballade in F, Schumann spoke of this one in G minor as
one of Chopin's wildest and most original compositions.
This expression leads Niecks to believe that Schumann, in
the letter quoted above, meant that the Ballade was
Chopin's " most spirited, most daring work, but not his
most genial, *i.e.*, the one fullest of genius." (The German
is certainly ambiguous, " sein *genialischtes*, nicht *genialstes*,
werk.")

Karasowski speaks of this Ballade as perhaps the best
known, and says it is inflamed by wild passion, and claims
special admiration for its finish of detail.

Klecyznski, in his " Chopin's Greater Works," analyses it
at considerable length and speaks of its strong dramatic
pathos : " while answering the requirements of æsthetic
beauty, it lacks neither grandeur nor seriousness." He
wastes considerable space over an absolutely apocryphal
anecdote of a mysterious Englishman who kidnapped
Chopin and kept him a prisoner for a month whilst he
taught his captor to play this Ballade.

It shares with the third Ballade in A flat an extreme of
popularity. Huneker says : " They (these two Ballades)
are hopelessly vulgarised ; they have been butchered to
make a concert-goer's holiday. The G minor, full of
dramatic fire and almost sensual expression, is a whirlwind ; unsexed by women and womanish men, it is a
byword and a reproach. Little wonder that Liszt
shuddered when asked to listen to this abused piece."

Elsewhere he says : " I am reminded of Andrew Lang's lines, ' the thunder and surge of the Odyssey,' when listening to the G minor Ballade. It is the Odyssey of Chopin's soul." He then gives a glowing but very fanciful description of what he sees in the music, and continues : " With such a composition any programme could be sworn to . . . That Chopin had a programme, a definite one, there can be no doubt. . . . The true narrative tone is in this symmetrically constructed Ballade. It is a logical, well-knit, and largely planned composition ; the closest parallelism may be detected in its composition of themes." He does not mention his authority for saying it is " after Konrad Wallenrod " (presumably one of Mickiewicz's poems).

The Ballade opens with a short introduction of seven bars, a cello-like phrase of recitative in unison, closed by a wonderful suspended chord with a dissonant E flat in the bass, which forms the subject of much dispute among the commentators. A comparison of a similar device in the thirty-fourth bar, however, leaves no doubt that the effect was intended by the composer. At the *moderato* the legend begins in a beautifully undulatory melody. This is followed at bar thirty-six by a more animated theme in the nature of an interlude between the first and second chief melodies, the latter beginning at bar sixty-eight (*meno mosso*). This is a theme of great beauty, broad and full of a delicious langour. Another interlude (bar eighty-two) leads back to the first theme in A minor with a dominant pedal E in the bass. At bar 106 this gives way to the second theme harmonically varied and strengthened, climaxing *ffz* with great power and followed by a sudden lull. A long and beautiful quaver passage leads to a third recurrence of the second theme followed by the interlude and a third return to the first theme. A sudden passionate phrase leads to the *coda* in common time, *presto con fuoco* concluding with weighty chords and brilliant scale passages.

Throughout the narrative and dramatic spirit is self-evident. The introduction seems to say, " Listen, I will tell you how it happened." Then the various themes and interludes, recurring in fuller and more developed forms, seem to tell the story ; one can almost follow the development of character from incident, and the *coda* seems to detail the inevitable catastrophe, which, however, does not appear wholly tragic for all concerned.

OPUS 24.—Four Mazurkas.

No. 1 in G. minor ; No. 2 in C. major ; No. 3 in A flat ; No. 4 in B flat major.

Dedicated to M. le Comte de Perthuis.
Published 1835.

No. 1 in G minor.

KLECZYNSKI calls this Mazurka " a wonderful poem in its simplicity and with its characteristic scale " (at the end of the first phrase of eight bars).

Huneker describes this scale as " an exotic scale of the augmented second," and says the Mazurka is a favourite because of its comparative freedom from technical difficulties. The same might be said of the whole set, which is certainly the easiest to play of any.

This Mazurka marks a return to the rustic feeling of the earlier numbers, and the trio is full of hearty country gaiety.

No. 2 in C major.

Here again Chopin indulges in an unusual scale. The fifteen bars from bar twenty-one are in the Lydian mode, which leaves a very curious effect of tonality on our ears. Huneker says : " The trio is occidental, and the entire piece leaves a vague impression of discontent ; the refrain recalls the Russian bargeman's songs utilised at various times by Tschaikowsky." The opening phrase, marked *sotto voce*, is highly original ; is used in an amplified form as a *coda* with extraordinary effect. This number is a favourite of Karasowski's.

No. 3 in A flat.

A beautiful little Mazurka of undeniable attractions. The pauses in the sixth and tenth bars are most effective, reminding one of the seventh prelude. Its chief charm is the exquisite *coda*, which dies away with ineffable sweetness.

No. 4 in B flat minor.

This is the most important of the set, and indeed marks another step in the evolution of the Mazurka in Chopin's hands. As Isaacs says, it contains some of Chopin's choicest melody, and is developed into a masterpiece. Huneker calls it a beautiful and exquisitely coloured poem.

The second edition in the major contains a phrase curiously prophetic of the third part of the valse, Opus 34, No. 1. The first theme is much elaborated in repetition, so much so that the unison, marked *sotto voce*, followed by simple chords comes as a relief. Then begins *con animo* the most beautiful melody forming the trio, after which the first theme recurs to be followed by a *coda* of extraordinary charm. It is one of those separate inspirations of Chopin which he occasionally reserves for the close of his pieces; it is a "dying away" *in excelsis*. The tone colour should be largely helped with the soft pedal. If any one could be in doubt as to the merits of Chopin's Mazurkas, this *coda* should convert them instantly.

OPUS 25.—Twelve Études.

No. 1, A flat major (The Shepherd Boy) ; No. 2, F minor (Presto) ; No. 3, F major (Allegro) ; No. 4, A minor (Syncopations) ; No. 5, E minor (Scherzo) ; No. 6, G sharp minor (double notes) ; No. 7, C sharp minor (Duo) ; No. 8, D flat (Rhythm) ; No. 9, G flat (Butterfly's Wings) ; No. 10, B minor (Octaves) ; No. 11, A minor (Winter Wind) ; No. 12, C minor (Arpeggios).

Dedicated to Mme. la Comtesse d'Agoult.
Composed 1830–1834.   Published 1837.

THIS is the second set of twelve studies (see Opus 10). Barbedette considers them more original than those of the first book : " In them Chopin's individuality developed itself." Schumann devoted an interesting article to these Études. Writing as Eusebius he says : " The name to which we have so often pointed, as to a rare star at a late hour of the night, must not be wanting in our museum. Whither its course may lead, how long may last its sparkling light, who can tell ? But it can always be distinguished whenever it shows itself, even by a child, for it always displays the same core of flame, the same deeply dark glow, the same brilliancy. And thus I remember that I have heard Chopin play nearly all of them, 'and very much *à la* Chopin he plays them,' whispers Florestan in my ear. Imagine that an æolian harp possessed all the scales, and that an artist's hand struck these with all kinds of fantastic, elegant embellishments, ever rendering audible a deep fundamental tone, and a softly flowing upper voice—and you will have some idea of his playing. . . . These studies are all models of bold, indwelling, creative force, truly poetic creations, though not without small blots in their details, but on the whole striking and powerful. Yet if I give my complete opinion, I must confess that his earlier large collection seems more valuable to me. Not that I mean to imply any narrowness in Chopin's artistic nature, or any deterioration, for these recently published studies were nearly all written at the same time as the earlier ones, and only a few were composed a little while ago— the first in A flat, and the last magnificent one in C minor, both of which display great mastership."

Stephen Heller was especially enthusiastic about this set of the Studies. Writing in the *Gazette Musicale* of February 24, 1839, he says : " What more do we require to pass one or several evenings in as perfect a happiness as possible ? As for me, I seek in this collection of poesy (this is the only name appropriate to the works of Chopin) some favourite pieces which I might fix in my memory rather than others. Who could retain everything ? For this reason I have in my note-book quite particularly marked the numbers 4, 5, and 7 of the present poems. Of these twelve much-loved studies (every one of which has a charm of its own) these three numbers are those I prefer to all the rest."

Reviewing the Chopin Études at the close of his interesting and exhaustive chapter, Huneker says : " Astounding, canorous, enchanting, alembicated, and dramatic, the Chopin studies are exemplary essays in emotion and manner. In them is mirrored all of Chopin, the planetary as well as the secular Chopin. When most of his piano music has gone the way of all things fashioned by mortal hands, these studies will endure, will stand for the nineteenth century, as Beethoven crystallised the eighteenth and Bach the seventeenth centuries in piano music. Chopin is a classic."

These Studies are dedicated to the Comtesse d'Agoult. This lady, who afterwards became known in literature as Daniel Stern, had left her husband, the Comte d'Agoult, in 1835 to live with Liszt. By this lady he had three children, one of whom, Cosima, became the wife of Von Bülow, and subsequently of Richard Wagner.

No. 1.—Étude in A flat.

We have Schumann's authority, presumably derived directly from Chopin, that this first Étude in the second set and the twelfth in C minor were composed later than the rest of the Opus, and presumably this brings the date of composition to 1834. Schumann, in reviewing this set, said : " No wonder then that we were charmed with the pieces at once, hearing them played by himself, and most of all with the first, in A flat major, rather a poem than a study. But it would be a mistake to suppose that he allowed us to hear every small note in it ; it was rather an undulation of the A flat major chord, brought out more loudly here and there with the pedal, but exquisitely entangled in the harmony ; we followed a wondrous melody in the sustained tones, while in the middle a tenor voice broke clearly from the chords, and joined the principal melody. And when the Étude was ended we felt as though we had seen a lovely form in a dream, and, half awake, we strove to seize it again ; but such things cannot be described, still less can they be fitly praised."

Of this Étude, Kleczynski tells us that Chopin explained to one of his pupils the manner in which this study should be executed. "I imagine," he said, " A little shepherd who takes refuge in a peaceful grotto from approaching storm. In the distance rushes the wind and the rain, while the shepherd gently plays a melody on his flute."

This is very interesting as being one of the few instances in which Chopin himself provided a programme; that is to say, he suggested a poetical and romantic idea, which an interpreter might bear in mind during the performance.

Niecks agrees with Schumann in the latter's estimate of the value of these studies, namely, that the total weight of Opus 10 amounts to more than that of Opus 25, and that of the latter set, Nos. 1 and 12 are the most important items. Of this one he says that the impression left upon us is that of a tremulous mist below, a beautiful breezy melody floating above, and once or twice a more opaque body becoming discernible within the vaporous element.

Von Bülow says that a frequent use and change of the pedal, even during one continuous harmony, is almost indispensable. A slight delay on the first note of each group; and secondly, a slight quickening of the other notes is not merely admissible, but even requisite to avoid a dryness in bringing out the melody.

Kullak says that the melodic and important tones must emerge, as it were, from within the sweetly whispering waves, and that the upper tones must be combined so as to form the real melody with the finest and most faithful shadings.

Moscheles has left on record his unlimited admiration of the manner in which Chopin played this study ; the melody is certainly one of the most entrancing sweetness ; at the same time it has a rain-washed freshness. The tenor melody, which appears at intervals, leaves a kind of feeling of the harmonies of nature. In this study, use of the pedal is all important. Huneker says " above all poetry, poetry and pedals. Without pedalling of the most varied sort this study will remain as dry as a dog-gnawed bone." He alludes to the twenty-fourth bar as being so Lisztian, that Liszt must have been benefited by its harmonies.

No. 2.—Étude in F minor (Presto).

Schumann heard Chopin play this Étude, and speaks of it as one " in which his individuality displays itself in a

F

manner never to be forgotten. How charming, how
dreamy it was ! Soft as the song of a sleeping child."

Von Bülow warns players " that all sentimentality
would be bad taste. The piece produces its most charming effect when played almost entirely without shading,
clearly, delicately, and, to a certain extent, dreamily."
It should be played completely without passion, and
without any *rubato.*

Huneker says : " There is little doubt this was the way
Chopin played it. Lizst is an authority on the subject,
and M. Mathias corroborates him. This study contains
much beauty, and every bar rules over a little harmonic
kingdom of its own. It is so lovely that not even Brahms'
distortion in double notes or the version in octaves can
dull its magnetic crooning. At times so delicate is its
design that it recalls the faint fantastic tracery made by
frost on glass."

Kullak says : " As the fundamental tone is *piano,* the
artistic delivery requires an accentuation so light that it
shall not force itself upon the attention, but make itself
more felt than heard. If one will, one may betake oneself
in fancy to a still, green, dusky forest and listen in profound solitude to the mysterious rustling of the foliage.
What, indeed—despite the algebraic character of the
tone-language—may not a lively fancy conjure out of, or
rather into, this Étude ? But one thing is to be held fast :
it is to be played in that Chopin-like whisper of which,
among others, Mendelssohn also affirmed that for him
nothing more enchanting existed."

No. 3.—Étude in F major.

Schumann heard Chopin play this Étude also. He said
that it was " fine again, but less novel in character ; here
the Master showed his *bravura* powers—but what are
words for all this ? " As executed by de Pachmann, this
Étude enjoys a popularity second to none. Kullak calls it
" a spirited little caprice, whose kernel lies in the simultaneous application of four different little rhythms to form
a single figure in sound, which figure is then repeated
continuously to the end. In these repetitions, however,
changes of accentuation, fresh modulations, and piquant

antitheses, serve to make the composition extremely vivacious and effective."

The *tempo* should be very lively ; it must be executed
with care but " amiable *bravura.*"

Von Bülow cautions performers against playing the
sforzati on the light staccato quavers in a sharp, cutting
manner. Huneker says : " What charm, buoyancy, and
sweetness there is in this caprice ! It has the tantalising,
elusive charm of a humming bird in full flight. The
human element is almost eliminated. We are in the open,
the sun blazes in the blue, and all is gay, atmospheric, and
illuding. Even where the tone deepens, where the
shadows grow cooler and darker in the B major section,
there is little hint of preoccupation with sadness. Subtle
are the harmonic shifts, admirable the ever changing
devices of the figuration."

No. 4.—Étude in A minor (Agitato).

This Étude was one of Stephen Heller's favourites, and
he points out that it reminds him of the first bar of the
Kyrie of Mozart's Requiem.

Kullak says this " study is more interesting from a
technical than a rhythmical point of view. It is a study
in syncopation, the chief beats of the bar are marked by
single notes only in the bass, whilst the secondary beats
are burdened with chords which have to be accentuated
in opposition to the regular beats of the bar. Associated
with the chords and seeming to grow out of them, there is
a melody in the upper part which begins on a weak beat
and produces numerous suspensions, which, in view of the
time of their entrance, appear so many retardations and
delayals of melodic tones. All these things combine to
give the composition a wholly peculiar colouring, to
render its flow somewhat restless and to stamp the Étude
as a capriccio, which might well be named ' Inquietude.'
With the exception of a *rallentando*, the Étude is to be
played strictly in time."

Huneker speaks of its breath-catching syncopations and
narrow emotional range, but admits that it has moments
of power and interest. This study should give the impression of agitation, but not of confusion, as, alas ! it so

often does in incompetent hands. On the first hearing it appears as, perhaps, the least attractive of all the Studies, but it has a curious fascination, and when properly performed, Heller's preference for it can be easily understood.

No. 5.—Étude in E minor (Vivace).

This Étude has the character of a Scherzo, but its difficulty is a terrible stumbling-block. It may not be as difficult as some to play, but the first part, which is repeated after the trio, sounds almost more difficult than anything that Chopin ever wrote.

Kullak says that a performer should possess a fine feeling for what is coquettish or agreeably capricious, and he will then understand how to heighten the charm of the chief part. The *piu lento* section, which is in E major, consists of a beautiful broad melody, which, "if soulfully conceived and delivered, will sing its way deep into the heart of the listener. Surrounding the melody as with a veil are arpeggios in triplets of semiquavers, which are to be played almost without accentuation. These die away till they become almost inaudible and then the chief part is repeated with piquant little changes. Chopin is just as admirable in the finest painting of details as where the problem is to design grand contours with bold strokes. There is a short *coda* with brilliant trills and arpeggios rising majestically in crotchets to the final tone. Huneker says it is safe to say that this study is less often heard in the concert-room than any one of its companions, " yet it is a sonorous piano piece, rich in embroideries and general decorative effect in the middle section. Perhaps the rather perverse, capricious, and not altogether amiable character of the beginning has caused pianists to be wary of introducing it at a recital. It is hugely effective and also difficult."

No. 6.—Étude in G sharp minor. (Allegro. Double notes).

More than any other this Étude shows Chopin's wonderful power of making a technical problem artistically interesting. The player should concentrate his attention on the passages for the left hand, leaving the treble to ripple on and look after itself.

Ehlert says of it : " Chopin not only versifies an exercise in thirds, he transforms it into such a work of art that in studying it one can sooner fancy oneself on Parnassus than at a lesson. He deprives every passage of all mechanical appearance by promoting it to become the embodiment of a beautiful thought, which in turn finds graceful expression in its motion."

Huneker considers that in "piano literature no more remarkable merging of matter and manner exists. The means justifies the end, and the means employed by the composer are beautiful. There is no other word to describe the style and architechtonics of this noble study. With the Schumann Toccata it stands at the portals of the delectable land of double notes. . . . This study is first music and then a technical problem."

It should be played throughout in the Chopin-like whisper which Kullak mentions in reference to the Étude in F minor, Op. 25, No. 2.

No. 7.—Étude in C sharp minor.

This very beautiful and poetic Étude is not so much concerned with technique in the ordinary sense of difficulty.

As Kullak says : " It was created to serve as a study in delivery, but one must be able to rise above the prose of ordinary feeling and perception and to enter fully and entirely into the rich and deep soulfulness of the divinely endowed composer."

It is sad throughout. Karasowski adopts as a kind of motto for it, " The heart has not lost *something*, it has lost *everything*."

The study is written throughout in a kind of duet, in which one seems to hear a human voice sustained by a violoncello *obligato*. A writer in *Temple Bar* says : " The appreciative listener may hear if he will a lover's quarrel, where love alternates with keen regrets and tender rebukes with stormy denunciations. The same idea seems to have occurred to Niecks, but he is more prosaic about it. He calls it ' A Duet between a He and a She,' cf whom the former shows himself more talkative and emphatic than the latter. It is indeed very sweet, but perhaps also somewhat tiresomely monotonous, as such *têtes-à-têtes* naturally are to third parties."

Kleczynski thinks it " one of the most dignified among the compositions of the Master," and says it should be numbered among the Nocturnes.

This study met with considerable contemporary appreciation. The English critic Chorley thought it was a masterpiece, original, expressive, and grand, whilst Heller said : " It engenders the sweetest sadness, the most enviable torments ; and if in playing it one feels one's self insensibly drawn towards mournful and melancholy ideas, it is a disposition of the soul which I prefer to all others. Alas ! how I love those sombre and mysterious dreams, and Chopin is the god who creates them."

The opening phrase reminds one of the beginning of the G minor Ballade, but it is more emphatically a 'cello phrase, and it is impossible to agree with Willeby in his dictum that " The requisite interpretation of this phrase could not be given by any other instrument than the piano."

Huneker finds it " both morbid and elegiac. It contains in solution all the most objectionable and most endearing qualities of the Master."

" Perhaps there is no more poetical *adagio* than what Chopin modestly calls the Étude in C sharp (Op.25, No. 7), which we may class with the Nocturnes. What a noble and elevated simplicity is observable in this duo ; what melancholy, what exquisite form in the melodious turns ! That this work is often played badly and with mannerism is not astonishing. To those who are not specially acquainted with Chopin's style it is very difficult. It requires deep perception, and notwithstanding its powerful dramatic character must not be rendered with undue roughness or sharpness. One must here consider the bass to be the chief melody. The right hand, in this duo, usually answers with a degree of discretion, though at the same time very expressively. It must be played very slowly, with much sadness and great simplicity. The execution of the accompaniment in the repeated chords should be extremely soft and poetical. At the end of the first part the performer must avoid affectation, into which he can easily fall on account of the beautiful turns of melody. It is extremely important that he should not caress their beautiful thoughts too much, but that he should play with naturalness and simplicity."

No. 8.—Étude in D flat (Double Sixths).

Von Bülow considers this study the most useful exercise in the whole range of Étude literature. "It might truly be called 'l'indispensable du pianiste,' if the term through misuse had not fallen into disrepute. As a remedy for stiff fingers and preparatory to performing in public, playing it six times through is recommended even to the most expert pianists."

Hadow, speaking of Chopin's independence of the conventional laws which governed harmony in his day, says that Chopin, like Grieg or Dvořák, "takes our recognised system of harmonic laws and literally honours it more in the breach than in the observance. Are consecutive fifths and octaves forbidden ? There is in one of the Études a delightful passage which consists exclusively of the prohibited intervals."

There is a delicious freshness and abandon about this study, and the concluding passage seems almost cheekily defiant of technical difficulty.

No. 9.—Étude in G flat (Butterfly's Wings).

This is one of the shortest, but at the same time one of the most graceful and attractive of the Études. The German professors affect not to think much of it.

Kullak calls it a charming little salon piece in Étude form, and says that it requires a graceful light touch, while Von Bülow considers it musically of little worth and that " the amiable commonplaceness of its melodic content reminds one of the style of the late Charles Meyer. It is, however, so deftly put together that by a neat performance it can still make a brilliant effect."

Huneker considers it if not deep, graceful and certainly very effective. "It has lately become the stamping-ground for the display of piano athletics. Nearly all modern *virtuosi* pull to pieces the wings of this poor little butterfly. They smash it, they bang it, and, adding insult to cruelty, they finish it with three chords, mounting an octave each time, thus giving a conventional character to the close, the very thing the composer avoids."

No. 10.—Étude in B minor (Octaves).

The last three studies of Opus 25 are of greater emotional importance. Von Bülow finds in this one a certain Asiatic wildness similar to the Chorus of Dervishes in Beethoven's "Ruins of Athens." Its technical end is the cultivation of *legato* octave playing.

Kullak says of it : " The chief part is wild and agitated. The secondary part should exercise a tranquillising influence. It fulfils, indeed, its technical end but it is somewhat far-fetched and forced in intention and leaves one cold, though it plunges on wildly enough to the end."

Niecks calls it "a real pandemonium. For a while holier sounds intervene but finally hell prevails."

Huneker says that because many pianists make little of it that does not abate its musical significance. "The opening is portentous and soon becomes a driving whirlwind of tone. Chopin has never penned a lovelier melody than the one in B, the middle section of this Étude. It is only to be compared with the one in the same key in the B minor Scherzo. There is a lushness about the octave melody. The tune may be a little over ripe but it is sweet sensuous music, and about it hovers the hush of a rich evening in early autumn."

No. 11.—Étude in A minor.

This is the longest and most important of the Studies. It is usually known as "The Winter Wind." It has not, however, a wintry chill about it. It is more a reflection of late autumn. The opening lines of George Meredith's magnificent poem seem to fit the music very closely :

> " The Great South-West drives o'er the Earth,
> And loosens all his roaring robes behind him
> Over moor and field."

Von Bülow says of it that "its particular merit is that while producing the greatest fulness of sound imaginable it keeps itself entirely unorchestral and represents pianoforte music in the most accurate sense of the word. To Chopin is due the honour and the credit of having set fast the boundary between pianoforte and orchestral music, which through other composers of the romantic school, especially Robert Schumann, has been defaced and blotted out to the prejudice and damage of both species."

Kullak says :—" It is a *bravura* study of the highest order ; and is captivating through the boldness and originality of its passages, whose rising and falling waves, full of agitation, overflow the entire keyboard ; captivating through its harmonic and modulatory shadings ; and captivating, finally, through a wonderfully invented little theme which is drawn like a ' red thread ' through all the flashing and glittering waves of tone, and which, as it were, prevents them from scattering to all quarters of the heavens."

The air is given out to commence with in single notes, then whispered again with fuller harmony. As in Opus 25, No. 6, attention should be given by the performer chiefly to the left hand passages which form the poetic content of the composition. The march-like rhythm must be played in strict time. The scale with which the Étude ends is a rare feature in Chopin's work.

Huneker says: "It takes prodigious power and endurance to play this work, prodigious power, passion and no little poetry. It is open air music, storm music, and at times moves in processional splendour. Small-souled men, no matter how agile their fingers, should avoid it."

No. 12.—Étude in C minor (Arpeggios).

Elemental warfare holds sway in this, the last and in some senses the greatest of the Studies. It seldom receives justice at the hands of performers.

As Niecks says : " In it the emotions rise not less than the waves of arpeggios which symbolise them."

The great billows of sound sway up and down like the ground swell of the ocean after some terrific storm. If one could imagine the first Study of Opus 10 in Arpeggios

in C major, No. 12 of Opus 10, the revolutionary Étude in
C minor, and No. 11 of Opus 25 in A minor, melted and
poured together in a crucible, one feels that the result
would be something like this study.

Willeby says that the sameness of the form of the
arpeggio figure causes a certain amount of monotony to be
felt, but this can only be the result of having heard it in-
adequately rendered.   As Huneker points out, it is only
monotonous in the sense that the thunder and spray of
the sea when it tumbles and roars on some sullen, savage
shore is monotonous.

" Beethovian in its ruggedness the Chopin of this C minor
study is as far removed from the musical dandyisms of
the Parisian drawing-rooms as is Beethoven himself.   It
is orchestral in intention and a true epic of the piano.
How Liszt must have thundered through this tumultuous
work.   Before it all criticism should be silenced that fails
to allow Chopin a place among the greatest creative
musicians.   We are here in the presence of Chopin the
musician, not Chopin the composer for piano."

One would think it was impossible to look upon this
emotional masterpiece prosaically, but Kullak only says of
it that it is a grand, magnificent composition for practice
in broken chord passages for both hands, which requires
no comments.

In Von Bülow's edition there are important hints as to
the proper rendering of this piece.   He warns performers
against allowing the strength of tone to degenerate into
hardness, and that in the poetic striving after a realistic
portrayal of a storm on the piano, the instrument as well
as the piece may come to grief.

The pedal is needful to give the requisite effect and
must change with every new harmony.

OPUS 26.—Two Polonaises.

No. 1, C sharp minor ; No. 2, E flat minor.

Dedicated to Mr. J. Dessauer.
Published 1836.

SIX years elapsed after the publication of Chopin's first
Polonaise (Opus 22, *q.v.*) before he gave these two to
the public. In the interval he had settled in Paris, had
suffered the loss of his "ideal" lady (Constantia Gladkowska), had loved and been refused by the pretty Marie
Wodzinska, had travelled, experienced disappointments at
his comparative non-success as a pianist before large
audiences, and had brooded much over the wrongs and
oppression of Poland. These two Polonaises show clearly
by their increased depth and emotional expression the
result on Chopin's character.

In the Polonaise in E flat major the composer was
occupied chiefly with its aspect as a dance, and the possibilities of providing an effective display of virtuosity
within the limits of the form. But just as he treated the
national dance form of the valse, turning it from a
brilliant dance into a lyric poem, so in these two
Polonaises we find the form modified until it becomes
a subtly expressive vehicle of emotion. Although the
rhythm is preserved the dancing character has disappeared. Whether Chopin so intended it one cannot
say, but certainly it is easy to read into this Polonaise a
complete love romance. The first four bars, *fortissimo*
and *allegro appassionato* are of superb strength and open
the piece with a grand rhythmical swing. The second
four bars are an earnest question delivered with emphasis
and insistence, and bars nine to twelve are quite as
clearly an answer, timid and hesitating. This section is
repeated, and then comes a rhythmical figure, at first
played *sotto voce* but constantly increasing to *fortissimo*,
and broken in upon by curious lightning-like flashes in
the right hand ; this is followed by a melody, simple and
tender, and then the question and answer of the opening
are repeated.

At the *meno mosso* the trio begins. Kleczynski says : " Here simplicity and exquisiteness are combined in a really Chopinesque and characteristic way." He also points out that bars nine to twelve gain immensely in effect if played with both loud and soft pedals, and that the beautiful modulatory bars should be played very *rubato*. The first part of the trio is a solo voice ; but in the second part a tenor joins the treble with expressive cantilena passages like a 'cello *obligato*. This Polonaise has no definite end, a peculiarity which is characteristic of much of Chopin's earlier work in all the dance forms. In the later works, however, whether mazurka, valse, or polonaise, the *codas* are often fresh inspirations of great beauty and form most effective endings.

No. 2—Polonaise in E flat minor.

This Polonaise forms a strong contrast to the preceding one. In it we seem to hear Chopin brooding over the wrongs and oppression of Poland. It opens with a phrase as of sullen murmurs of discontent, and the fact that it is played *pianissimo* when the natural pianistic interpretation would be *forte*, gives a curious feeling of suppression. The very numerous *ritenutos* and *accelerandos* serve to mark the unsettled state of feeling throughout the piece.

Niecks says that it " speaks of physical force and self-reliance. It is full of conspiracy and sedition. The ill-suppressed murmurs of discontent, which may be compared to the ominous growls of a volcano, grow in loudness and intensity, till at last, with a rush and a wild shriek, there follows an explosion, the thoughts flutter hither and thither, in anxious, helpless agitation. Then martial sounds are heard—a secret gathering of a few, which soon grows in number and boldness. Now they draw nearer ; you distinguish the clatter of spurs and weapons, the clang of trumpets (D flat major). Revenge and death are their watchwords, and with sullen determination they stare desolation in the face (the pedal F with the trebled part above). After an interesting transition the first section returns. In the *meno mosso* (B major) again a martial rhythm is heard ; this time, however, the gathering is not one for revenge and death, but for battle and victory. From the far-off distance the winds carry the message that tells of freedom and glory. But what is this (the four bars before the *tempo* I.) ? Alas ! the awakening from a dream. Once more we hear those sombre sounds, the shriek and explosion, and so on. Of the two Polonaises, Op. 26, the second is the grander, and the definiteness which distinguishes it from the vague first shows itself also in the form."

Huneker, who says that this Polonaise is variously known as the Siberian or the Revolt Polonaise, calls it an awe-provoking work. " The episode in B major (*meno mosso*) gives pause for breathing. It has a hint of Meyerbeer. But again with smothered explosions the Polonaise proper appears, and all ends in gloom and the impotent clanking of chains."

To Karasowski it is " mysterious, gloomy, and shudder-ing. It seems to picture the suffering Poles banished in chains to Siberia."

Kullak says that " the beginning of the second part seems to silence for a moment the mental struggles. It sounds like military (cavalry) music passing by, and is to be kept strictly in time, but this is only a passing moment and does not hinder the previous disconnectedness and passionateness from resuming sway. Calm and peace are afforded by the secondary subject only, which also sounds like military music."

This Polonaise, unlike the preceding one, has a short but definite and very expressive *coda*.

OPUS 27.—Two Nocturnes.

No. 1. in C sharp minor, Larghetto ; No. 2 in D flat, Lento sostenuto.

Dedicated to Mme. la Comtesse d'Appony.
Published May 1836.

THESE two Nocturnes are amongst the most interesting of the whole group, being only equalled by the two forming Opus 37 and the No. 1 of Opus 48. Of the first in C sharp minor Huneker says : " It is the gloomiest and grandest of Chopin's moody canvasses. Its middle section is Beethovian in breadth."

Kleczynski thinks that it marks the culminating point of Chopin's creative genius. "An entire world separates us here from Field ; the thought of a poetry profoundly felt clothes itself in magic form." Willeby considers it the most dramatic of all the Nocturnes, and Huneker says it is a masterpiece and the great essay in the form. "The wide meshed figure of the left hand supports a morbid persistent melody that grates on the nerves." Niecks has nothing to say of it except to remark on this accompaniment figure as its most noteworthy feature. It certainly is wonderfully in keeping with the anxious and distressed character of the opening theme, and the way in which it changes to support the agitation of the middle section is masterly. At the close we have one of those marvellous *codas* of Chopin which constantly make the endings of his compositions so interesting and beautiful, that they appear to be separate inspirations, and one regrets that they are not the basis of a new work to be developed and amplified at leisure. Kullak speaks of it as ecclesiastic in colouring, and beneficent and conciliatory in effect. He finds in this Nocturne a psychological resemblance to Meyerbeer's song "The Monk." "The chief subject is gloomy in colouring ; it is like the melancholy lament of one who is done with life. In the secondary subject, bar twenty-nine, *piu mosso*, silent resignation gives way to bitterness and resentment, which, after climaxing in the first two strophes (bars twenty-nine to fifty-three and fifty-four to sixty-four, in the third (bar sixty-five *con anima*) veers to extremes, to covetous desires, to passionate longing for the pleasures of the world. To greatest ecstasy succeeds, weak and exhausted, the repetition of the chief subject " (bar eighty-four *tempo primo*).

This is the train of ideas that this Nocturne suggests to Kullak, and it is interesting to compare it with Kleczynski's somewhat melodramatic impression of its meaning. It appears to him "to be the description of a calm night in Venice, when, after a scene of murder, the sea closes over a corpse and continues to serve as a mirror to the moonlight."

The music is certainly very moving and dramatic, and

every one will have their own ideas as to its possible meaning. It is very interesting to see how it appeals to different temperaments, resulting as it does in very wide variations of reading. There is no doubt that Finck is right when he says " that it embodies a greater variety of emotion and more genuine dramatic spirit in four pages than many operas in four hundred."

No. 2.—Nocturne in D flat (Lento sostenuto).

Just as the Nocturne in E flat (Op. 9, No. 2) is the favourite of the amateur, so this one in D flat is the *cheval de bataille* of the professional. It exhibits in an extreme form all the sweetness, the refinement, the exquisite ornamentation and the luscious melody of which Chopin was capable. At the same time it demands very perfect technique and consummate taste for its adequate rendition. There are two chief subjects in it which are each repeated in strophes three times in transposed and enriched forms. There is a lavish use of sixths in the right hand, and a profusion of delicate fioriture. Kleczynski is of opinion that the leading theme should be played *piano* and repeated the second time *pianissimo* with both pedals, and the third time should be taken *forte*, in opposition to the markings in the music of some of the older editions. He objects, however, to the cadenza in the seventh bar of the third repetition being taken *con forza*, as directed, and thinks it should be played *con delicatezza*. It should really be a matter of choice, depending on the reading of the piece as a whole. It remains for every performer to be able to convince his audience that his particular reading is the right one. It is for him to make his version—(that blessed word of musical criticism)—" convincing."

Kleczynski quotes Fontana, Chopin's friend and publisher, in support of his theory that the third repetition of the theme loses all effect after the *crescendo* of the second repetition, unless it is taken *forte*. He considers it " an immensely rich composition, possessing distinction of form independently of the nobility of its main conception." Elsewhere he says, that it " has been compared to the highest creations of contemporary poets. His concluding bars are inimitable, they are sighs with truth stamped upon them, which rise in the air to lose themselves in the entrance of the heavens. The whole work shows the full development of the composer's youthful dreams and enchantments."

Huneker says: " It contains but one subject and is a song of the sweet summer of two souls, for there is obvious meaning in the duality of voices. It is a lovely imploring melody, and harmonically most interesting."

In Klindworth's edition, attention is drawn in the fourth bar of the second repetition of the leading theme to one of the harmonically interesting points that lay concealed in the unchanged homogeneous figure of the accompaniment. If the D flat, D natural, and E flat are lightly dwelt upon, a very original and beautiful effect is disclosed.

Kullak's otherwise very interesting edition does not draw attention to this or similar points.

Niecks has a word of caution about its enervating style. " Nothing can equal the finish and delicacy of execution, the flow of gentle feeling lightly rippled by melancholy, and spreading out here and there in smooth expansiveness.   But all this sweetness enervates, there is poison in it. We should not drink in these thirds, sixths, &c., without taking an antidote of Bach or Beethoven."   The Professor is right ; beautiful and entrancing as is the melody, it is with a feeling of relief, as of coming out into the open air from a conservatory, that we turn to the fresh, broad, and noble sweep of such a theme as the leading subject of Beethoven's *Appassionata Sonata*, the towering strength of the first movement of the *Eroica* symphony, or the simple majesty of the pianoforte trio, Opus 97.

OPUS 28.—Twenty-four Preludes.

No. 1, C major (Agitato) ; No. 2, A minor (Lento) ; No. 3, G major (Vivace) ; No. 4, E minor (Largo) ; No. 5, D major (Allegro Molto) ; No. 6, B minor (Lento Assai) ; No. 7, A major (Andantino) ; No. 8, F sharp minor (Molto Agitato) ; No. 9, E major (Largo) ; No. 10, C sharp minor (Allegro Molto) ; No. 11, B major (Vivace) ; No. 12, G sharp minor (Presto) ; No. 13, F sharp (Lento) ; No. 14, E flat minor (Allegro) ; No. 15, D flat (Sostenuto) ; No. 16, B flat minor (Presto con fuoco) ; No. 17, A flat (Allegretto); No. 18, F minor (Allegro Molto) ; No. 19, E flat (Vivace) ; No. 20, C minor (Largo) ; No. 21, B flat (Cantabile) ; No. 22, G minor (Molto Agitato) ; No. 23, F major (Moderato); No. 24, D minor (Allegro Appassionato).

Dedicated " À Son Ami Pleyel " and to Mr. J. C. Kessler (in the German Edition).
Published September 1839.

Twenty-four Preludes.

AS Niecks says in discussing the title Preludes, no one name could adequately describe the infinitely varied contents of this Opus. He writes : " This heterogeneous collection of pieces reminds me of nothing so much as of an artist's portfolio, filled with drawings in all stages of advancement, finished and unfinished, complete and incomplete compositions, sketches and mere memoranda, all mixed indiscriminately together."

When examined carefully, however, it will be seen that each Prelude is a musical thought absolutely rightly expressed, never a line too long or a bar too short. They are quatrains and lyrics perfectly finished, rounded and polished, never fragmentary or incomplete. There are twenty-four in the twenty-four different keys from C major to D minor, a fact which in itself seems rather to tell against Niecks's theory of a fortuitous concourse of atoms.

Rubinstein calls them the pearls of Chopin's work ; and Huneker says : " The twenty-five Preludes alone would

G

make good Chopin's claim to immortality. Such range, such vision, such humanity! All shades of feeling are divined, all depths and altitudes of passion explored. If all Chopin, all music, were to be destroyed I should plead for the Preludes." This is also Finck's choice, and would probably be the choice of the majority of pianists, for it would be difficult to find any music of the same length which contains so much that would harmonise with every possible mood and in which grace, beauty, distinction, and interest were so happily blended.

Schumann, in reviewing them, said : "I must signalise the Preludes as most remarkable. I will confess that I expected something quite different, carried out in the grand style, like his Études. It is almost the contrary here ; these are sketches, the beginnings of studies, or, if you will, ruins, eagles' feathers, all wildly, variegatedly intermingled. But in every piece we find, in his own refined hand, written in pearls, 'This is by Frederic Chopin'; we recognise him even in his pauses, and by his impetuous respiration. He is the boldest, the proudest, poet-soul of to-day. To be sure, the book also contains some morbid, feverish, repellent traits ; but let every one look in it for something that will enchant him. Philistines, however, must keep away."

Finck says of them : "There are among Chopin's Preludes a few which breathe the spirit of contentment and peace or of religious grandeur ; but most of them are outbursts of the saddest anguish and heartrending pathos. If tears could be heard they would sound like these Preludes."

But this seems to me only another attempt to force upon the memory of Chopin this hard-to-kill tradition of effeminate sentimentality. Carried away by a facile phrase Finck labels these Preludes wholesale. But what is really the case ? Fourteen out of the twenty-four are expressions of happiness, content, and gaiety. Seven depict conflict, protest, impulse, even rage. Only three are really sad or sorrowful, and even in these it is a manly self-contained grief, nothing hysterical or morbid.

Rightly does Niecks speak of the "almost infinite and infinitely varied beauties collected in this treasure trove."

Much has been written about the probable date of

their composition, and many are the disputes as to which of them, if any, were composed during the winter that Chopin and George Sand spent together at Majorca. A careful study of Chopin's letters, in which there are references to the Preludes, leads one to believe that the majority of them were composed in 1837 and 1838, before the journey to the island. It is just possible, however, that three or four may have been written at Palma or Valdemosa ; whilst it is certainly the case that Chopin revised the whole Opus at the latter place before forwarding it to his publisher, Camille Pleyel, who had paid him 2000 francs for the copyright. It is on record that Chopin said : " I sold the Preludes to Pleyel because he liked them," and that Pleyel exclaimed on one occasion " These are my Preludes."

The term Prelude, which strictly signifies an introduction or a piece played before a more important composition, is however frequently used in music for a work of intrinsic and independent value, and it is in the latter sense that we must look at the title as used to describe these varied tone poems.

Kullak says of them that " Chopin's genius nowhere reveals itself more charmingly than within narrowly bounded musical forms. The Preludes also are in their aphoristic brevity masterpieces of the first rank."

Liszt comments on the unassuming nature of the title " Preludes," and adds : " Yet the compositions which are thus modestly named are none the less types of perfection in a mode which he himself created, and stamped, as he did all his other works, with the deep impress of his poetic genius. Written when his career was only just beginning, they are marked by a youthful vigour not found in some of his later works even when they are more elaborate and finished, and richer in combinations."

The meeting with George Sand would seem to have at first hindered the composer in his work, as the Preludes are the only publication of the year 1839. It is noteworthy that the next six Opus numbers were all published in 1838. This in itself would seem to prove that most of the Preludes were composed in 1837 and 1838.

No. 1.—Prelude in C major (Agitato).

This beautiful little impromptu has perhaps more the nature of a prelude than any of the others, and therefore is particularly in place as the first of the twenty-four.

Kleczynski recommends that it should be played twice, the first time with less, the second with greater haste in the middle part, the speed becoming slower towards the end.

Huneker says, after speaking of the Bach Preludes, that although this one is not Bach-ian, yet it could have been written by no one but a devout Bach student. " The pulsating, passionate, agitated, feverish, hasty qualities of the piece are modern ; so is the changeful modulation. It is a beautiful composition, rising to no dramatic heights, but questioning and full of life."

No. 2.—Prelude in A minor (Lento).

Kleczynski dismisses this Prelude very briefly and in a most arbitrary fashion. He thinks it "ought not to be played, as it is bizarre" ; but this is a most gratuitous and unfounded assertion. It is difficult also to agree with Huneker, who finds it desperate, exasperating to the nerves, ugly, despairing, almost grotesque and discordant. He says : " A small figure is repeated in descending keys until hopeless gloom and depraved melancholy are reached in the closing chords. Chopin now is morbid ; here are all his most antipathetic qualities. There is aversion to life—in this music he is a true lycanthrope. A self-induced hypnosis, a mental, an emotional atrophy are all present."

This Prelude appears to have an extraordinary effect upon Huneker, for in his " Mezzotints in Modern Music " he says : "No. 2, with its almost brutal quality and enigmatic beginning, is for a rainy day—a day when the soul is racked by doubts and defeats. It is shuddersome and sinister. About it hovers the grisly something which we all fear in the dark but dare not define."

It is a piece that will appeal differently to varying temperaments, and it certainly is of extreme originality. It has by some commentators been seized upon as an evidence that Chopin must have written the Preludes during his illness at Majorca, because it is so morbid and febrile in tone, but the evidence of Tarnowski proves clearly that it was written before that time.

Notwithstanding its eccentric reputation it will be found by no means the least interesting of the Preludes.

No. 3.—Prelude in G major (Vivace).

The contrast of the fresh and delicate grace of this Prelude, compared with the gloom of the preceding number, is most characteristic. No two pieces could be more unlike, and yet one of the salient features of these Preludes is that when they are played consecutively as a whole there appears to be a distinct relationship running through them. One feels, for instance, that if in playing them through, one of the Nocturnes or one of the Études was inserted that it would at once appear strange and throw out the balance of the work.

Huneker speaks of the rippling rain-like figure of the accompaniment, " graceful and gay ; the G major Prelude is a fair reflex of Chopin's sensitive and naturally buoyant nature. . . . A ray of sunshine, but a sun that slants in the West, is this Prelude."

Willeby thinks the flowing semiquaver figure of the accompaniment is essentially French. Some commentator, badly equipped with imagination, has given this delicate little study the curiously ill-chosen name of " Le Ruisseau." This kind of publisher's title, when bestowed without the most sensitive care, is only misleading.

This Prelude is a fleeting vision of beauty, barely apprehended before it floats away. It passes like thistledown on a summer breeze.

No. 4.—Prelude in E minor (Largo).

This Prelude with No. 6 was played at Chopin's funeral service in the Madeleine. Niecks calls it " a little poem, the exquisitely sweet languid pensiveness of which defies description. The composer seems to be absorbed in the narrow sphere of his *ego*, from which the wide, noisy world is for the time being shut out."

It is one of the three Preludes which can truly be called sad, and it certainly justifies Shelley's line :

"Our sweetest songs are those that tell of saddest thought."

As Willeby says, the melody seems literally to wail and its sadness is exquisite.

Karasowski refers to it as a real gem which alone would immortalise the name of Chopin as a poet.

Huneker thinks that it must have been this number that impelled Rubinstein to assert that the Preludes were the pearls of Chopin's work. "Its despair has the antique flavour, and there is a breadth, nobility, and proud submission quite free from the tortured, whimpering complaint of the second prelude. The picture is small, but the subject looms large in meanings."

No. 5.—Prelude in D major (Allegro Molto).

This short Prelude is seldom heard in public. It is very difficult and curiously intricate in accent and phrasing. It is like some beautiful fabric, shot with gold thread in a curious arabesque pattern, which is waved before our eyes and whisked away before we have had time to apprehend its mazy texture. For Huneker " it is Chopin at his happiest, spinning his finest, his most iridescent web, and reveals musicianship of the highest order."

No. 6.—Prelude in B minor (Lento Assai).

With No. 15 this is perhaps the most played of the Preludes. With amateurs this is probably on account of their being two of the easiest.

In George Sand's "Histoire de ma Vie" the authoress narrates that they were detained and their lives placed in considerable danger by a heavy storm. Arriving late at the monastery at Valdemosa they found the composer seated at the piano playing this Prelude. The rain had just ceased, but heavy drops were falling steadily from the eaves, and the depressing and monotonous sound is supposed to be reflected in the reiterated dropping notes of this Prelude. George Sand says : " When I called his attention to those drops of water which were actually falling upon the roof he denied having heard them. He was even vexed at what I translated by the term imitative harmony. He protested with all his might, and he was right, against the puerility of these imitations for the ear. His genius was full of mysterious harmonies of nature."

Kleczynski points out that if this idea is taken as the musical foundation of the piece it is only fully developed in the Prelude No. 15, in B flat, compared with which the present example is a mere sketch. Liszt, again, who tells the same story in a different way, connects the same idea with Prelude No. 8, in F sharp minor, but certainly with less foundation. George Sand said of this one that "it precipitates the soul into frightful depression." Huneker thinks it doleful and pessimistic, although classical in its repression of feeling and its pure contour. For Willeby it expresses prostration of soul.

Though certainly sad it will hardly convey to most people such an exaggerated feeling of gloom, and there is no disputing its extreme beauty.

No. 7.—Prelude in A major (Andantino).

Set like a gem between the sorrow of the sixth and the feverish agitated anxiety of the eighth Preludes, this little miniature of a Mazurka never fails to exercise an enthralling charm. As Huneker says : "It is a mere silhouette of the national dance, yet in its measures is compressed all Mazovia."

No. 8.—Prelude in F sharp minor (Molto Agitato).

"How wonderfully the contending rhythms of the accompaniment and the fitful jerky course of the melody depict a state of anxiety and agitation." (Niecks.)

All through as far as the climax (the *fortissimo* after the *stretto*) this Prelude displays a feverish, agitated anxiety, which, however, dies down and is succeeded by calmer feelings.

It is noteworthy how Chopin, though using throughout a recurrent figure of semiquavers, has avoided monotony. Hadow considers it the most astonishing instance in music of this form of decorative effect.

No. 9.—Prelude in E major (Largo).

Multum in parvo. Though only four lines long this is one of the biggest and broadest pieces of music ever written. It is as majestic and as sonorous as Tennyson's Alcaics :

> " O mighty-mouth'd inventor of harmonies,
> O skilled to sing of Time or Eternity,
> 　God-gifted organ-voice of England,
> 　Milton, a name to resound for ages."

It has the grandeur of a cathedral aisle. Barbedette says that it is an evocation of sovereign majesty.

Willeby thinks it might almost be termed Schumannish, but admits that it shows all over it the individuality of its creator. Huneker finds in it a measure of grave content, with hints of both Brahms and Beethoven.

No. 10.—Prelude in C sharp minor (Allegro Molto).

The next, No. 10, must surely have been the one which suggested to Schumann the simile of eagles' feathers that he used in reviewing the Preludes. He said that on each one was written in pearls, " This is by Frederic Chopin " ; " we recognise him even in his pauses, and by his impetuous respiration."

This sentence seems to apply more to this short Prelude than to any other.

No. 11.—Prelude in B major (Vivace).

This Prelude is a miracle of concentrated grace and beauty, but it is so short that it is gone almost before one has time to enjoy it. Huneker calls it "another gleam of the Chopin sunshine ; " and Willeby says : " No one who hears the first four bars could help exclaiming, ' That is Chopin.' "

No. 12.—Prelude in G sharp minor (Presto).

After the sunshine of the last Prelude storm-clouds gather in this. Barbedette dwells on its passionate character. In its position between the sunny charm of the last and the calm beauty of the next this Prelude passes like a summer storm on the Lake of Como.

No. 13.—Prelude in F sharp major (Lento).

The most exquisite peace reigns in this Prelude. The opening section is devotional, almost prayerful. The *più lento* expresses an almost ecstatic happiness, while the modulations in the *coda* are so strangely original, unexpected, and beautiful that they are of perennial interest. Willeby exclaims : "Here is the most beautiful of all," and brackets it with No. 15 as his choice. Niecks thinks it beautifully melodious, and Kleczynski recommends that it should be played in almost religious style.

No. 14.—Prelude in E flat minor (Allegro).

There is a superficial resemblance in this Prelude to the finale of the B flat minor Sonata, inasmuch as it is in unbroken triplets, but instead of "sweeping by cold and unfriendly like the wind over a newly-made grave," this Prelude is hot with anger, and should be played with powerful emphasis. Huneker speaks of its sinister key and its heavy sullen-arched triplets. " The heat of conflict is over it all."

No. 15.—Prelude in D flat major (Sostenuto).

This is by many considered the most beautiful of the Preludes. The opening phrase is only to be matched by such melodies as those of the F sharp and D flat Nocturnes, while the middle section is impressively dramatic.

Niecks says that in hearing it there " rises before one's mind the cloistered court of the monastery of Valdemosa, and a procession of monks chanting lugubrious prayers, and carrying in the dark hours of the night their departed brother to his last resting-place. It reminds one of the words of George Sand that the monastery was to Chopin full of terrors and phantoms. This C sharp minor portion of No. 15 affects one like an oppressive dream ; the re-entrance of the opening D flat major, which dispels the dreadful nightmare, comes upon one with the smiling freshness of dear, familiar nature—only after these horrors of imagination can its serene beauty be fully appreciated."

Kleczynski thinks that in this Prelude Chopin elaborated the idea of the constant falling of rain drops which appeared in the sixth Prelude, and throughout the dominant pedal is almost continually used. It must have been the middle section of this Prelude of which George Sand was thinking when she said : " Some of them create such vivid impressions that the shades of the dead monks seem to rise and pass before the hearer in solemn and gloomy funeral pomp."

No. 16.—Prelude in B flat minor (Presto con fuoco).

This Prelude was a great favourite with Rubinstein, who used to play it with extraordinary fire and *bravura*.

It is a marvellous expression of determined impulsiveness. The first six chords sound like the declaration of some fixed intention, followed by a pause of concentration on the aim in view. Then an impetuous rush of resistless energy in the treble passages of unbroken semiquavers, supported by a dogged persistent rhythmic figure in the bass. At the *stretto*, the left hand, as it were, stops for a moment to shout encouragement in spreading chords, once more resumes its active support, gives a final rousing cheer, and then both hands rush upwards together in successful attainment.

For Huneker this is the boldest of the set. It is Chopin in riotous spirits. " The introduction is like a madly jutting rock from which the eagle spirit of the composer precipitates itself."

No. 17.—Prelude in A flat major (Allegretto).

This is another general favourite. With this Prelude Chopin won over Moscheles, who was at first not quite sympathetic to the composer. We read in his " Memoirs," " I called on him according to agreement with Charlotte and Emily, who are also quite enthusiastic about him, and who were particularly struck with the Prelude in A flat major, in the $\frac{6}{8}$ time, with the ever-recurring pedal A flat.

" His *ad libitum* playing, which with the interpreters of his music degenerates into disregard of time, is with him only the most charming originality of execution ; the dilettantish harsh modulations which strike me disagreeably when I am playing his compositions no longer shock me, because he glides lightly over them in a fairy-like way with his delicate fingers ; his *piano* is so softly breathed forth that he does not need any strong *forte* in order to produce the wished-for contrasts."

Kleczynski calls this Prelude a beautiful romance, and Niecks thinks it akin to Mendelssohn's " Songs Without Words," but when some one spoke slightingly to Mendelssohn about it the generous composer replied with unusual warmth, " I love it ! I cannot tell you how much, or why, except perhaps that it is something which I could never at all have written."

As Huneker says, the eleven booming A flats on the last page are historical, but this effect is often grossly exaggerated in performance.

No. 18.—Prelude in F minor (Allegro Molto).

There is a curiously close resemblance in this Prelude to Schumann's " Aufschwung" (Soaring). Huneker finds it " dramatic almost to an operatic degree, sonorous, rather grandiloquent, it is a study in declamation. This page of Chopin's, the *torso* of a larger idea, is nobly rhetorical."

No. 19.—Prelude in E flat major (Vivace).

> " What is so rare as a day in June ?
> Then if ever come perfect days."

These lines of Lowell's would be a fitting poetical motto for this exquisite Prelude.

It is the expression of contented happiness ; the melody goes singing along in unbroken triplets, with but a single sudden pause, as if to allow the soul to recognise that most exquisite of all joys, the conscious realisation that one is happy, a golden moment of life ; and then again back to the complete abandonment, to the enjoyment of the hour with just the delicate change of accent towards the end, by which Chopin seems to indicate that in this ideal happiness there is no shade of monotony or satiety. Not all tears are sad, for, as Edgar Allan Poë said : " Beauty of whatever kind in its supreme development inevitably excites a sensitive soul to tears " ; and this Prelude is supremely beautiful and happy enough to excite the tribute of emotion.

No. 20.—Prelude in C minor (Largo).

Twelve bars of some of the most beautiful chords ever written make up the sum of this Prelude. Barbedette says that it is a magnificent Chorale which would make a great effect on the organ. Commencing *fortissimo* it dies away to a *piano*, and the second half is repeated in a whisper.

Willeby finds a comparison with Schumann's " Nachtstuck," Opus 23, No. 1, interesting. There is a curious resemblance in form, but it is only a coincidence, and it would be unfair to Schumann to carry the comparison further, as the " Nachtstuck " is distinctly inferior in scope and power to this Prelude.

No. 21.—Prelude in B flat major (Cantabile).

Once again, as in No. 15, we have in this Prelude a melody difficult to match even from the Elysian fields of the Nocturnes. Specially interesting, too, is the novel diverging quaver figure of the accompaniment, which halfway through is taken up by both hands. Huneker thinks it superior in content and execution to most of the Nocturnes, while in feeling it belongs to that form.

Niecks says it is one of the finest of the collection.

No. 22.—Prelude in G minor (Molto Agitato).

This Prelude represents a short but triumphant struggle. It is in wonderful contrast to the calm beauty of the preceding one, and the delicate grace and fancy of the next. In fact, in studying these Preludes consecutively, one cannot but be struck by the genius which which Chopin has used contrast to heighten the effect of his work.

The octave passages in the bass are most effective.

No. 23.—Prelude in F major (Moderato).

For delicate graciousness and airy charm this Prelude must carry off the prize. As in No. 19, exquisite happiness is here again the note, not so buoyant perhaps, but quite as contented, with just a sudden touch of vagueness and elusiveness in an E flat in the last bar, that seems to float the melody off into infinity, one of those convincing touches of genius that hallmarks everything that Chopin wrote.

Huneker says : " It deliciously colours the close, leaving a sense of suspense, of anticipation, which is not totally realised, for the succeeding number is in a widely divorced key ; but it must have pressed hard the Philistines. Aerial, imponderable, and like a sun-shot spider-web oscillating in the breeze of summer, its hues change at every puff. It is in extended harmonics and must be delivered with spirituality. The horny hand of the toilsome pianist would shatter the delicate, swinging fantasy of the poet."

No. 24.—Prelude in D minor (Allegro Appassionato).

With this last Prelude we go back to a mood akin to that of the C minor Étude (Op. 10, No. 12), and the fall of Warsaw, to which it is a companion picture. It is the protest and struggle of a nation against oppression ; the sense of conflict is in the wide stretching figure in the bass, while the passionate melody continually urges to renewed strife. Just before the final outburst, in a phrase of unmatched and eloquent beauty, we feel the foreboding of ultimate defeat and the pathos of fruitless struggle, whilst all through, and in the three concluding sullen single notes, we seem to hear, as did Longfellow in the " Arsenal at Springfield," " the loud diapason of the cannonade."

THE IMPROMPTUS.

CHOPIN wrote four Impromptus, and in this small group of pieces his genius is displayed as convincingly as in any of his other compositions. The term

Impromptu, has been used so often by composers to describe works which are nothing if they are not laboured and obviously carefully thought-out compositions, that it is refreshing to find in Chopin's Impromptus that their leading features are spontaneity and untrammelled development ; they are Day pieces as opposed to Nocturnes ; they are not narrative in form as the Ballades ; they have no kinship with the national dance forms ; they have not the technical purpose of the Études, nor the personal revelation of the Scherzi ; they are and could be nothing but Impromptus.

Niecks finds their contents of a more pleasing nature than the Scherzi, and speaks of their charming lovable waywardness.

Huneker points out that " with all the freedom of an improvisation the Chopin Impromptu has a well-defined form.   There is a structural impulse although the patterns are free and original."   Later on he says : " Not one of these Impromptus is as naïve as Schubert's ; they are more sophisticated and do not smell of nature and her simplicities."

The fourth of the group, which was published posthumously by Fontana, has been called by him a Fantaisie-Impromptu, though it is difficult to guess the reasons which led him to affix the term Fantaisie to a piece already sufficiently distinguished by the term Impromptu, and so obviously belonging to the same class of piece as the others of that name.   It was written in 1834, which makes it the first of the group in point of time, the next, Opus 29, not being written till late in 1837.

OPUS 29.—Impromptu.   A flat major.

Dedicated to Mlle. la Comtesse de Loban.
Published January 1838.

KULLAK excuses himself from giving an analysis of the structure of the Impromptus in his annotated edition of Chopin's works, " because the small dimensions of these charming and emotional pieces facilitates their survey."

But although these Impromptus have not the length and importance of the Ballades or Scherzi, Ben Jonson's lines occur to us as we survey the exquisite balance and perfect grace of this little masterpiece :

"In small proportions we just beauties see ;
And in short measure life may perfect be."

The perusal of this Impromptu moved Schumann to write: "Chopin will soon be unable to write anything more without making people cry out, at the seventh or eighth bars already, 'That is indeed by him.' People have called this mannerism, declaring that he makes no progress. They should be less ungrateful. Is not this the same original force that dazzled you so surprisingly in his first works, that in the first moment perplexed and then enraptured you? And now that he has given you a succession of rare creations, and that you understand him more easily, do you ask something different from him ? That would be like cutting down a tree because it produces the same fruit every year. But his productions are not alike ; the trunk is indeed the same, but its fruits vary wonderfully in growth and flavour. The above Impromptu so little resembles anything in the whole circle of his works that I can scarcely compare it with any other Chopin composition ; it is so refined in form ; its cantilena is from beginning to end so enclosed in charming figuration ; it is nothing more nor less than so unique an Impromptu that it cannot be placed beside any of his other compositions."

The opening phrases are of amazing spontaneity and freshness. Du Maurier made Trilby sing this piece under the hypnotic influence of Svengali, and certainly for a vocalist to sing such phrases as these perfectly requires supra-normal influence.

Niecks says : " This Impromptu has quite the air of a spontaneous unconstrained outpouring. The first section with its triplets bubbles forth and sparkles like a fountain on which the sunbeams that steal through the interstices of the overhanging foliage are playing. The F minor section is sung out clearly and heartily, with graces as beautiful as Nature's. The song over, our attention is again attracted by the harmonious murmuring and the changing light of the water."

Willeby, who considers this Impromptu one of the most spontaneous and beautiful of Chopin's works, draws attention to the peculiar whirring effect obtained by the use of the D natural against the dominant E flat in the left hand. Wagner has obtained the same effect in his Spinning-Wheel chorus in the "Flying Dutchman" by the same means.

Huneker notes the relief to the ear of the strongly contrasted rhythms of the first and second parts. "The simple duple measure, so naturally ornamented, is nobly, broadly melodious."

Rubato should be very freely employed in the rendering of this section. Kleczynski says : "Here everything totters from foundation to summit, and everything is, nevertheless, so beautiful and so clear."

OPUS 30.—Four Mazurkas.

No. 1 in C minor ; No. 2 in B minor ; No. 3 in D flat major ; No. 4 in C sharp minor.

Dedicated to Mme. la Princesse de Wurtemberg, *née* Princesse Czartoryska.
Published January 1835.

No. 1 in C minor.

SCHUMANN reviewed this set of the Mazurkas. He said : "Chopin has elevated the Mazurka to a small art form ; he has written many, yet few among them resemble each other. Almost every one contains some poetic trait, something new in form and expression."

Of the first, Huneker says it is "another of those wonderful heartfelt melodies of the master."

The passage marked *con anima* is especially beautiful. This Mazurka is short but full of intense feeling.

No. 2 in B minor.

The special feature of this Mazurka is its curious insistence, especially in the trio where Kleczynski, whom we suppose wrote with authority, mentions that the constantly recurring phrase " perfectly realised the character of Ujejeski in his little poem ' The Cuckoo.' "

Huneker says : " It is sprightly and with the lilt, notwithstanding its subtle progressions, of Mazovia."

No. 3 in D flat major.

This Mazurka introduces us to a brighter, fuller tone than any that have gone before. Chopin is here in his aristocratic, almost ceremonious mood.   For once the nation or the nation's joys and sorrows are abandoned. There is a wholly French ring about this brilliant and elaborate dance ; although the alternate major and minor betrays its Polish origin.   At the very end, just as one has decided that Chopin means to end in the minor, he startles us with an abrupt return to the major.   Huneker terms this witty and epigrammatic, and says : " One can see Chopin making a mocking *moue* as he wrote it. Tschaikowsky borrowed the effect for the conclusion of the Chinoise in a miniature orchestral suite."

No. 4 in C sharp minor.

Again, as in the two preceding books, the last of the set is the most important.   Huneker says : " The sharp rhythms and solid build of this ampler work give it a massive character.   It is one of the big Mazurkas, and the ending, raw as it is—consecutive bare-faced fifths and sevenths—compasses its intended meaning."

OPUS 31.—Second Scherzo.   B flat minor.

Dedicated to Mlle. la Comtesse Adéle de Furstenstein. Published December 1837.

THIS is the best known and most popular of the four Scherzi.   A survey of the programmes of the Saturday to Monday Popular Concerts from 1851 to 1891 shows that this Scherzo enjoyed nine performances against seven of the B minor, and none of Opus 39 and Opus 54.

Schumann in reviewing it said : " The impassioned character of the Scherzo reminds us more of its predecessors ; it is a highly attractive piece, so overflowing with tenderness, boldness, love and contempt, that it may be compared, not inappropriately, to a Byron poem. Such a one does not please every one to be sure."

It opens with a very striking phrase, *presto* and *sotto voce*, which Niecks quotes as an instance of scorn in music. Von Lenz, however, tells us that Chopin himself taught that it was a question, and the second phrase is as distinctly an answer. "For Chopin it was never question enough, never *piano* enough, never vaulted (*tombé*) enough, never important enough. It must be a charnel-house," he said on one occasion.

These personal reminiscences of the composer's ideas are extremely valuable. If this phrase is studied carefully in the light of this teaching the right spirit of the opening movement can hardly be missed. It is a weighty question, a question of the riddle of existence asked of fate with bated breath by some perplexed soul standing in a vaulted antechamber to the grave. The answer is indeed scornful, and though the succeeding mood is lighter, even its most beautiful phrases are, as Niecks points out, clouded with sadness.

The melody, marked *con anima*, is so beautiful that it was probably the cause of Ehlert's exclamation, that " this Scherzo was composed in a blessed hour !" Huneker speaks of its winning distinction, and says : " It has a noble tone, is of a noble type."

The trio, or middle section in A, marked *sostenuto*, reminds Niecks of Leonardo da Vinci's " La Gioconda." " It is a pondering and wondering, full of longing."

This and the continuing episode in C sharp minor must be taken slower than the first part, and when the arpeggio passage in E major, marked *leggiero*, enters the former pace may be resumed. As in the B minor Scherzo it is permissible to shorten this one by omitting the repetition of the secondary subject.

The *coda* is of superb strength and energy. It has in it a ring of triumph. The questioning phrase recurs in an altered form, followed by the answer ; but this time we feel that the two are in accord, the scorn has vanished, the question is answered, and one of Chopin's greatest and most original works comes to a brilliant and satisfying end.

" How supremely welded is the style with the subject ! What masterly writing, and it lies in the very heart of the piano ! A hundred generations may not improve on these pages." (Huneker.)

" A very important composition, richer and more varied in emotional incidents than the other works of Chopin which bear the same name." (Niecks.)

" More highly finished than the Scherzo in B minor and equally impassioned, Chopin never loses the feeling of equilibrium ; always refined, he feels that passion should never descend to the prose of realism. He suffers, he has his fits of madness, but he never forgets to preserve his dignity ; he knows that it is not for him to exhibit to strangers the extreme depths of his heart." (Kleczynski).

OPUS 32.—Two Nocturnes.

No. 1 in B major (Andante Sostenuto) ; No. 2 in A flat major (Lento).

Dedicated to Mme la Baronne de Billing.
Published 1837.

IN these two Nocturnes there is a kind of reaction from the dramatic height and melodic beauty of the two forming Opus 27. They are seldom played. Neither in Willeby's list of Chopin's works performed at the " Pops," nor in the programmes of the Hallé concerts at Manchester, do they appear, and this is a fairly representative test of their popularity. It was, however, with Chopin a case of *reculer pour mieux sauter*, for in Opus 37 he touches the high-water mark of his efforts in this line.

There are three Nocturnes in this key of B major, but of the three by far the most celebrated is Opus 62, No. 1, fantastically known as the " Tuberose " Nocturne. To identify this one, therefore, the Opus number should be

quoted on programmes. The prevailing notes of this
Nocturne are sweetness, dreaminess, and simplicity.
Kleczynski says it should be played as simply as an air
by Mozart, and with very little pedal. A feature throughout is the way the melody is broken off and interrupted
by a sudden pause several times, after which a beautiful
cadence leads us to the close of the phrase. The point,
however, which lends the greatest interest to this Nocturne
is the abrupt introduction of a *coda*, dramatic in form and
of powerful energy. As Huneker says, it is the best part
of the piece. "It is in the minor, and is like the drum-
beat of a tragedy. The entire ending, a stormy recitative,
is in stern contrast to the dreamy beginning."

Kullak says : "The Nocturne expresses feelings, such
as awaken in quiet hours of solitude far from the noisy
world, when one is absorbed in thought and reverie and
dear familiar images arise in memory. The tender lyric
mood continues to the *coda*. The latter is strangely and
overpoweringly dramatic in effect. It is as if something
coming from without (perhaps repeated strokes of the
clock, or a rapping at the door) suddenly made an end of
all reveries. In correspondence with the prevailing mood
of the Nocturne, the delivery must be tenderly dreamy
and tranquil throughout. The more passionate outpourings
must be rendered with moderation so as to avoid
glaring contrasts. The *coda* is to be executed drama-
tically (*recitativo*).

Niecks thinks that both these Nocturnes are pretty
specimens of Chopin's style of writing in the tender, calm,
and dreamy moods. He prefers the quiet pellucid first
one. "It is very simple, ornaments being very sparingly
introduced. The quietness and simplicity are, however,
at last disturbed by an interrupted cadence, sombre
sounds as of a kettle drum and a passionate recitative
with intervening abrupt chords."

No. 2.—Nocturne in A flat.

Here again we have simplicity as the dominant note (see
Opus 32, No. 1), but when the second subject appears, the
mood changes and works up to a stormy and passionate
expression of emotion. This passes and the first theme

recurs, but it now swells and surges as if still under the influence of the stormy mood. It is some time before it recovers its calm tenderness and dies away with a *pianissimo* repetition of the two opening bars, the spreading chords of which thus form both an introduction and a *coda*.

Kleczynski recommends that a more drawing-room style should be employed in this Nocturne in contrast to the Mozartian simplicity recommended for the preceding one. The ornaments in the fourteenth and twenty-second bars should be played rapidly and very softly. He urges caution against the excessive use of the *tempo rubato* in the middle section.

There is in this Nocturne a distinct reversion to the Field type, the opening reminding us of that master's Nocturne in B flat, which is the reason possibly why Huneker, notwithstanding the dramatic nature of the second section, finds the work in its entirety a little tiresome.

Niecks dismisses it briefly as having less originality and pith than its companion. Nevertheless, it forms a very clear and definite picture of a mental mood, and there will be times when it will appeal irresistibly to nearly every one.

OPUS 33.—Four Mazurkas.

No. 1 in G sharp minor ; No. 2 in D major ; No. 3 in C major ; No. 4 in B minor.

IN reviewing these Mazurkas Schumann wrote : " His forms seem to grow ever brighter and lighter—or are we becoming accustomed to his style ? These Mazurkas will charm every one instantly, and seem to us more popular in character than his earlier ones."

As a whole they are perhaps simpler in emotional content, and brighter than any other set.

No. 1 in G sharp minor.

This is a simple and plaintive melody. Huneker calls it moody but tender-hearted, epithets which describe it far more accurately than others he employs, " curt and rather depressing."

It is brief, but the phrases are well rounded, and it is not really melancholy.

No. 2 in D Major.

A vocal setting of this bright, brilliant, and taking Mazurka has ensured it even a wider popularity than it would in any case have attained. The song, arranged by Viardot-Garcia, is a favourite of light sopranos of the French School. There is a curious intermezzo where the same phrase is repeated sixteen times, giving, as Kleczynski remarks, a character of determined enjoyment, dancing, notwithstanding misery and trouble or of childish naiveté with constant returning to and moving round one idea.

Huneker describes this Mazurka as " bustling, graceful, and unrestrained vitality—bright and not particularly profound."

It fairly bubbles with high spirits, and has such a lilting, babbling character that it is not to be wondered at that it attracted attempts to set it vocally. It is almost the only instance of a Chopin transcription being more than moderately successful.

No. 3 in C major.

Short but very beautiful, this Mazurka is best known as having been, according to Van Lenz, the cause of a sharp quarrel between Chopin and Meyerbeer. The latter, entering Chopin's room while the composer was playing this Mazurka, remarked that it was in $\frac{2}{4}$ time ; " $\frac{3}{4}$," replied Chopin flushing angrily, and Meyerbeer insisting, the two actually quarrelled about this trifling matter. Meyerbeer must, however, have been rather offensive in his manner, as a similar remark is chronicled by Charles Hallé as having been made by himself. " Chopin denied it stoutly, until I made him play, and counted audibly four in the bar, which fitted perfectly. Then he laughed and explained that it was the national character of the dance which created the oddity." Hallé explains that the illusion arose from his dwelling so much longer on the first note of the bar.

No. 4 in B minor.

There is a distinct vein of humour in this Mazurka, for which two "programmes" have been put forward. It inspired a Polish poet, Zelenski, to write a comic poem, which, however, like the anecdote of the little Jew is pointless and coarse and totally unfitted for association with the delicate charm and quaint turns of the music. Kleczynski associated it with a poem called "The Dragoon," by another poet, Ujejeski, which again seems even less fitted to the music, although less unworthy in subject.

It is perhaps not unnatural that an attempt should have been made to foist a story on to this Mazurka, for it has a narrative tone. It seems to express some comedy of peasant manners, a half-humorous, half-cynical outlook on life ; but such an interpretation is yet to seek.

OPUS 34.—Trois Valses Brillantes.

No. 1, A flat (Vivace) ; No. 2, A minor (Lento) ; No. 3, F major (Vivace.   The Cat Valse).
Published 1838.

No. 1.—A flat.
Dedicated to Mlle. de Thun-Hohenstein.

HERE, as Niecks says, " We find ourselves face to face with true dance poems. How brisk the introductory bars of the first of these three Valses ! And what a striking manifestation of the spirit of that dance all that follows ! We feel the whirling motions ; and when at the seventeenth bar of the second part, the quaver figure enters, we think we see the flowing dresses sweeping round. Again what vigour in the third part, and how coaxingly tender the fourth. And lastly, the brilliant conclusion, the quavers intertwined with triplets."

Of these three Valses also Schumann writes enthusiastically. He says they "will delight above all things, so different in type as they are, from the ordinary ones, and of such a kind as only Chopin dared to venture on or even invent, while gazing inspired among the dancers whom he has just called up by his Preludes, and while thinking of far different things than those that are to be danced there. Such a wave of life flows through them, that they seem to have been improvised in the dancing-room.

Huneker considers that this Valse may be danced as far as its *coda* which he calls "dithyrambic," and he draws attention to a passage in the *coda* (bars eighteen-twentyfour) which resembles one in the Préamble of Schuman's Carnival. He calls it a debt that Schumann owes Chopin, but considering that the Carnival was written in 1834, and the Valse in 1838, the debt is presumably the other way.

At the commencement of the Valse after the introduction, some editions have *dolce* and some *forte* as the expression mark. Klindworth and Kullak, however, agree that the latter is preferable as harmonising in mood with the brilliantly climaxing passages of the introduction. This Valse whilst equally brilliant, shows more inspiration and poetic quality than the first, Opus 18 in E flat.

No. 2.—Valse in A minor (Lento).
Dedicated to Mme. d'Ivri.

Stephen Heller told Niecks an interesting anecdote about this Valse. Chopin was at his publishers (Schlesingers) when Heller came in and ordered all the Valses. The composer asked him which he liked best. Heller mentioned this one, and Chopin said, "I am glad you like that one, it is also my favourite," and he straightway invited Heller to lunch with him at the Café Riche.

It is the least valse-like of all the Valses, which perhaps accounts for Chopin's preference. The opening is a contemplative, melancholy, slow valse ; there is nothing danceable about it. At the thirty-seventh bar the *tempo* should be quickened, the rhythm here becoming more that of a Mazurka than a Valse, but at the change of key to A major (*sostenuto*, bar fifty-three) the melody which Huneker describes as of "exceeding loveliness," should be played as slowly as the opening section. At bar sixty-nine, the echo of this melody in the minor has a peculiarly haunting effect. The different sections recur with continually increasing charm, and as Huneker says, " It is elegiac in tone even unto the Mendelssohn point." The *coda* commences with a fascinating quaver passage in the left hand, which should be played in rather quicker time and with exquisite attention to the gradations of tone.

There is no occasion to force the sentiment here, the phrases sing themselves naturally, and the Valse closes with the opening passage in dreamy melancholy. As Niecks says : " The composer evidently found pleasure in giving way to this delicious languor, in indulging in these melancholy thoughts full of sweetest, tenderest loving and longing."

No. 3.—Valse in F major (Vivace).
Dedicated to Mlle. A. d'Eichthal.

"Improvised in the ball-room." This saying of Schumann's might perhaps more appropriately be written over this Valse than any of the others. At the same time, it is an improvised " dance poem " and not a valse to dance to. There is so much energy about the introduction, such a wild whirling and turning when the melody enters at bar seventeen, that Barbedette terms it savage and fantastic, a veritable inspiration " *à la* Weber." A greater contrast to the tender melancholy of the preceding Valse could hardly be imagined. The *appoggiatura* passage in the fourth section is probably responsible for the somewhat absurd nickname occasionally bestowed on this piece, " the Cat Valse." The legend is that Chopin's cat leapt upon the keyboard as he was composing, and running up and down gave him the idea of this particular phrase ; possibly the similarity of the quaver passage at the commencement to that at the beginning of the well-known " Dog Valse," coupled with the amateur's preference for some title by which to identify a composition more easily than by key or Opus number, is equally responsible for its name.

Keeping up its character of an improvisation, this Valse is very brief ; it is over in a flash of energy and high spirits. Huneker calls it " a whirling wild dance of atoms. It has the *perpetuum mobile* quality, and older Masters would have prolonged its giddy arabesques into pages of senseless spinning. It is quite long enough as it is. The second theme is better, but the *appoggiaturas* are flippant. It buzzes to the finish."

OPUS 35.—Sonata in B flat minor.

Composed 1838 ; published 1840.

ABOUT this B flat minor Sonata, Opus 35, which contains the celebrated Funeral March as a slow movement, there are as many opinions as men. Schumann is often quoted, or rather misrepresented by partial quotation, in support of the theory that Chopin was not great enough to master the Sonata form. This theory causes Finck, original and daring as ever, to flash out : " Chopin not great enough ! The fact is, that the Sonata form could not master him." What Schumann really said was, " that the idea of calling this work a Sonata was a caprice, if not a jest, for Chopin has simply bound together four of his wildest children, to smuggle them under this name into a place to which they could not else have penetrated."

But surely Schumann never meant to say that these four wildest children were not related and were only bound together fortuitously ; it is the calling the work a Sonata that he describes as a jest, not the juxtaposition of the four movements. It is true that later on he says an adagio in D flat would have been more effective than the Funeral March, which has some repellant points, and that the finale sounds more like a joke than a piece of music. To one of Schumann's morbid temperament the March may have been unendurably poignant, so that we are bound to consider the personal equation in considering his epithet repellant, whilst his dictum as to the finale must be read with the context. He goes on to say : " Yet we must confess that even from this joyless, unmelodious movement, an original, a terrible mind breathes forth, the preponderance of which annihilates resistance, so that we listen, fascinated and uncomplaining, to the end—for this is not music. The Sonata commences enigmatically and closes with an ironical smile—a sphinx."

This last quotation is a curious commentary on what he said at first, namely, that the finale was a joke ; and when Schumann says it is not music, it fills one with a haunting fear that never can a critic, even when himself a man of genius, keep abreast of the *Zeitgeist*, the first breath of which is always felt in the work of that most sensitive of electric recorders, the brain of a musician. For which of us, with Wagner or Richard Strauss in our minds, will venture to deny that this finale is music, and music of the highest poetical value. But it must be heard in its right place at the end of this so-called Sonata, which is not a Sonata in the classical sense, but *is* an organic and indivisible whole, a tone poem, a reading of life on earth, even such a life as that of Chopin himself. An inner life of strenuous fighting against drawbacks, over-sensitiveness, ill-health, and physical weakness, starting from the first, as it were, with a sigh, almost a groan, of resignation, then conflict and struggle, but not without moments of rest and perfect happiness, this extending through the two first movements, which all admit are organically connected with each other. Then comes the stumbling-block, the sudden abrupt clang and toll of the funeral march, just as we might have been looking for the fruition of the earlier stress and striving. After all, what is it but the too oft repeated tale of untimely death. There had been no hint of the catastrophe in the idyllic close of the second movement. As ever, death came suddenly, blighting the fairest promise, and though in the trio sweet memories of the past blend with hopes of immortality or the everlasting peace of Nirvana, for the survivors there is only, as in Chopin's own version of the meaning of the finale, the subdued talk of surface trifles, which masks the aching heart below ; or as Kullak more poetically, but metaphorically suggests : " The autumn wind whirling away the withered leaves over the fresh grave." " It must be played," he says, " gloomily, and with self-absorbed expression. It must rush by, cold and unfriendly. Then, to be sure, it will not enrapture the hearer, but no one will fail to perceive the logic of its connection with the Funeral March." It is

> " The ground whirl of the perished leaves of hope,
> The wind of death's imperishable wing."

All Chopin's commentators and biographers have written at such length about this Sonata that exigencies of space prevent full quotation. This work, is perhaps the most interesting, and certainly the most discussed, of Chopin's works.

The first movement opens with a brief introduction of four bars marked *grave*, passing at the double bar to an agitated accompaniment figure in the bass *doppio movimento*, and after four more bars the main theme enters marked *agitato*. After a climax *ff*, with a strong syncopated accent, the second theme enters *piano sostenuto*. Chopin by this time certainly understood the value of contrast of themes in Sonata writing. It is a beautiful broad melody, demanding, as Kullak points out, a quieter *tempo* than the anxious haste of the first theme. At the *stretto* the time is quickened up again to the repeat.

The working out, commencing *sotto voce*, is exquisite in detail, and leads to a resumption of the second theme in B flat major. The movement comes to a brilliant and exciting close with a powerful *stretto* and a brief *coda* of twelve bars.

The Scherzo opens with an impetuous gloomy and powerful movement with swirling crescendos demanding enormous wrist power. At the double bar the ascending chromatic passages on chords of the sixth are wonderfully suggestive of the whistling of the wind, and with a series of crashing chords and octaves, the storm dies down and is succeeded by a melody of heavenly beauty, *più lento*. The first movement returns and is closed with a marvellous effect by a brief *coda* formed from the melody of the trio. The storm and calm represented are, however, contrasts of human emotion ; notwithstanding the wind-like passages no one could mistake this music for a transcript of nature.

Then follows the well-known Funeral March. Schumann's idea that the March is not an integral portion of the Sonata obtains some justification from a letter written by Chopin from Nohant in the summer of 1839.

"I am composing here a Sonata in B flat minor, in which will be the Funeral March which you have already. There is an Allegro, then a Scherzo, in E flat minor, the March, and a short finale of about three pages. The left hand *unisono* with the right hand are gossiping after the March."

This March is too well known to require detailed description. Kullak considers the bass of the first part is an imitation of the tolling of the bell with which the funeral *cortège* begins to move, and even suggests that the left hand may play two bars of the bass alone before the theme of the March commences. Karasowski says : " Such a funeral march could only have been written by him, in whose soul the pain and grief of the entire nation resounded as an echo."

There are chords and harmonies here which tear the heart strings, but the melody of the trio with its peculiar detached serenity brings calmness and consolation in its train.

The resumption of the March once more precipitates us into the very luxury of woe ; as the last bars die away we are left in the mood to appreciate the weird poetry of the finale. It would be a waste of words to try and make any one see the poetic value of this wonderful movement, to whom it does not at once appeal as the only possible end to the work. (Mendelssohn, for instance, when asked his opinion of it, said briefly, " Oh, I abhor it.")

Kullak has hit upon exactly the right terms to describe how it should be rendered if the effect is not to be missed. It " is to be played gloomily and with self-absorbed expression without special regard to the Étude-like brilliancy. It must rush by cold and unfriendly." The rest of the comment has already been quoted above.

This Sonata is one of the priceless possessions of music. It must for ever rank with the masterpieces of all ages. It may not be, it is not, a model of classical form, but in depth and beauty of poetic content it is second to none.

OPUS 36.—Second Impromptu.   F sharp minor.

Composed 1838.   Published 1840.

THIS is an Impromptu suggested by memory rather than
anticipation.   There is a touch of the Ballade-like
quality of narration about it, a suggestion of the sensuous
contemplation of the Nocturnes.

Niecks and Huneker differ as to its relative importance.
The former, while admitting its tender sweetness and
euphony ; finds it inferior to the first, having less pith in
it, while the latter considers it of more moment than the
other three.   Both of them however feel the obviously
dramatic nature of the poetic content.

To Huneker, " its nocturnal beginning with the caril-
lon-like bass recalling Hauptmann's 'Sunken Bell,' the
sweetly grave close of the section, the faint hoof-
beats of an approaching cavalcade, with the swelling
thunders of its passage, surely suggest a narrative, a
programme."

Niecks says that " without such assistance (a programme) the D major section of the Impromptu is
insignificant.   We want to see, or at least to know, who
are the persons that walk in the procession which the
music accompanies."

Both commentators notice the very curious modulation
from D major to F major, two bars which Huneker
happily describes as " creaking on their hinges."

The *coda* is celebrated for what the French call " *le jeu
perlé* " of the scale passages in the treble, but Von Bülow
cautions players against exhibiting their skill by playing
them too fast when he says the " *jeu perlé* " becomes the
" *jeu cochonné.*"

Kullak says : " This piece makes greater demands upon
the imitative poetic fancy of the player than the other
Impromptus.   The dreamy, song-like beginning ; the
immediate contrast with which the march in D major
enters ; the fantastic retrogression to the afterwards varied
first theme ; finally, the passages quietly gliding away, with
their expressive accompaniment—all these things bear the
impress of an improvisation seemingly suggested by

scenes from real life. Symmetry of musical form is wholly abandoned."

It is certainly less in the nature of an Impromptu than any of the others ; but perhaps for that very reason it is musically of greater importance.

OPUS 37.—Two Nocturnes.

No. 1 in G minor (Andante Sostenuto) ; No. 2 in G major (Andantino).

Composed 1838 and 1839. Published in 1840.

THE actual date of the composition of these two Nocturnes is a moot point. They are often attributed to the winter of 1838, when Chopin spent November and December with George Sand. Niecks says : " They may have had their origin in the days of Chopin's sojourn in the Balearic island, although a letter of Chopin's written from Nohant in the summer of 1839 leaves scarcely room for such a conjecture."

" I have a new Nocturne in G major, which will go along with the Nocturne in G minor, if you remember such a one."

It is probable, however, that the first in G minor was composed in the summer of 1838, and that the second, in G major, even if, owing its inspiration, as has been suggested, to the impressions of the calm, warm voyage to Majorca, was not actually finished till after his return.

Niecks says of them that they " are two of the finest ; I am inclined to say, the two finest of this class of Chopin's pieces. The first and last sections of the one in G minor are plaintive and longing, and have a wailing accompaniment ; the chord progressions of the middle section glide along hymn-like. Were it possible to praise one part more emphatically than another without committing an injustice, I would speak of the melodic exquisiteness of the first motive. But already I see other parts rise reproachfully before my repentant conscience."

Kleczynski suggests for it the title of " *Heimweh*,"

unromantically translatable in one word only as "Home-sickness."

"The poet weeps at the remembrance of his native soil, a remembrance which we perceive in the middle part of the piece in the form of a prayer played upon the organ of a country church. This prayer soothes the mind of the artist, who concludes with a last modulation into G major."

Karasowski speaks of it as "keeping up a ceaseless moan, as of harping on some sad thought, until interrupted by a church-like movement in chords, whose sadly comforting strains resemble the peacefulness of the grave."

Huneker does not admire it "inordinately." It has a complaining tone, and the chorale is not noteworthy. This particular part, so Chopin's pupil, Gutmann, declared, is taken too slowly, the composer having forgotten to mark the increased *tempo*.

The Nocturne consists of a chief and secondary subject, followed by a repetition of the first theme and a brief *coda* of two bars closing in the major key. It is interesting to compare this composition with the Nocturne No. 3 of Opus 15 (*q.v.*) Kullak says : "Here, too, the chief subject is the expression of deep melancholy, though in comparison with the passion of the former Nocturne, the present one discloses a touch of still resignation. In both there follows a secondary subject of religious character, which moves along full of nobility and dignity, and bestows comfort and tranquillity. Opus 15 closes with its secondary subject. In the present Nocturne, on the other hand, the chief subject is repeated. This is indeed justifiable in point of form, but at the same time, it weakens the poetic contents of the work ; for the secondary subject, with its beautiful intimation, that for deep suffering of soul religion is the best and highest consolation, is lowered to a merely passing moment."

On this occasion, the worthy pedagogue's theological views have interfered with his artistic insight. Just as in the Opus 15, the opening movement could not have been repeated after the completely satisfying and final close of the second section, so here it would have been just as impossible to finish with the chorale. In the most natural manner the mood of the opening theme returns, and the inevitable close is reached by the *coda* modulating into the major.

In the middle section a beautiful and organ-like effect is produced by putting down the pedal and taking it up between each chord (Kleczynski).

Schumann reviewed these two Nocturnes, and his luminous criticism is of such value in its bearing on all Chopin's work, that it is appended in full.

" Chopin may now publish anything without putting his name to it ; his works will always be recognised. This remark includes praise and blame ; that for his genius, this for his endeavour. He possesses such remarkable original power that, whenever it displays itself, it is impossible to be for a moment uncertain as to its source ; and he adds to this an abundance of novel forms that astonish us as much by their tenderness as their boldness. But, though ever new and inventive in the outward forms of his compositions, he remains the same within ; and we are almost beginning to fear that he will not rise any higher than he has so far risen. And although this is high enough to render his name immortal in the modern history of art, he limits his sphere to the narrow one of pianoforte music, when, with his powers, he might climb to so great an elevation, and from thence exercise an immense influence on the general progress of our art. But we must fain content ourselves. He has already created such noble things, he gives us so much at present, that we ought to be satisfied ; for we should certainly congratulate any artist who could accomplish merely the half of what he has accomplished. It is not necessary to write thick volumes to deserve the name of poet ; two true poems are enough for that, and Chopin has written many more. The above named notturnos are also poems ; they are essentially distinguished from his earlier ones by simpler decoration and more gentle grace. We all know how Chopin was formerly strewn with pearls, spangles, and golden trinkets. He has altered and grown older ; he still loves decoration, but now of that nobler kind under which poetic ideality gleams more transparently. We must allow that he possesses the most refined taste possible, but it will not be understood by thorough bassists, for they give their thoughts entirely to the

detection of consecutive fifths, and every succession of
these exasperates them.   But even they may learn much
from Chopin, about consecutive fifths above all."

No. 2.—Nocturne in G major (Andantino).

If we adopt the theory that this Nocturne was written
in Majorca, there is a passage in Georges Sand's diary
describing the voyage thither, which might well serve as a
programme to the work.

" The night was warm and dark, illumined only by an
extraordinary phosphorescence in the wake of the ship ;
everybody was asleep on board except the steersman, who,
in order to keep himself awake, sang all night, but in a
voice so soft and so subdued that one might have thought
that he feared to awake the men of the watch, or that he
himself was half asleep.   We did not weary of listening to
him, for his singing was of the strangest kind. He observed
a rhythm and modulation totally different from those we
are accustomed to, and seemed to allow his voice to go at
random, like the smoke of the vessel carried away and
swayed by the breeze.   It was a reverie rather than a
song, a kind of careless floating of the voice, with which
the mind had little to do, but which kept time with the
swaying of the ship, the faint sound of the dark water, and
resembled a vague improvisation, restrained nevertheless
by sweet and monotonous forms."

This excellent translation is by Miss Eleanor d'Esterre-
Keeling, who goes on to say : " Any one who plays the G
major Nocturne after reading this passage will be struck
by the singular likeness that the music bears to the written
description of the scene.   The swaying of the double notes
over the undulating bass accompaniment, suggests the
gliding motion of the vessel, while the richness of the harmonies carry out the idea of the brilliancy of the water
scintillating with phosphorescent lights.   Then comes the
vague song of the steersman, rather a reverie than a song.

" The mind has indeed little to do here, but the pulse of
the poet throbs through every note.   The song dies away
and the boat floats over the sea once more, then we hear
the steersman again ; this time he starts on a lower tone,
and the melody is worked up chromatically to a truly

Chopinesque climax ; that done, to quote old Herrick, it sinks down again into a silvery strain, and makes us smooth as balm and oil again ; then more repetition of the swaying motive, and as the vessel passes out of sight we hear in the dim distance the murmuring song of the steersman across the dark waters."

The melody of the second subject is, according to Kleczynski, possibly taken from the motive of a French song sung in Normandy ; perhaps the steersman came from the northern coast. In any case, whether entirely original or not, Karasowski considers it " the most beautiful melody Chopin ever wrote, to which one can never listen without a sense of the deepest emotion and happiness." In this Huneker agrees with him, and although we know that Chopin personally thought he had never written another such a melody as that of the Étude in E major, Opus 10, No. 3, yet it is probable that if a vote could be taken on the subject, the theme of the second part of this Nocturne would be adjudged the prize.

Huneker says : " Painted with Chopin's most ethereal brush, without the cloying splendours of the one in D flat, the double sixths, fourths, and thirds are magically euphonious. It is in true barcarolle vein, and most subtle are the shifting harmonic tones. Pianists usually take the first part too fast, the second too slowly, transforming this poetic composition into an Étude."

Speaking of the second section, Willeby says : " It is a very lovely theme this, and if we look into it we find it is simplicity itself. I think a careful study of such works of Chopin's as these Nocturnes will go far to do away with a very prevalent notion that his musical thoughts were complicated ; on the contrary, we find here, as with many others of the masters of music, that the most beautiful are frequently the most simple."

Niecks finds in this Nocturne " a beautiful sensuousness, it is luscious, soft, rounded, and not without a certain degree of languor. But let us not tarry too long in the treacherous atmosphere of this Capua—it bewitches and unmans."

OPUS 38.—Second Ballade in F major.

Dedicated to Mr. R. Schumann.
Composed 1838.   Published 1840.

THIS is one of the compositions mentioned in Chopin's
letters written from Majorca.   There was some
question as to whether this Ballade or the Preludes
should be dedicated to Pleyel or Schumann.   Ultimately
the Preludes were allotted to Pleyel and the Ballade to
Schumann.   It was sold to the publishers for 500 or 600
francs.   Schumann in reviewing it said : " We must
direct attention to the Ballade as a most remarkable
work.   Chopin has already written one composition of
the same name—one of his wildest and most original
compositions ; the new one is different, a less artistic
work than the first, but equally fantastic and intellectual.
Its impassioned episodes seem to have been afterwards
inserted.   I recollect very well when Chopin played the
' Ballade ' here ; it finished in F major, now it closes in A
minor.   He then said that he had been inspired by some
poems of Mickiewicz to write this Ballade.   On the other
hand, his music would inspire a poet to write words to it.
It thrills one's inmost heart."
    The point as to the way Chopin altered this composition
is interesting as showing the care with which he revised
his work before finally giving it to the public.   Hadow
instances the change of key from F major to A minor as
an instance of the way Chopin occasionally deliberately
strays away from a logical conclusion.   If Schumann is
right in thinking that " the impassioned episodes " were
inserted as an afterthought, Chopin must have changed
the whole tenour of the piece.   After the shuddering
terror and tragedy of the *coda*, this Ballade could no
longer have ended in the major in this fashion.
    " The second Ballade possesses beauties in no way
inferior to those of the first.   What can be finer than the
simple strains of the opening section !   They sound as if
they had been drawn from the people's storehouse of
song."
    How any one can write of this marvellous, vivid,

pathetic poem in the cold, slighting, pedantic fashion adopted by Willeby is amazing. The only possible explanation is that he has never heard an adequate interpretation of the work. He is not even correct as to the key, which he gives as F minor. Undoubtedly its technical difficulty, as in the case of the fourth Ballade in F minor, has prevented it becoming so well known and overplayed as the first and third.

Rubinstein in his " Conversations on Music " has left us his own interesting idea of the poetic content of this Ballade. " Is it possible," he says, " that the interpreter does not feel the necessity of representing to his hearers a field flower caught by a gust of wind, a caressing of the flower by the wind ; the resistance of the flower, the stormy struggle of the wind, the entreaty of the flower which at last lies there broken ; and paraphrased—the field flower a rustic maiden, the wind a knight, and so almost in every instrumental composition."

Kleczynski analyses this Ballade at some length and gives useful hints as to the proper phrasing. According to Huneker, Chopin admitted that it was written under the direct inspiration of Mickiewicz's poem, " Le Lac de Willis." He says : " The episodical nature of this Ballade is the finest of the esoteric moods of its composer. It follows a hidden story and has the quality of great, unpremeditated art."

The first theme, Andantino, is described by all the commentators as " idyllic." Barbedette even says "pastoral," and undoubtedly this Ballade is a story of the country, a love tragedy, with a betrayal, and a terribly tragic ending.

The theme dies away and we are left pondering on a softly reiterated A natural. Suddenly and without the slightest warning the storm bursts *ff*, *presto con fuoco*. Its first onslaught is, however, brief, and the first theme recurs. "But life is never the same again," and the innocent simplicity of the beginning never returns. Other moods follow in rapid succession, thoughtful, argumentative, passionate, and then once more the storm, but this time culminating with sullen rolling of thunder in the terrific shuddering catastrophe of the *coda*.

An abrupt sudden pause like a catch of the breath, and

then the sobbing broken reference to the first theme with its questioning close, and the deep, deep sigh of the closing bars—" But yet the pity of it, O, the pity of it."

OPUS 39.—Third Scherzo in C sharp minor.

Dedicated to Mr. A. Gutmann.
Composed 1838–39.   Published 1840.

EARLY in the winter of 1839 Moscheles called on Chopin in Paris.   Describing his visit in a letter, he wrote, " Chopin's excellent pupil Gutmann played his master's manuscript Scherzo in C sharp minor."

This is one of the few pieces of which Chopin speaks in his letters from Majorca.   It was undoubtedly begun during his stay on the island, but was not finished till his convalescence in the summer of 1839.   " Do not speak to any one of the Scherzo, I do not know when I shall finish it, for I am still weak and cannot write."   This he wrote to Fontana on March 17, 1839.

Niecks calls it " the peevish, fretful, and fiercely-scornful Scherzo," and says it is " quite in keeping with the moods one imagines the composer to have been in at the time." He speaks elsewhere of its capricious starts and changes, its rudderless drifting, and considers the name *capriccio* would be more suitable to this than to any of the other Scherzi.   Hadow however speaks of " its short, clear-cut phrases and exact balance ; an exactitude due to an intense desire for clearness and precision," which he considers a national Polish characteristic, and especially Chopinesque.

The two opinions seem somewhat hard to reconcile, but although the form of its phrases is precise, its harmonies and modulations are intensely original and unexpected. Karasowski speaks of " its demonianism and drastic power," and Willeby calls it " fitful " if not exactly capricious.   Huneker writes about this Scherzo at considerable length ; he considers it " the most dramatic, the most finely moulded of the six.   It is capricious to madness but the dramatic quality is unmistakable.   It seethes

with scorn, if such an extravagant figure is permissible.
It is all extravagance, fire, and fury, but it signifies something."

The *tempo* is marked *presto con fuoco*, but Kullak is
never tired of pointing out that for modern pianos Chopin's
extremely quick *tempi* should be moderated, or else with
the increased power and heavier action of modern grands
there is a tendency to blur the outlines and to lose power.
If this Scherzo is started too fast there will be a sense of
effort, and a lack of contrast on arriving at the *coda*, which
should be played as fast as possible.

Kullak calls the introduction "more prelude-like than
independent in character." The use of four crotchets in
triple time is an instance of the caprice of which Niecks
speaks. The sixth bar is a tremendous crashing chord,
and von Lenz says that Chopin dedicated this Scherzo to
Gutmann because, with his immense power, he was able to
"knock a hole in the table" with this chord. The leading
subject (bar 25) is of great energy and power ; at bar 57
the second section is perhaps more like Beethoven than
anything else of Chopin's. At the change of key to D
flat, marked *meno mosso*, the chief subject is a kind of
chorale ; every four bars it is interrupted by a lace-like
fall of broken *arpeggios*. Through their delicate veil the
last chord of each section of the chorale must be heard
sounding, being sustained by the continuation pedal.

Kleczynski warns us against too great an equality of
rhythm, "a matter wherein *virtuosi* err so often, playing
as they do, the chords too slow and the subsequent
passages too quick."

The second section (marked *leggiero*) is especially
beautiful. The sweeping *arpeggios* of changing harmonies
are like

"The lovely laughter of the wind-swept wheat,"

and the return to the chorale seems an expression of
gratitude for so much beauty. The impetuous first theme
is repeated, with its Beethoven-like trio. Then there is a
resumption of the chorale, and at the thirty-third bar after
the *piu lento*, there is a weird and most fascinating modulation stranger than anything in Grieg or Wagner, which
leads to an episode, fifteen bars further on, of ravishing

beauty. A wild *stretto* leads to a *coda* of superb frenzy, closing in the major key, which, as Huneker says, "is a surprising conclusion considering all that has gone before. Never to become the property of the profane, the C sharp minor Scherzo, notwithstanding its marked asperities and agitated moments, is a grand work of art. Without the inner freedom of its predecessors, it is more sober and self-contained than the B minor Scherzo."

OPUS 40.—Two Polonaises.

No. 1 in A major ; No. 2 in C minor.

Dedicated to Mr. J. Fontana.
Composed 1838. Published 1840.

THIS is throughout the most consistently bright and brilliant piece that Chopin ever wrote. Both the first and second subjects are of the same proud, bold, military character, and the whole piece should be played in strict time. It reminds Kullak of Weber's Polacco in E major, and he says "it is full of festal uproar without romanticism." It is a striking contrast to the following number in C minor.

Rubinstein said that for him these two Polonaises were synonymous with Poland's greatness and Poland's downfall.

According to Kleczynski the appearance of this Polonaise marked an epoch. Liszt used to play it at all his concerts. "In this dance, which may be called glorious in the full significance of the word, the Polish type appears in all its sumptuousness and with a splendour somewhat theatrical. Each note, each accent, glows with life and power."

He points out that the triplet in the second bar should always be accented, and says that the sudden modulation to C sharp in the fifth bar is gorgeous. It certainly has an electrifying effect. The seventh and eighth bars are important as showing the characteristic robustness of the Polonaise. "Each of the six quavers has a solid weight of its own, an accent, a significance . . . the *tempo* of this 'march' ought to be buoyant indeed, but never too fast or too flying, as we should then entirely lose the accents in the two last bars. . . . In the third part trumpets are heard and the music in general deceives the ear. The piano seems to change into an orchestra, but it is curious that this part when arranged for an actual orchestra shows to least advantage."

The eighth bar of this part should imitate the rolling of a drum. It is a great pity that Chopin wrote no *coda* for this Polonaise, as, owing to its brilliant character, this deficiency seems more marked than usual. The approach of the ending should be indicated by a *rallentando*.

A Polish painter, Kwiatkowski, told Niecks that it was this Polonaise to which the following anecdote is attached, although it has often been mentioned in connection with the A flat major Polonaise. The story goes, that Chopin, while playing it one evening when alone, was so carried away by the ideas that it evoked that he had a vision of a train of Polish ladies and nobles suddenly entering his room. These phantoms were so real to him that he rushed from the apartment in terror and dared not return the whole night.

It is possible that Chopin composed this Polonaise during his stay at Majorca. He certainly mentions it often in his letters from there, but it is quite possible that, like the Preludes, it was only revised at that time. Niecks says : "If the sadly ailing composer really created and not merely elaborated and finished in Majorca the superlatively healthy, vigorously-martial, brilliantly-chivalrous Polonaise in A major, we have here a remarkable instance of the mind's ascendency over the body, of its independence of it." Later, he speaks of it as the simplest, though not the easiest, composition of Chopin, and says that it is the most popular of the Polonaises. " The mind of the composer is fixed on one elating thought. He sees the gallantly advancing chivalry of Poland, determination in every look and gesture ; he hears rising above the noise of stamping horses and the clash of arms their bold challenge scornfully hurled at the enemy."

No. 2 in C minor (Allegro maestoso).

In the dignified but gloomy colouring of this Polonaise Rubinstein saw a picture of Poland's downfall. Seldom has fortitude under suffering found such poignant expression as in the noble melody of the first theme in the bass. Kullak says it should be executed with dignity, melancholy, nobility, and strictly in time.

Niecks sees in it the mind of the composer turning from one depressing or exasperating thought to another. "He seems to review the different aspects of his country's unhappy state, its sullen discontent, fretful agitation, and uncertain hopes." He draws attention to "the chafing agitation of the second part, the fitful play between light and shade of the trio-like part in A flat major, and the added wailing voice in the recurring first portion at the end of the piece."

For Huneker it is "a noble, troubled composition, large in accents and deeply felt. The trio in A flat with its kaleidoscopic modulations produces an impression of vague unrest and suppressed sorrow. There is loftiness of spirit and daring in it."

Willeby's criticism is that though the whole piece presents more variety of emotion than the preceding Polonaise the second portion in A flat major is wanting in conciseness, and he finds its continuous inharmonic changes somewhat irritating.

OPUS 41.—Four Mazurkas.

No. 1 in C sharp minor ; No. 2 in E minor ; No. 3 in B major ; No. 4 in A flat.

Dedicated to Mr. E. Witwicki.
Composed 1835–39.   Published 1840.

"YOU know that I have four new Mazurkas : one from Palma in E minor, three from here. They seem to me pretty, as the youngest children usually do when the parents grow old."

Chopin wrote thus to Fontana in the summer of 1839, and his opinion of this set is more than justified. Again we have the most complete contrast of moods, fascinating modulations, exquisite unexpected harmonies, and the whole gamut of human emotions.

No. 1 in C sharp minor.

Huneker calls this Mazurka the apotheosis of rhythm, and it certainly requires less *rubato* than any other of the Mazurkas. " Its scale is exotic, its rhythm convincing, its tune a little saddened by life, but courage never fails. This theme sounds persistently in the middle voices, in the bass, and at the close in full harmonies, unisons, giving it a startling effect. Octaves take it up in profile until it vanishes."

This "exotic scale" is one of the most original and fascinating of Chopin's devices, and its bold use coupled with the quality of the melody, such wonderful passages of modulation and tone-colour as the one marked *tranquillo*, *una corda*, and the grand climax make this one of the greatest of the Mazurkas.

No. 2 in E minor.

This is the Mazurka that Chopin himself tells us he wrote at Palma, in Majorca, and it is hardly to be wondered at that it should reflect the somewhat melancholy episodes of the composer's stay in the island. Huneker calls it " sad to the point of tears." The first three lines are full of a feeling of self-pity, but the second section brings with a lovely change a happier mood. It is a gem, and compared with these two the next are uninteresting.

No. 3 in B major.

This is one of the least interesting and least distinguished of the Mazurkas. Huneker calls it " a vigorous sonorous dance." The persistent recurrence of the rather heavy-footed opening phrase becomes monotonous. There is comparatively little to dwell on here.

No. 4 in A flat.

This, again, although prettier and more graceful, can hardly rank with the other Mazurkas of this period of Chopin's development. Huneker styles it "playful and decorative, but not profound in feeling." The rhythm is almost valse-like, and the ending is unsatisfactory.

OPUS 42.—Valse in A flat major.

Published in 1840.

THIS is one of the few pieces of Chopin's with no dedication. Schumann says of it that "like his earlier Valses it is a salon piece of the noblest kind"; if he played for dancers, Florestan thinks "half the ladies should be countesses at least." And he is right, for Chopin's Valse is aristocratic through and through.

Huneker calls this Valse Chopin at his dancing best, and with its combination of duple and triple rhythm (bar 9), the constantly recurring *ritournelle*-like passage (bar 41), and the lilting melody marked *sostenuto*, it would make a most fascinating dance for those who can appreciate the subtleties of rhythmic accent.

Later on Chopin employed a similar combination of duple and triple rhythm in the fourth Scherzo, Op. 54. To Niecks this device is "indicative of the loving, nestling and tender embracing of the dancing couples. Then after the smooth gyrations of the first period, come those sweeping motions, free and graceful like those of birds (the *ritournelle* passage) that intervene again and again between the different portions of the Valse."

The professor describes this passage as "a self-surrendering heaven and earth-forgetting joyousness"; and instances as a stroke of genius as delightful as it is clever, the way in which Chopin breaks off from the sentimental ardour of the passage marked *sostenuto*, and plunges back into the abandon of the *ritournelle*.

For Huneker this Valse is a "marvellous epitome, the best rounded specimen of Chopin's experimenting with the form. The prolonged trill on E flat, summoning us to the ball-room, the suggesting intermingling of rhythms, duple and triple, the coquetry, hesitation, passionate avowal, and the superb *coda* with its echoes of evening, have not these episodes a charm beyond compare ! Only Schumann in certain pages of his ' Carnival ' seizes the secret of young life and hope ; but his is not so finished, so glowing a tableau."

OPUS 43.—Tarantelle in A flat major.

Published 1841.

CHOPIN wrote in a letter from Nohant, in 1841 : " I send you the Tarantella. Please to copy it, but first go to Schlesinger, or better still to Troupenas, and see the collection of Rossini's songs published by him. In it there is a Tarantella in F. I do not know whether it is written in $\frac{6}{8}$ or $\frac{12}{8}$ time. As to my composition, it does not matter which way it is written, but I should prefer it to be like Rossini's." The composer finally decided on $\frac{6}{8}$ time, which is fortunate, for Niecks justly remarks that " this is a characteristic instance of Chopin's carelessness in the notation of his music ; to write his Tarantella in $\frac{12}{8}$ or common time with triplets would have been an egregious mistake. How Chopin failed to see this is inexplicable to me."

Schumann reviewed this Tarantella : " This is in Chopin's most daring manner ; we see the madly-whirling dancers before us, until our own senses seem to reel. We can scarcely term this lovely music, but we willingly forgive the Master for the wildness of his imagination, the night side of which he may certainly be allowed to display sometimes. However, Chopin did not write this for severe reviewers. A correct first understanding of the piece is rendered still more difficult from the press errors with which the edition swarms."

Niecks, however, protests against Schumann saying that it is not beautiful music. He says " that it is full of life, indeed, spirited in every respect, in movement, and in boldness of harmonic and melodic conception. The *Tarantelle* is a translation from Italian into Polish, a transmutation of Rossini into Chopin, a Neapolitan scene painted with opaque colours, the south without its transparent sky, balmy air, and general brightness. That this composition was inspired by impressions received from Rossini's Tarantella, and not from impressions received in Italy (of which, as has already been related, he had a short glimpse in 1839), is evident. A comparison of Chopin's Op. 43, with Liszt's glowing and intoxicating transcription of Rossini's composition, may be recommended as a study equally pleasant and instructive."

" Composed at Nohant, it is as little Italian as the Boléro is Spanish. Chopin's visit to Italy was of too short a duration to affect him, at least in the style of dance. It is without the necessary ophidian tang, and far inferior to Heller and Liszt's efforts in the constricted form. One finds little of the frenzy ascribed to it by Schumann in his review. It breathes of the North, not the South, and ranks far below the A flat Impromptu in geniality and grace." (Huneker.)

There is no doubt that this Tarantella, although not without a certain measure of excitement, leaves one cold. The form was not a sympathetic one to Chopin, and it is only too evident that the inspiration to compose it came to him at second hand. It is evidently not the result of the direct impression produced by his brief visit to Italy in 1839, when, however, he did not go further south than Genoa. The references in his letters to Rossini's Tarantella show that it was composed as the result of his admiration of the great Italian's work.

OPUS 44.—Polonaise in F sharp minor.

Dedicated to Mme. la Princesse Charles de Beauvau. Published 1841.

THIS, and the better-known Polonaise in A flat major, Opus 53, are Chopin's two greatest compositions in the Polonaise form. This one is not as well known as the latter, as it is much less often played. It is of colossal difficulty, and requires a giant's strength to do it justice. Even the strongest wrists and fingers are apt to flinch before the end. It opens with a rush of exasperation and surprise—an indignant pause—and then a roar of defiance —a tossing sea of emotion, conflict, strain, and stress ; then a dream-like change, and we are on a battlefield ; cannon shots boom out with rhythmical insistence, while a curious figure of reverberating overtones completes a page that is purposely rasping to the nerves. For Chopin, as if to accentuate our gloom and distress, now introduces a Mazurka, pure, idyllic, tender and graceful as a flower, of which Liszt says, that " so far from effacing the memory of the deep grief which has gone before serves by the bitter irony of contrast to augment our painful emotions." Then, with the insistence of a nightmare, back comes the first passionate rush and the thunderous and lurid theme of the Polonaise. After a wild flight upwards of two octaves in the bass, the music dies away suddenly, and ends with a single loud octave like a convulsive shudder.

Liszt says "the whole production is one of great originality, and excites us like the story of some broken dream, told after a night of restless wakefulness, in the first dull, grey, cold, leaden rays of a winter sunrise. It is a dream poem, in which impressions and objects follow each other with startling incoherence and with the wildest transitions. . . ."

Huneker considers that there is no greater test for the poet-pianist than the F sharp minor Polonaise. " It is profoundly ironical—what else means the introduction of that lovely Mazurka, a flower between two abysses ? . . . No sabre dance this, but a confession from the dark depths of a self-tortured soul. . . . To me the piece far surpasses in grandeur all of Chopin's Polonaises, even the ' Heroic,' with its thunderous cannon and rattling of horses' hoofs. It may be morbid, but it is also magnificent."

Niecks writes rather unsympathetically about this Polonaise. He says that " what we find in it cannot be art ; we look in vain for beauty of melody and harmony. Dreamy unisons, querulous melodic phrases, hollow-eyed chords, hard progressions and modulations throughout

every part of the Polonaise proper. We receive a pathological rather than æsthetical impression. Nevertheless,
no one can deny the grandeur and originality that shine
through this gloom."

OPUS 45.—Prelude in C sharp minor.

Dedicated to Mlle. la Princesse Elisabeth Czernicheff.
Published November 28, 1841.

IN one of Chopin's letters to his friend Fontana, undated,
but written from Nohant in 1841, we read: "For
Schlesinger * I have composed a Prelude in C sharp
minor, which is short, as he wished it. It is well modulated, and I can send it without hesitation. He ought to
give me 300 francs for it, *n'est-ce-pas*."

And in a second letter he begs Fontana to ask the
governess of the young Princess Elisabeth Czernicheff,
to whom he wanted to dedicate the piece, how the name is
spelt.

The Prelude is certainly beautifully modulated, and a
rare bargain for £12. It stands isolated from the twenty-
four Preludes of Opus 28, and is the only other composition of Chopin to which he has given this name.

When no other generic title that he was wont to use
fitted his composition Chopin apparently called it a Prelude. Niecks thinks it more like a Prelude than any of
the twenty-four, but says he would rather call it an
Improvisata. "It seems unpremeditated, a heedless outpouring when sitting at the piano in a lonely dreamy hour,
perhaps in the twilight."

It opens with a phrase curiously reminiscent of one of
Mendelssohn's "Lieder Ohne Wörte" (No. 2), and then
goes on with a melody that, both in quality and treatment,
is a great deal more like Brahms than anything that
Chopin ever wrote. This Prelude vindicates Chopin's
reputation as a path-finder in harmony. Huneker has
also been struck by this resemblance, and says of this
melody that it is "Oh, so Brahmsian, that bitter-sweet

* The Paris music-publisher

lingering, that spiritual reverie in which the musical idea is gently propelled, as if in some elusive dream."

Towards the end there is a wonderful cadenza, played *pianissimo* and *a piacere*, the last two bars of which anticipate by some fifteen years a *leitmotiv* of Wagner's. It is almost identical with the phrase that accompanies the threatening gesture of Alberich just before the rays of the rising sun strike upon the Rheingold.

The concluding bars modulate from C sharp minor to D major and back again in a passage of haunting though elusive beauty.

It is not one of the composer's most popular works, for it is too uncommon, and one requires to be very familiar with it before one can appreciate its subtle charm.

OPUS 46.—Allegro de Concert in A major.

Dedicated to Mlle. F. Muller.
Composed 1841.   Published January 1842.

SCHUMANN states possibly that this Concert Allegro (which he describes as having the complete form of a first movement of a Concerto) was originally written with an orchestral accompaniment. Presumably he had his information direct from the composer. Niecks thinks it probable that it is worked up from sketches for a Concerto for two pianos that Chopin in a letter, written from Vienna in December 1830, said he would play in public with his friend Nidecki if he succeeded in writing it to his satisfaction. It is significant also that the composer, when sending the manuscript of the work to Fontana, calls it a Concerto. Schumann says further : " A fine middle melody is wanting, though the cantilena is rich in new and brilliant passages ; but it floats past us too restlessly, and we feel the absence of a slow after movement, an adagio —for the entire plan suggests a complete Concerto in three movements. The idea of raising the pianoforte to the highest point of independence possible, and of rendering the orchestra unnecessary, is a favourite one with young composers, and it seems to have influenced Chopin

K

in the publication of his Allegro in this form ; but this
new attempt again proves the difficulty of the task, though
it will by no means serve as a warning against future
endeavour."

Kleczynski, who says it is full of life and gaiety, finds
some resemblance to the introduction to the Fantaisie on
National Airs which was composed in 1828.   Niecks says
that " the principal subject and some of the passage work
remind one of the time of the Concertos ; other things
again belong undeniably to a later period."

Nicodé has published an arrangement for piano and
orchestra, but both Niecks and Huneker condemn this,
especially his addition of seventy bars of a working-out
section.

Huneker calls this Allegro a " truncated Concerto, much
more so than Schumann's F minor Sonata, called *Concert
sans Orchestre*.   While it adds little to Chopin's reputation, it has the potentialities of a powerful and more
manly composition than either of the two Concertos."
The Mlle. Friederike Muller, to whom it is dedicated,
was one of the most gifted of Chopin's pupils, and assisted
Carl Mikuli in the preparation of his edition of the Works.

Kullak in his annotated edition marks the passages
which are evidently orchestral in intention with the direction, *Tutti ;* but the veriest tyro could tell with his eyes
shut when the orchestra is supposed to be playing and
when the solo instrument enters, which it does at the
eighty-seventh bar with an elaborate cadenza.   It is the
second theme of this solo part which has the most important share in the development of the movement.   It is a
bright, tuneful melody, exceedingly characteristic of
Chopin's earlier period, and it is preceded by some of his
most modern-sounding harmonies.   One passage might
certainly have given Wagner the idea of the fire music of
Loge, and immediately preceding the air there are four
bars exactly like the music in " Siegfried," where Mime is
terrified by the flickering of the sunlight through the trees
outside his forge.   After much brilliant passage work, a
long shake ushers in a brief resumption of the *Tutti*, to be
followed by the main theme in the minor, which mode
suits it wonderfully.   Then back it goes to the major, and
still more brilliant passages lead up to a prolonged and

elaborate trill, and a magnificent ascending climax lands us in a triumphant closing *Tutti*.

Niecks rather under-estimates its value, and certainly its interest, which, owing to the circumstances of its composition, is absorbing. It is astonishing that it is so neglected by modern *virtuosi;* nothing that Liszt has written surpasses it in pianistic brilliance ; it is difficult enough to make it interesting even to the greatest technician, and it gives scope for the highest artistic intelligence in its rendering. Huneker says : " The Allegro is one of Chopin's most difficult works. It abounds in risky skips, ambuscades of dangerous double notes, and the principal themes are bold and expressive. The colour note is strikingly adapted for public performance."

OPUS 47.—Third Ballade in A flat major.

Dedicated to Mlle. P. de Noailles.
Composed 1841.   Published January 1842.

THE distinguishing characteristic of this ballade is its high-spirited light-heartedness as compared with the three other compositions in this form. Schumann says, " This Ballade, Chopin's third, differs in a striking manner, in form and character, from his earlier ones, and must be counted among his most original creations. The finely intellectual Pole accustomed to move in the most courtly circles of the French capital, will be distinctly recognised in it. We shall not attempt to analyse its poetic atmosphere any further."

Niecks speaks of its fundamentally caressing mood, and says, " It does not equal its sisters in emotional intensity, at any rate, not in emotional tumultuousness. The fine gradations, the iridescence of feeling, mocks at verbal definition. Over everything in melody, harmony, and rhythm there is suffused a most exquisite elegance. A quiver of excitement runs through the whole piece. The syncopations, reversions of accent, silences on accented parts of the bar (sighs and suspended respiration, felicitously expressed), which occur very frequently in this Ballade, give much charm and piquancy to it."

Willeby, who is much more sympathetic in dealing with this work than he is with the F major Ballade, draws attention to the similarity of the opening bars to a phrase in the fourth Scherzo, Op : 54. These bars " contain a complete question and answer ; while the syncopations which follow are essentially characteristic of the whole Ballade throughout which they are maintained. Especially is this so with the lovely theme in F major, one of the most delicate and idealistic to be found even amongst the many idealities he has given us."

A pseudonymous writer " Israfel," in an extinct periodical called " The Dome," says, " One of Chopin's compositions has never ceased to puzzle me. Under what alien influence did he write it—the Ballade in A flat?— It is so peculiarly unlike himself in its boyish swagger and its gallant light-heartedness ; it is so young, so cocksure, and so successful, drawing to a logical happy close, instead of ceasing gloomily in the customary manner."

Huneker says this Ballade is too well known to analyse. " It is the schoolgirl's delight, who familiarly toys with its demon, seeing only favour and prettiness in its elegant measures. Graceful, charming, it appeals even to the lovers of music-hall ditties (and like the G minor), it too has been worried to death. It is aristocratic, gay, graceful, piquant, and also something more. Even in its playful moments there is delicate irony, a spiritual sporting with graver and more passionate emotions."

Only Kleczynski reads into this Ballade anything approaching a tragedy. He says it is evidently inspired by Mickiewicz's poem of Undine. He finds in the concluding pages " a picture of dark horror, increasing in intensity, suggestive of a whirlpool," and so on. But this is beside the mark. The triumphant song of the last pages is but the first naïvely poetic cheerful theme, broadened and ennobled and in the concluding phrases a certain happy frenzy reigns rather than any suspicion of a tragedy. Any one adopting Kleczynski's view of this Ballade must produce a very distorted, ill-proportioned reading.

The first eight bars bring us at once to the main theme, two questions and two distinct answers. Then a second section in which we are given at once the characteristic rhythm of the whole piece ; the accent is transferred to the third and sixth quaver, which, in the F major section mentioned above, leaves us, as Oscar Bie points out, to the enjoyment of a wonderful, pseudo-rhythm, wavering deliciously between two time emotions. Chopin both in this and the opening sections nowhere loses sight of the narrative feeling, the distinguishing characteristic of the Ballade form. At the change of key to C sharp minor there is a contrast of mood, and an elaborate bass passage, which is followed by the melody in the left hand under a dominant pedal in the treble. At the return to the major the *coda* commences to work up to a final outburst, in which it is almost difficult to recognise the simple charm of the opening bars, so transfigured as it is by a noble and triumphant emotion. The *stretto* works up to an almost frenzied but intensely happy conclusion.

OPUS 48.—Two Nocturnes.

No. 1 in C minor ; No. 2 in F sharp minor.

Dedicated to Mlle. L. Duperré.
Composed 1841. Published January 1842.

THESE two Nocturnes belong to the period of Chopin's most mature genius.* The first in C minor is the grandest of all the Nocturnes. It is quite as dramatic as the C sharp minor, and although less agitated is full of a more noble emotion. Karasowski considers it " most imposing, with its powerful intermediate movement, which is a thorough departure from the Nocturne style."

It is almost a Ballade, and Huneker says : " the ineluctable fact remains that this is the noblest Nocturne of them all. Biggest in conception, it seems a miniature music drama. It requires the grand manner to read it adequately and the *doppio movimento* is exciting to a dramatic degree. A fitting pendant is this work to the C sharp minor Nocturne. Both have the heroic quality, both are free from

* See Opus 49.

mawkishness and are of the greater Chopin, the Chopin of the masculine mode."

Barbedette considers these Nocturnes two masterpieces, and speaks of the first as epic in its proportions and grandiose in style.

Against these opinions we have Niecks, who denies them a foremost place amongst their companions, and Willeby, who somewhat inexplicably finds them sickly when not laboured, instancing the *doppio movimento* as an example of the latter quality. But this it is not when properly played. It should not be hurried.

Kullak says : " It is not best to hold too literally to the designation *doppio movimento*, for then it would remain only to choose between inartistic precipitation in the chief subject, or a no less critical dragging of the secondary subject." He proposes a metronome marking of 96 for a crotchet, and also says that the octave passages in triplets in the elaboration of the second subject should be played strictly in time, to retain the march-like character of the theme.

The brief *coda* is one of Chopin's happiest inspirations, and comes like a breath of ineffable peace after the stormy agitation of the repetition of the chief theme.

In his lectures on Chopin's greater works, Kleczynski devotes several pages to a lucid and instructive description as to how this Nocturne should be played. He says : " This dignified and expressive work is very often played coldly and phrased colourlessly or falsely. Yet every note in this composition is full of meaning. I do not know if the legend be true that this Nocturne represents the contrition of a sinner. The reproaches of conscience are, according to this idea, followed in the middle part by heavenly harps and angelic choirs, and later on by a growing disquietude ending with death and a yearning flight to heaven."

Kullak says : " The design and poetic contents of this Nocturne make it the most important one that Chopin created ; the chief subject is a masterly expression of a great powerful grief, for instance at a grave misfortune occurring to one's beloved fatherland. Upon such an occasion and in such a mood, it is but a step to self-sacrificing deeds. The secondary subject makes upon me an impression as if heroic men had banded themselves together and solemnly went forth to the holy war to conquer or die for their native land.

"In correspondence with the character of a grand heroic march, the harmonic masses finally tower aloft in imposing splendour and majesty."

Schumann reviewed these Nocturnes, but for once his opinion seems to have been rather perfunctory : "These Notturnos must be placed, from their melancholy and graceful manner, among Chopin's earlier ones. The second especially will speak to many hearts."

We may agree with the judgment on the second, but the first belongs distinctly to Chopin's most mature period of development.

No. 2.—Nocturne in F sharp minor.

This Nocturne has not the importance of the preceding one. It is peculiarly Chopinesque, particularly in the introductory bars, which recall the opening of the A flat Nocturne, Opus 32, No. 2, and also in the chief theme, the commencement of which is closely paralleled in the succeeding Nocturne, Opus 55, No. 1. It is in a soft elegiac mood, and Niecks speaks of its *flebile dolcezza* (tear-laden sweetness).

Barbedette refers to it as "*d'une tristesse navrante.*" The first theme is repeated twice, transposed and enriched, and then the second subject enters. This is marked *più lento*, and is very different in character.

Willeby says it is fragmentary, and the relief is not sufficient, but Niecks considers it is much finer, "in it we meet again, as we did in some other Nocturnes, with soothing simple chord progressions." When Gutmann studied it with Chopin, the master told him the middle section should be played as a recitative, "a tyrant commands" (the first two chords), he said, "and the other asks for mercy." Kullak says : "The short, concentrated phrases of the new subject, the change of key (major instead of minor) and of time, all indicate a change of mood. In place of weeping and lamentation, appears the resolve to endure courageously and nobly."

In a letter Chopin tells us he sold the French rights of

these two Nocturnes with the Allegro de Concert, the F sharp minor Polonaise, and the Fantaisie for two thousand francs.

OPUS 49.—Fantaisie in F minor.

Dedicated to Madame la Princesse L. de Souzzo.

THIS Fantaisie ranks by general consent as one of the highest expressions of the composer's genius.

It was written at George Sand's Château at Nohant in 1841, the time when his friendship with the authoress was at its happiest. As Niecks says : " Chopin's genius had now reached the most perfect stage of its development and was radiating with all the intensity of which its nature was capable."

Of this particular work, he says : " It is one of his best compositions ; nothing more common than the *name* of Fantaisie, here we have the *thing*." The very flower of the great imaginative works, it is the nearest akin to the Ballades, but in those the narrative feeling is so strong that you realise that Chopin is telling you some old-world legend or romance that he has heard.

The triple time common to all the Ballades, and that seems inseparable in music from the idea of a story told, is here replaced by common time, with the result that, although it is unmistakably narrative in form, we feel that Chopin is revealing to us some dramatic and moving incident in his own life. It is not a revelation of personal moods as are the Scherzi, but a narrative of events in which the composer himself has borne a part. It has more of the universal and less of the Polish national feeling than the Polonaises.

It opens with a march-like theme of serene gravity : according to Chopin, if we may credit the statements at third-hand of Liszt, the actual exciting cause of this com- position was a quarrel and reconciliation between the com- poser and George Sand. The first two bars represent the knocking at the door of the room in which the composer is dreaming at the piano, and the next two stand for his invitation to come in. Enter George Sand with Liszt, Madame Camille Pleyel, and other friends ; she kneels for pardon ; then come scenes of intercession, reproaches, piteous appeals, and finally reconciliation.

Very possibly Chopin may have had some such episode in his mind, but this is music into which everybody will read their own meaning ; the themes are of such self-sufficing beauty and variety that no programme is necessary for its full enjoyment.

The treatment of this introduction is full of interest and novelty. Hadow has pointed out how Chopin leaves us in doubt as to whether he intends "the melody to be entirely homogeneous in style, and whether the concluding strain of the stanza can possibly get back without awkwardness to the key from which it has strayed. Both these doubts are solved in the most masterly fashion in the concluding line, which not only carries the modulation with consummate ease, but completes the organic outline of the melody with the daintiest delicacy and finish."

In the next section a series of ascending triplet passages gradually increasing in force and velocity usher in an agitated theme (bar sixty-eight *agitato*) which leads to a very beautiful passage, the proper interpretation of which is much discussed (bar seventy-seven).

In the "Klindworth" Edition it is marked *dolce*, but Kullak says that he does not consider this "authentic, nor does it correspond with the heroic, highly dramatic character of the subject."

Huneker calls it "that heroic love-chant erroneously marked '*dolce*,' and played with the effeminacies of a *salon*. Three times does it resound, yet not once should it be caressed ; the bronze fingers of a Tausig are needed." It is emphatically a case where every player should be guided by his own feeling as to what is right. It remains for him to convince his hearers by the artistic completion of his reading of the whole piece that the way in which he has played the passage is the only possible rendering.

These various themes recur several times in different keys, and then, after three dropping *pianissimo* octaves, there comes a heavenly melody in B major (*Lento sostenuto*), a reverie which after dreaming along for twenty-four bars is broken in upon by a sudden *sforzando* with dramatic effect).*

The former themes are repeated ; two bars reminiscent of the *lento* ushers in a sweet and plaintive recitative, soft billowy arpeggios swell up and die away ; then two crashing chords once more bring us back with a start to every-day life.)†

" In the Fantaisia we again meet with the bold stormy tone-poet, as we have learnt to know him. It is filled with genial traits in detail, though the whole did not choose to subject itself to the limits of a fine form. We can only make suppositions as to the figures that floated before Chopin when he wrote this, but the pictures were certainly not cheerful ones." (Schumann.)

" This work is one of Chopin's best compositions—unfettered by the scheme of a definite form such as the Sonata or the Concerto, the composer develops his thought with masterly freedom. There is an enthralling weirdness about this work, a weirdness made up of force of passion and an indescribable fantastic waywardness. The music falls on our ears like the insuppressible outpouring of a being stirred to its heart's core, and full of immeasurable love and longing. Who would suspect the composer's fragility and sickliness in this work ? Does it not rather suggest a Titan in commotion ? There was a time when I spoke of the Fantaisia in a less complimentary tone, now I bow down my head regretfully and exclaim *peccavi.*" (Niecks.)

" It parades a formal beauty—not disfigured by an excess of violence, either personal or patriotic, and its melodies, if restless by melancholy, are of surprising nobility and dramatic grandeur. Without including the Beethoven Sonatas, not strictly born of the instrument, I do not fear to maintain that this Fantaisie is one of the greatest of piano pieces. Never properly appreciated by pianists, critics, or public, it is, after more than half a century of neglect, being understood at last." (Huneker.)

* *Cf.* Scherzo in B minor. End of lento section, Opus 20.
† *Cf.* End of Opus 61. Polonaise Fantaisie.

OPUS 50.—Three Mazurkas.

No. 1 in G major ; No. 2 in A flat major ; No. 3 in C sharp minor.

Dedicated to M. Léon Szmitkowski.
Composed 1841.   Published 1842.

CHOPIN published this and the next three books of Mazurkas in sets of three, possibly because, taking them as a whole, from now on, the form shows a greater amount of development, and on an average, greater length and importance.

No. 1 in G major.

This is a beautiful, melodious, happy-hearted Mazurka, straightforward in treatment, calling for no special comment.
Klindworth marks the close *pianissimo*, while Kullak prefers *forte*. It is unimportant, the method of playing it being entirely a question of the mood of the moment.
Huneker says, "healthy and vivacious, good humour predominates."

No. 2 in A flat major.

This Mazurka is even more melodious, more interesting and more beautiful than its predecessor.   Huneker calls it "a perfect specimen of the aristocratic Mazurka."   The trio in D flat, with its episode in B flat minor, and its decisive rhythm, is a well marked contrast to the lightness and grace of the opening theme.

No. 3 in C sharp minor.

Harmonically this is one of the most interesting, but emotionally one of the least so of the Mazurkas.   There is a curious classical feeling about its opening section. Chopin's careful study of, and his predilection for Bach, here appear unmistakably.   Von Lenz says of this piece : "It begins as though written for the organ, and ends in an exclusive *salon ;* it does him credit, and is worked out more fully than the others. Chopin was much pleased when I told him that in the construction of this Mazurka, the passage from E major to F major was the same as that in the Agatha aria in ' Freischütz.' " Huneker refers to the Bach-like imitations of the opening : " The texture of this dance is closer and finer spun than any we have encountered. Perhaps spontaneity is impaired, *mais que voulez-vous ?* Chopin was bound to develop, and his Mazurkas, fragile and constricted as is the form, were sure to show a like record of spiritual and intellectual growth."

OPUS 51.—Third Impromptu (Allegro vivace) in G flat major.

Dedicated to Mlle. la Comtesse Esterhàzy.
Composed 1842.   Published 1843.

THIS is the least known of the Impromptus ; Huneker even says it is practically undiscovered.

It opens with two bars that Von Bülow directs should be played as an improvisation, " at first somewhat *ritenuto,* so that the allusion they contain to the opening passage in the Impromptu Opus 29 (which is assuredly not unintentional) may be perceptible. Then a slight *accelerando* leading into the lively *Tempo giusto,* which however must not be too lively ; *giusto* to be understood in contrast to *rubato.*"

The opening phrase has a most curious effect of winding and twirling. Huneker describes the curves in triplets as ophidian, and speaks of their tropical colouring and rich morbidity. The trio in E flat minor has the melody in a cello-like passage in the bass, recalling the C sharp minor Etude.

Niecks speaks of its feverish restlessness and faint plaintiveness. " After the irresolute flutter of the relaxing and enervating chromatic progressions and successions of thirds and sixths, the greater steadiness of the middle section, more especially the subdued strength and passionate eloquence at the D flat major has a good effect. But here, too, the languid, lamenting chromatic passing and auxiliary notes are not wanting, and the anxious, breathless accompaniment does not make things more cheerful. In short, the piece is very fine in its way, but the unrelieved, or at least very insufficiently relieved, *morbidezza* is anything but healthy."

Huneker, too, feels this " morbidity." He says : " It is neither so fresh in feeling nor so spontaneous in utterance as its companions. There is a touch of the faded, *blasé*, and it is hardly healthy in sentiment. The absence of simplicity is counterbalanced by greater freedom of modulation and complexity of pattern. The impromptu flavour is not missing, and there is allied to delicacy of design a strangeness of sentiment ; that strangeness which Edgar Poe declared should be a constituent element of all great art."

OPUS 52.—Fourth Ballade in F minor.

Dedicated to Mme. la Baronne C. de Rothschild.
Composed 1842. Published 1843.

AS Niecks says : " It would be foolish and presumptuous to pronounce this or that one of the Ballades the finest ; but one may safely say that the fourth is fully worthy of her sisters."

Karasowski tells us that contemporary critics, who, with the exception of Schumann, unanimously condemned Chopin's larger works, made a fierce onslaught on this Ballade. He holds, however, that : " It displays the most poetry and intelligence of them all ; and for a satisfactory interpretation of its manifold beauties, not only considerable mechanical skill, but also subtle musical perception are required."

Kleczynski is less sympathetic to it. Apparently its technical difficulties repelled him, for he speaks of the final passages containing ostentation of difficulties rather than organic development of the idea, and passes over its many obvious beauties with almost slighting brevity. It is throughout as sad and melancholy as the preceding

Ballade in A flat is light-hearted and cheerful. Niecks says : "The emotional keynote of the piece is longing sadness, and this keynote is well preserved throughout ; there are no long or distant excursions from it. The variations of the principal subject are more emphatic restatements of it ; the first is more impressive than the original, the second more eloquently beseeching than either of them."

Huneker writes of this masterpiece with characteristic hyperbole, but he understands and appreciates its value. It is to him a sanctuary : "Its inaccessible position preserves it from rude and irreverent treatment ; it is a masterpiece in piano literature as the Mona Lisa and Madame Bovary are masterpieces in painting and prose. Its melody, which probes the very coverts of the soul, is haunting in its chromatic colouring. . . . The narrative tone is missing after the first page, a rather moody and melancholy pondering usurping its place."

It is undoubtedly more introspective than the other Ballades. There is perhaps in it an almost personal note, as if Chopin had been reminded by something in the story of some event in his own life and had abandoned himself to the mood of the moment.

The opening seven bars form a kind of introduction, the main theme has, as Huneker puts it, "the elusive charm of a slow, mournful valse, that returns twice, bejewelled, yet never overladen."

A close analysis of this masterpiece would be of little value without an annotated edition of the music to follow it with, but attention must be drawn to the second theme with its wonderful modulations, to the elaborate but brief little cadenza, with its telling pauses, the harmonic progressions at the *stretto* before the furious and passionate *coda*, and the *pianissimo* chords descending softly and ending in a long sustained suspension before the final outburst.

OPUS 53.—Polonaise in A flat major.

Dedicated to Mr. A. Leo.
Published 1843.

THIS Polonaise is called the eighth on the original title-page, but to arrive at this number it is necessary to include the Polonaise Opus 3 for piano and violoncello. It is usually known as the " Heroic " Polonaise.

Niecks says : " Only pianoforte giants can do justice to this m: tial tone-picture. The physical strength of the composer certainly did not suffice."

Chopin's pupil, Gutmann, said that " in this Polonaise Chopin could not thunder forth in the way we are accustomed to hear it. As for the famous octave passages which occur in it, he began them *pianissimo* and continued them without much increase in loudness. And then, Chopin never thumped." Would that we could say the same of some of our modern *virtuosi !* But this is a piece that constantly tempts many of them to extravagance.

Sir Charles Hallé in his interesting reminiscences tells us that Chopin resented sharply any deliberate misreading of his compositions. " I remember how, on one occasion, in his gentle way he laid his hand upon my shoulder, saying how unhappy he felt because he had heard his ' Grande Polonaise ' in A flat, *jouée vite !* thereby destroying all the grandeur, the majesty, of this noble inspiration. Poor Chopin must be rolling round and round in his grave nowadays, for this misreading has unfortunately become the fashion."

It is the descending semiquaver octave figure in the bass which *virtuosi* usually play too fast, making too prominent what is only an accompaniment figure, and thereby destroying the essential nobility of the theme in the right hand. Niecks, Karasowski, Huneker, and Willeby all give currency to the idea that in this passage Chopin meant to suggest the trampling of horses. If, however, the passage is played in correct time it will be found that there is no such suggestion. It is not in the right rhythm, as will be seen on comparing it with the wonderful orchestral interlude at the commencement of the third

scene in the last act of Lohengrin.   Kleczynski's analysis
of this Polonaise and the remarks he makes incidentally
about programme music in connection with it form the
most valuable portion of his lectures on Chopin's Greater
Works.   He says that even among Chopin's compositions
this Polonaise is a culminating point.   " It exhibits a most
majestic and finished style.   It is a glorious apotheosis of
the past."   He points out the dignity that the opening
theme takes on when each quaver in the bass is given its
full value and accent.   Between the Trio and the resumption of the first part there are " strange and most
charming passages whose connection with the main idea
is not easily perceptible and which present no little difficulty of style to the performer . . .   What are the
particular principles of this phrase of the Polonaise ?   In
the right hand a creeping passage sufficiently representing
quiet and monotonous movement ; in the left hand the
rhythm of the Polonaise constantly asserts itself and does
not stop for a moment.   Moreover, the movement of the
right hand becomes gradually more and more silent, as
though dying away in the distance, while in the last few
bars, with a kind of assault and in a very rapid *crescendo*,
it returns and bursts out with the principal theme.   But
what is this part doing in the whole picture ?   Imagine a
gorgeous castle of ancient structure, with many towers,
halls, passages and bridges.   In it, in the centre ball-
room, a fine band plays a majestic Polonaise.   The
couples in national dress, war-like with swords, glide
dignified, accentuating with the step the rhythm.   In the
middle part, E major, we may see the approach of a
cavalcade, may be after a triumph ; no matter, we shall
only give our attention to that part of the Polonaise where
all the buoyant march following the first couple passes
gaily into adjacent halls, then glides over the distant
bridges, enters the park, and only after such an excur-
sion when they all seem lost, do we hear them approaching by another entrance, and with them the strains of
triumphal music.   Does not this explanation help us
to play the piece ?   Do we not feel more sure of
our way in consequence of it ?   Shall we not shade
the *pianissimo* passages with a more charming delicacy,
knowing the significance of the music, and will not the

the *fortissimo* phrases appear afterwards with greater splendour ? "

There is no doubt that Kleczynski is right in his powerful plea that there is much in modern music which we cannot understand and therefore render intelligible without an exercise of our imagination. " It is imagination which must create in our soul a certain whole which will bring into harmony the various contrasts, a whole with which the parts are sometimes connected only obliquely, by a combination of sounds only."

It is on record that in the trio Tausig used to hold down the loud pedal for a length of time without interruption. Kleczynski points out that this is only allowable in grand *crescendos*, when the sonority of the instrument attains prodigious proportions. At the seventeenth bar of the trio, where the key suddenly changes again into A flat, there is a very curious effect. The first eleven bars of the octave passage are *pianissimo*, then as if one heard the procession approaching without seeing it, there is a rapid *crescendo*, and at the change of key the whole body of sound is dropped a semitone, which gives exactly the effect of the cavalcade having just rounded a corner and come suddenly into view.

OPUS 54.—Scherzo No. 4 in E major,

Dedicated to Mlle. J. de Caraman.
Published 1843.

IF we look upon the Scherzi as affording a more personal revelation of Chopin than any other of the composer's works, we shall be consoled to find that, notwithstanding his increasing ill-health, we find him here in a happier, lighter-hearted, more contented frame of mind than eight years before, when he published his first Scherzo in B minor. The mood too is quite different from that of the fierce scorn of the third Scherzo. Here a delightful independence replaces defiance, and a gentle raillery reigns instead of the sarcasm and invective of the earlier work. It is a delightful composition, so full of charm and delicate

L

beauty of detail that it is impossible to agree with Willeby, who finds it of inordinate length.

He draws attention to the similarity of the ascending phrase at bar seventeen, to the opening of the Ballade in A flat, on which he bases the statement that he finds the Scherzo more valuable for its exquisite treatment of detail than for its absolute originality of idea.

The resemblance is, however, more striking on paper than in performance, for in tonality, rhythm, and feeling, the two phrases are widely distinct.

Kullak draws attention to the fact that this Scherzo differs from the others inasmuch as the rhythmic animation, peculiarly appropriate to the Scherzo style, is much less prominent than the long drawn out, soft *cantilenas*.

Niecks does not seem to have been in a very happy frame of mind when he set down his opinions of this genial work. He finds that "although less closely wrapped (like the other Scherzi) it wears dark veils," and he considers it inferior to its brothers, and to have the appearance of being laboured, painfully hammered and welded together. However, he acknowledges the beauty of many of the details ; "indeed, the harmonic finesses, the melodic cunning, and rhythmical piquancy, are too potent to be ignored. The resting-place and redeeming part of this Scherzo is the sweetly-melodious second section, with its long, smooth, gently and beautifully curved lines."

Karasowski speaks of its "kindlier face ;" and Huneker, as usual, does it full justice, seizing the character of the work, and mirroring it, as it were, in the style of his description. He says it "can be described by no better or more commonplace a word than delightful. It is delightful sunny music, and its swiftness, directness, and sweep are compelling. The five preluding bars of half-notes, *unisono*, at once strike the keynote of optimism and sweet faith. What follows is the ruffling of the tree-tops by warm south winds." He tells us that the ascending passage at the seventeenth bar has been boldly utilised by Saint-Saëns in the Scherzo of his G minor piano concerto, and draws attention to the episode in E of contrasted duple and triple rhythm which is reminiscent of the A flat valse, Op. 42. Elsewhere he says : "Built up by a series of cunning touches and climaxes, and without the mood, depth, or variety of its brethren, it is more truly a Scherzo than any of them. It has tripping lightness, and there is sunshine imprisoned behind its open bars. Here is intellectual refinement and jesting of a superior sort ; I find the fairy-like measures delightful after the doleful mutterings of some of the other Scherzi. There is the same spirit of opposition, but of arrogance none. It seems to be banned by classicists and Chopin worshippers alike. The agnostic attitude is not yet dead in the piano-playing world."

It certainly would be as well if some of our drawing-room *virtuosi* would give the G minor and A flat Ballades a rest, and devote some attention to making this delightful work more familiar to the general run of amateurs. It is full of beauties, which are, however, so obvious that they require no special comment. One may, however, particularise the *stretto*, and recitative-like passage leading up to the beautiful *cantabile* melody marked *più lento*, the re-entry of the first subject with the double pedal-point, and the fascinating *coda* with its billowy ascending passage, the contrasted vigour of the closing phrases and its silvery concluding scale.

OPUS 55.—Two Nocturnes.

No. 1 in F minor ; No. 2 in E flat major.

Dedicated to Mlle. J. W. Stirling.
Published in 1844.

THESE two Nocturnes are distinctly less interesting than any of the others ; the first is well known to amateurs, as it is one of the least difficult, but the second is the most unfamiliar of the whole group.

Kullak finds the chief subject of the first gloomy and melancholy, but Niecks refers to its *flebile dolcezza* (tear-laden sweetness). Kleczynski gives elaborate directions how this Nocturne should be played. He opposes the theories of Hanslick—who pronounces music to be power-less for the production of sentiments—and declares that if

the work is to be grasped in its entirety it is necessary to
" apply it to the words of an imaginary poem created by
our own mind ; the details will then come spontaneously
and without difficulty."

To him this Nocturne represents " a sadness which
rises by different degrees to a cry of despair, and is then
tranquillised by a feeling of hope."

Kullak acting on this theory says : " We may be per-
mitted to imagine a wanderer, who goes his way solitary
and sad, after taking leave of his beloved home and all his
dear ones."

The second section, which Niecks considers inferior,
though more impassioned, is " march-like in character, as
if the wanderer had resolved henceforth to go on more
courageously."   In the ninth bar of the second subject the
movement becomes more passionate and excited.   A
passage in the treble which seems like an abandonment to
despair should be played *molto rubato*, and leads through
an effective passage *stretto* to a resumption of the first
subject.   This, however, breaks off into an agitated movement, which gradually calms down and floats off into a
passage that rises over a firmly-held chord in the bass,
and is played always softer and faster till it seems to
vanish.   Two beautiful chords lead from the minor to the
major, and three arpeggio chords, " strong, long, and
majestic, as though proceeding from an organ," bring the
Nocturne to a grateful close.

Kullak says, the *coda* sounds to him like " Thank God,
the goal is reached."

Huneker says : " It is the relief of a major key after
prolonged wanderings in the minor.   It is a nice Nocturne,
neat in its sorrow, yet not epoch-making."

No. 2 Nocturne in E flat.

This Nocturne does not lend itself easily to analysis.
Kullak says " that it makes the impression of an improvisation.   One and the same mood breathes through the
entire piece, but the ideas follow each other as in free
improvisation, following the impulse of the moment only,
and paying no heed to strict laws of form in either
articulation or arrangement."

Niecks draws attention to its difference in form from the other Nocturnes in " that it has no contrasting second section, the melody flowing onward from beginning to end in a uniform manner, the monotony of the unrelieved sentimentality does not fail to make itself felt. One is seized by an ever-increasing longing to get out of this oppressive atmosphere, to feel the fresh breezes and warm sunshine, to see smiling faces, and the many-coloured dress of Nature, to hear the rustling of leaves, the murmuring of streams and voices which have not yet lost the clear, sonorous ring that joy in the present and hope in the future impart."

The fact is the commentators seem to have become a little tired of their detailed examination of the group of Nocturnes, for Huneker only says, " it has the merit of being seldom heard," and Kleczynski merely remarks that " the style is somewhat grandiose, by reason of an extended phrasing." Barbedette speaks of it as written in a style " un peu tourmenté."

It will, however, repay careful study, being full of interesting harmonic details. The *coda* is a gem ; beginning from the twelfth bar from the end, there is a wonderful modulation to the eleventh bar, followed by a phrase as original, distinguished and beautiful as anything Chopin ever wrote. The fame, however, of this Nocturne in E flat is quite eclipsed by the more popular one in the same key, Opus 9, No. 2.

These two Nocturnes were offered, with the three Mazurkas forming Opus 56, to a Paris publisher for 600 francs, and they are dedicated to Miss Stirling, the kind and generous Scotch friend and pupil to whom Chopin owed it that his last months were not spent in poverty.

OPUS 56.—Three Mazurkas.

No. 1 in B major ; No. 2 in C major ; No. 3 in C minor.

Dedicated to Mlle. C. Maberly.
Published 1844.

ON the whole this set shows a falling off in Chopin's inspiration, and in this particular it is curiously matched by the two Nocturnes Opus 55, which, written about the same time, are decidedly the least interesting of the pieces of that group.

No. 1 in B major.

This is one of the most elaborate of the Mazurkas. Huneker calls it " very virtuoso-like, but not so intricate as some of the others.   There is decoration in the *ritornelle* in E flat, and one feels the absence of a compensating emotion despite the display of contrapuntal skill."

No. 2 in C major.

Karasowski selects this Mazurka as the one which illustrates most strikingly the way in which Chopin displays "a tinge of melancholy, as if the composer had only indulged in a momentary diversion and narcotic intoxication to return the more sadly to his original gloom."

Huneker says : " There is the peasant in the first bars in C, but the A minor which follows soon disturbs the air of *bonhomie*.   Theoretical ease is in the imitative passages; Chopin is now master of his tools."

No. 3 in C minor.

This Mazurka is a pendant to No. 1 of the set.   It shows the same elaboration and somewhat monotonous, insufficiently relieved length.

Huneker thinks it does not give the impression of a whole : " with the exception of a short break in B major, it is composed with the head, not the heart, nor yet the heels."

Some of the harmonies are quite Wagnerian.   It suits

some moods, especially if one has leisure for contemplation. It rather grows on one.

OPUS 57.—Berceuse in D flat major.

Dedicated to Mlle. Elise Gavard.
Composed 1844.   Published 1845.

THIS Berceuse is perhaps the most marvellous instance of " filagree " work in music.   Chopin, starting with two bars of a simple rocking figure in the bass, takes a naïve little melody of four bars, and with these two phrases performs miracles.   The bass remains in unaltered rhythm throughout the whole seventy bars, on the tonic and dominant harmonies, except at the twelfth and thirteenth bars from the end, when the chord of the subdominant gives a moment's change.

After the first four bars, the melody is joined by what Niecks happily styles " a self-willed second part," and thence onwards every repetition of the phrase is the subject of some exquisite variation, of such delicate beauty and charm that the senses become hypnotised, and in listening to it we pass into a kind of trance.   Alexandre Dumas felt this charm, and wrote in the *Affaire Clemenceau :* " This muted music (*musique en sourdine*) which penetrated little by little the atmosphere and enveloped us in one and the same sensation, comparable, perhaps, to that which follows a Turkish bath, when all the senses are confounded in a general *apaisement*, when the body, harmoniously broken, has no longer any other wish than rest, and when the soul, seeing all the doors of its prison open, goes wherever it lists, but always towards the Blue, into the Dreamland."

The " fineness, subtlety, loveliness, and gracefulness " of the " *fioriture, colorature* and other trickeries " remind Niecks of Queen Mab, and Shakespeare's fairy-like passage describing her coach in " Romeo and Juliet."

Willeby thinks that " never was music written more happily bearing out its title," and in the last eight bars sees " the nurse, who has been rocking the child, herself succumbing to the drowsy influence of the music."

But a finer appreciation is that of " Israfel" writing in the *Dome*. He calls it "a little wrought ivory piece of exquisiteness just sufficiently trivial, which is, however, so delicately and ecstatically amorous that it misses its mark as a cradle song." It is hardly a Berceuse in the sense of a lullaby ; it is rather the reverie of a young mother over the cradle of her child, more occupied with her own dreams and eloquent fancies than the lulling of the infant. Kullak evidently finds the same thing, for in his directions as to performance he says : " The melody at the beginning is to be played very tenderly, in keeping with the character of a cradle song ; the following passages in that dreamy, half-vanishing way which suggest picture on picture to the fancy without sketching a single one in firmer outlines."

Huneker speaks of its "modulations from pigeon-egg blue to pale green, most misty and subtle modulations that dissolve before one's eyes, and for a moment the sky is peppered with tiny stars in doubles, each independently treated. Within a small segment of the chromatic bow Chopin has imprisoned new, strangely dissonant colours. It is a miracle, and after the drawn-out chord of the dominant seventh and the rain of silvery fire ceases, one realises that the whole piece is a delicious illusion, but an ululation in the key of D flat, the apotheosis of pyrotechnical *colorature*." Elsewhere he speaks of the " delicate and aristocratic child " that must be the recipient of such a lullaby, and contrasts it with the homelier but no less precious babe of Brahms' music in the same style.

Kleczynski thinks this Berceuse should be numbered with the Nocturnes. This seems rather a superficial and undiscriminating classification. Its one ideal fanciful, and contemplative quality differentiates it radically from the more varied lyric and dramatic strength of the Nocturnes. It is interesting to compare this masterpiece with the first variation of the Polish folk song in the Fantaisie on National Airs, Op. 13, when the idea of the unchanged rocking bass with the variations on the air above is clearly foreshadowed.

OPUS 58.—Sonata in B minor.

Dedicated to Mme. la Comtesse E. de Perthuis.
Composed 1844.   Published June 1845.

"THE psychology of the Sonata form is false," says
Finck. "Men and women do not feel happy for
ten minutes as in the opening *allegro* of a Sonata, then
melancholy for another ten minutes as in the following
adagio, then frisky as in the scherzo, and finally fiery
and impetuous for ten minutes as in the *finale*. The
movements of our minds are seldom so systematic as this.
Sad and happy thoughts and moods chase one another
incessantly and irregularly, as they do in the compositions of Chopin, which, therefore, are much truer echoes
of our modern romantic feelings than the stiff and formal
classical Sonatas. And thus it is that Chopin's habitual
neglect of the Sonata form, instead of being a defect,
reveals his rare artistic subtlety and grandeur."

The same writer, in his admirable essay on Chopin,
quotes Dr. Hanslick, the celebrated German critic, as
saying of Chopin : " This composer, although highly and
peculiarly gifted, was never able to unite the fragrant
flowers which he scattered by handfuls into beautiful
wreaths."

Finck says Hanslick intends this as censure, but he
regards it as the greatest compliment Chopin could have
been paid. " A wreath may be very pretty in its way, but
it is artificial. The flowers are crushed, and their fragrance
does not blend."

Chopin certainly put enough flowers into the wreath of
this Sonata. The first movement contains such a profusion of themes and such a wealth of details that two
movements might be made out of them.

Karasowski says : " The composer seems to have found
it difficult to keep the profusion of thought within due
proportions. In the development of the first theme there
is a want of repose which is only made up for by the
wonderful *cantilene* in D major." Huneker calls this
melody " an *aubade*, a Nocturne of the morn. There is a
morning freshness in its hue and scent, and when it bursts

a *parterre* of roses." All the commentators regret the confused wealth of material and the tropical luxuriance of its handling that intervenes between the clear-cut opening phrases and the exquisite melody of the second subject.

But this reproach cannot be brought against the graceful, airy, restrained perfection of the scherzo. A beautiful quaver figure winds in and out, up and down untiringly and without pause till the trio is reached, which is delicious in contrast, but yet in exquisite accord with the mood of the first section.

Huneker speaks of it as " vivacious, charming, light as a harebell in the soft breeze. It has a clear ring of the scherzo, and harks back to Weber in its impersonal, amiable hurry." Elsewhere, in comparison with the great Scherzi, he speaks of it in a more slighting tone, and says : " The resolution is not intellectual and is purely one of tonality. It might go on for ever. It must be considered as an intermezzo, and also as a prelude to the lyric measures of the beautiful largo that follows. This largo is one of Chopin's less happy inspirations. The melody has a ring of the commonplace, and the accompanying figure in the bass is jerky and in ill accord with it."

Kullak speaks of the self-absorbed, religious character of the second subject in E major. It is so self-absorbed that it goes on too long with its almost unbroken quaver figure and unrelieved sweetness. It must be taken as a typical instance of what Liszt said when he spoke of Chopin's efforts in the larger forms as showing *plus de volonté que d'inspiration.*

The *finale*, however, is brilliant, or should be so when properly played. It takes a giant's strength to play it, and is probably responsible for Professor Hans Schmidt of the Vienna Conservatoire placing this Sonata at the head of all Chopin's compositions for technical difficulty. The other two Sonatas and the Allegro de Concert share the next three places in this interesting classification. It opens with eight bars of a vigorous introduction, and then the melody enters marked *agitato*. Twice again we get this fine theme. The first time it is accompanied in the bass by quavers in groups of three ; the second time the quavers are in groups of four ; and at the last *reprise* the melody is in octaves accompanied by galloping groups of six semiquavers. Between each section there are wonderful pages of brilliant passage work, and the *coda* in B major is of thrilling *brio*, and brings the whole work to an aboundingly happy conclusion.

It is a magnificent Sonata taken as a whole, but nothing like as poetical as Opus 35, although more of a Sonata in the usual classical sense.

OPUS 59.—Three Mazurkas.

No. 1 in A minor ; No. 2 in A flat major ; No. 3 in F sharp minor.
Published January 1846.

AFTER the halt in interest and inspiration of the Mazurkas forming Opus 56, it is refreshing to find Chopin's genius again leaping forward ; and as we could compare the uninteresting Nocturnes of Opus 55 with that set of Mazurkas, we can now compare the success of the present set with the rich and melodious mood of the Nocturnes forming Opus 62.

No. 1 in A minor.

This Mazurka contains some of Chopin's most self-willed and original modulations. If Rellstab wanted to tear up Opus 7, what would he have not done to this wild and wayward composition of Chopin's prime ?

Huneker compares it with its quality of sturdy affirmation to the one in C sharp minor No. 1 of Opus 41. It is quite as strange in its harmonies, but much less decided and consistent. Huneker says : "That Chopin did not repeat himself is an artistic miracle. A subtle turn takes us off the familiar road to some strange glade wherein the flowers are rare in scent and odour. This Mazurka, like the one that follows, has a dim resemblance to others, yet there is always a novel point of departure, a fresh harmony, a sudden melody, or an unexpected ending."

No. 2 in A flat major.

"Perhaps the most beautiful of all the Mazurkas," says Hadow, and the majority of people will agree with him. It may not be the strongest, the most original, or the most fascinating, but it certainly is the most exquisitely tuneful and graceful.

Huneker says: "There is no gainsaying the fact that this is a noble composition." It appeals to him as an amplification of the lovely Mazurka in the same key, Opus 50, No. 2.

The leading melody is exquisite, and the trio worthy of it, and the passage marked *marcato* where the air is given to the left hand is entrancing. At the *à tempo* fresh charm is added by the sub-melody of the top notes of the chords in the bass, as indicated by Klindworth.

No. 3 in F sharp minor.

Huneker raves, and deservedly, about this Mazurka : "Chopin is at the summit of his invention. Time and tune that wait for no man, are now his bond slaves. Pathos, delicacy, boldness, a measured melancholy, and the art of euphonious presentment of all these, and many factors now stamp this Mazurka a masterpiece."

It is intensely characteristic and interesting throughout. The *coda* is a gem ; it has humour, freshness, spontaneity. It is one of those separate inspirations of Chopin that, as in the Nocturnes, he occasionally reserves with prodigal extravagance for his *codas* only.

OPUS 60.—Barcarolle in F sharp major.

Dedicated to Mme. la Baronne de Stockhausen.
Published 1846.

THIS is Chopin's only essay in the popular and essentially Venetian form of the Barcarolle. The word means a boat song, and is used to designate pieces written in imitation of the songs of Venetian *barcaroli* as they urge their gondolas along the silent canals. The essential characteristic of the form is the alternation of a strong and light beat in $\frac{6}{8}$ time ; Chopin's Barcarolle is an exception, being written in $\frac{12}{8}$ time. A triplet figure pervades the entire composition, the object being to convey the idea of the rise and fall of the boat, or the regular rhythmic strokes of the oars. There is a certain amount of local colour in this piece, and the melody is of such a character that we are reminded of Schumann's saying that Chopin in his melodies leans sometimes over Germany towards Italy.

But even in this purely local form Chopin is occupied not so much with a transcript of nature, a rendering of the charm of the canals and lagoons of Venice, with their shifting, opalescent light and colours, as with human emotions. He concentrates our attention on what is evidently a dramatic duet between two lovers in a gondola, absorbed in themselves and their own affairs. This piece requires consummate skill in handling, otherwise the unbroken long-breathed rhythm and the want of contrast in the middle section will make it appear rather long, and, in spite of the great beauty of much of the detail, monotonous. This was the view held by Von Lenz until he heard the great virtuoso Tausig play the piece when they were alone together. He had offered to do so, saying : " That is a performance which must not be undertaken before more than two persons ; I shall play you my own self (*meinen menschen*). I love the piece, but take it up only very rarely." He describes the piece as a continuous tender dialogue with a two-part *cantilena* superimposed on a lightly-rocking theme in the bass.

Kullak says the melody of the chief subject should be graceful and fragrant in delivery, but that the second subject at the change to A major requires more definite treatment. The bass here in contrast to the soft wavelike motion of the first part has the monotonous steadiness of oar-strokes.

Tausig considered that the affairs of the lovers came to a crisis at the cadenza-like phrases marked *dolce sfogato* (softly breathed out), which he took to symbolise an embrace and a kiss. Certainly after this the melody is resumed with an emotion somewhat heightened and filled, as it were, with a sense of love triumphant.

The *coda* dies away in a happy dream, and closes with *fortissimo* octaves, a favourite device of Chopin's, who sought thereby to bring his hearers back from his music-dreamland to the world of every day.

Hallé in his memoirs narrates how he heard Chopin play this Barcarolle at his last public concert in Paris, when, on account of his lack of physical strength owing to increasing illness, Chopin " played it from the point when it demands the utmost energy, in the opposite style *pianissimo*, but with such wonderful nuances that one remained in doubt if this new rendering were not preferable to the accustomed one."

OPUS 61.—Polonaise Fantaisie in A Flat.

Dedicated to Mme. A. Veyret.
Published 1846.

IN this wonderfully beautiful and interesting piece Chopin still further emancipated himself from adherence to the strict form of the Polonaise, so much so that the qualifying title " Fantaisie " became absolutely necessary. The distinguishing rhythm of the Polonaise, although prominent in the leading subject, often becomes disguised and is frequently absent altogether ; but the piece remains very distinctly Polish in character and feeling. Chopin here is in an entirely different mood to that of the F sharp minor Polonaise (Op. 44) and the A flat Polonaise (Op. 53). His mood here is more contemplative, and an elegiac sadness pervades the greater part of the piece. It is practically his last important work, and throughout we seem to see the shadow of his approaching end. The introduction with its abrupt pause and its contemplative cadenzas is strikingly original. The chief and secondary subjects are full of character and charm. The *più lento* in the B major episode is as beautiful as the slow movement in the great F minor Fantaisie. The succeeding page becomes certainly more Fantaisie than Polonaise, with its chain of shakes, its references to the slow movement and its return to the introduction. There is a curious indecision at the change of key to A flat ; but then, as if suddenly inspired, Chopin breaks off, and the hesitation and uncertainty vanish in a triumphant outburst, in which we seem to hear Chopin prophesying the ultimate recovery of freedom by his oppressed country ; and in the contented contemplation of this the music dies away, getting softer and softer, until a single loud chord brings us back to the world of every day. Niecks calls this the most affecting composition among all the productions of Chopin, but he reads into it " unspeakable, unfathomable wretchedness—boundless desolation —lamentations and cries of despair," and he says that on account of its pathological contents the work stands outside the sphere of art. This, however, is a very extreme view. The Professor seems to have been infected by some of Liszt's exaggeration. The great pianist, after reading into the work restless, feverish anxiety and a kind of hysterical despair, says that " such pictures as these are of little value to art. They only serve to torture the soul, like all descriptions of extreme moments, of agonies, of death rattles," and so on.

This work has received scant justice at the hands of nearly all the critics, but Huneker says: " It is one of the three great Polonaises, and is just beginning to be understood. It unites the characteristics of superb and original manipulation of the form, the martial and the melancholic." Elsewhere he compares it with Poe's poem " Ulalume," with its haunting harrowing harmonies :

> " Then my heart it grew ashen and sober,
>   As the leaves that were crispèd and sere—
>   As the leaves that were withering and sere."

OPUS 62.—Two Nocturnes.

No. 1 in B major (Andante) ; No. 2 in E major (Lento).

Dedicated to Mlle. R. de Könneritz.
Published in 1846.

THERE seems to be a consensus of opinion amongst the critics that these two last Nocturnes of Chopin's are lacking in spontaneity, and reflect to a certain extent the ravages that illness had made upon his constitution.

Niecks says, "that they seem to owe their existence rather to the sweet habit of activity than to inspiration ; at any rate, the tender flutings, trills, roulades, syncopations, &c., of the first in B major and the sentimental declarations and confused monotonous agitation of the second in E major do not interest me sufficiently to induce me to discuss their merits and demerits." Kleczynski sees in them the evidences of a broken spirit, and thinks that by their somewhat too affected form, they "furnish an indication of the ravages made upon the heart of the poet by deception and physical suffering."

Willeby finds the "opening two bars of the first sufficiently original, and the melody which follows, although hardly one of the best, inexpressibly sweet."

Considerable harmonic cunning is evinced in this Nocturne, but the whole lacks that spontaneity which so distinguishes some of the earlier ones.

Huneker is warmer in his appreciation. He calls it the "Tuberose Nocturne," and says : "It is faint with a sick rich odour. The climbing trellis of notes, that so unexpectedly leads to the tonic, is charming, and the chief tune has charm, a fruity charm. It is highly ornate, its harmonies dense, the entire surface overrun with wild ornamentation, and a profusion of trills. Although this Nocturne is luxuriant in style, it deserves warmer praise than is accorded it. Irregular as its outline is, its troubled lyrism is appealing, is melting, and the A flat portion, with its hesitating, timid accents, has great power of attraction."

Finck, however, always daring and unconventional as a critic, "speaks out loud and bold." He says it is the sublimest of the Nocturnes, and waxes eloquent on the wonderful modulation from B major to A flat, and later about the delicious series of chords in the fourth and fifth bars after the *tempo primo*, which lead to the final section (14 bars from the end).

There are three Nocturnes in this key of B major of which this is the most celebrated, and as it offers considerable technical difficulties in the proper execution of the chain of trills which are such a feature of the last part, it is now often played at concerts, although for many years it was unaccountably neglected. Kullak says : "The

Nocturne is like a beautiful lyric poem created in a conse-
crated hour free from trouble. The chief subject reminds
one of Opus 32, No. 1. In the secondary subject, with the
change of key, a change of mood is perceptible ; it
becomes a shade more earnest, but also more elevated and
serene. On the return of the chief subject it appears
arrayed in such a profusion of chain trills and *fiorituras*
that its effect, when executed with taste and elegance, is
magical."

If this Nocturne has a fault it is that the two chief
subjects are not sufficiently contrasted, and therefore
there is a slight tendency for the sweetness of the melodies
to become monotonous. It is night in this Nocturne, a
warm moonlit, tree-shaded night in an Italian garden, with
the heavy scent of daturas on the air, and the nightingale
singing in " full-throated ease."

No. 2.   Nocturne in E major (Lento).

NOTWITHSTANDING the depreciatory remarks of
some critics (see Op. 62, No. 1) there is no falling off
in either power or charm in this last Nocturne from
Chopin's pen. Karasowski says that " although written
shortly before Chopin's death (really three years before),
it is full of refinement of harmony, sweet melody and
reverie ; " and Barbedette considers that " both in harmony
and counterpoint it offers an infinite amount of interest."

Huneker defends it, and says that it is not at all sentimental, as Niecks avers, unless so distorted in the playing.
"It has a Bardic ring, its song is almost declamatory.
The intermediate portion is wavering and passionate like
the middle of the F sharp major Nocturne. It shows no
decrease in creative vigour or lyrical fancy."

The chief subject recalls distinctly the beginning of the
Nocturne in C minor, Opus 48, No. 1. It leads through
an interlude to a second subject which " is more passionate and animated in character. The upper and bass
voices form a sort of dialogue in lively controversy. The
incidental imitations are to be made prominent in delivery.
The Nocturne is no less rich in fine points of harmony
and melody, than all preceding works of the same
species " (Kullak).

M

There is a lingering pathos about the *coda*, as if Chopin was loth to end what he perhaps felt would be his last inspiration in this form.

OPUS 63.—Three Mazurkas.

No. 1 in B major ; No. 2 in F minor ; No. 3 in C sharp minor.
Dedicated to Mme. la Comtesse L. Czosnowska.
Published 1847.

IN 1847 there appeared the three last works that Chopin published during his life.   Niecks finds it strange that the last book of Mazurkas should have something of the early freshness and poetry of the composer.   Why strange ?   With the exception of Opus 55 and 56, which apparently marked only a passing phase, there is no evidence of any falling-off in the inspiration of Chopin's later works.   There is especially in the first of these Mazurkas a winning charm, whilst the contrapuntal skill displayed in the third is evidence of the development of Chopin's technical resources.

No. 1 in B major.

Huneker speaks of this as " full of vitality "—sufficiently various in figuration and rhythmical life to single it out from its fellows.
The opening theme is vivacious, bright and full of freshness of feeling ; the trio is quaint and curiously reminiscent of the persistent monotonous music we are accustomed to associate with the Savoyards.

No. 2 in F minor.

" Brief and not difficult of matter or manner is this dance ; it has a more elegiac ring," says Huneker.   Elegiac happily expresses the dominant expression of this slightly mournful Mazurka.

No. 3 in C sharp minor.

Ehlert was so much impressed with the technical skill displayed at the close of this Mazurka that he was moved to say : " A more perfect *canon* on the octave could not have been written by one who has grown grey in the learned art."

Huneker says it is of winning beauty ; he calls it a pendant to the C sharp minor valse, and defies any one to withstand its pleading, eloquent voice.

OPUS 64.—Trois Valses.

No. 1 in D flat major (Molto vivace) ; No. 2 in C sharp minor (Tempo giusto) ; No. 3 in A flat major (Moderato). Published 1847.

No. 1 in D flat major.
Dedicated to Mme. la Comtesse Potocka.

THIS is the best known, easiest and most popular of all the Chopin valses, indeed it is so familiar that if one hears it badly played one is tempted to apply to it the term " hackneyed."

But properly handled, and when not used merely as a vehicle for the display of agility, this little valse with its banal anecdotal title " Valse du petit chien," is still as attractive and graceful as ever. The story goes that George Sand had a little dog that used to run after its own tail, and one evening she said to the composer, " If I had your talent I would improvise a valse for that dog," and Chopin promptly sat down to the piano and played this fascinating little improvisation.

It was a piece peculiarly suited to show off Chopin's technique, and when he played it at his last concert in Paris in 1848, a lady asked, " Quel est le secret de Chopin pour que les gammes fussent si *coulées* sur le piano ? "— " *coulées* " being an adjective that expresses more exactly than any single word in English the exact quality of

Chopin's scale technique so often admiringly described by his contemporaries.

Huneker, who had the advantage of hearing it played by Mathias, one of Chopin's favourite pupils, says that the first section is nearly always played too fast and the second too slow, and with sloppy sentiment. Mathias said that " the Master took the *tempo* rather moderately, making an *accelerando* on the up run, ending with a little *sforzando* click on the B flat."

The *cantabile* section is perhaps the most graceful and spontaneous melody in the whole range of the valses.

A comparison of the treatment of the cadence in the eighth and twenty-third bars of this section will give some idea of the originality, delicate variety and charm of Chopin's handling of detail. The valse has no *coda*, but ends with a rapid run, a deliciously unexpected amplification of a quaver passage that concludes each section. It is Parisian in its grace, coquetry and playful defiance. The end reminds one of the rhythmic tap of the foot with which some graceful dancer concludes a cleverly executed *pas*.

No. 2 in C sharp minor.   Tempo giusto.
Dedicated to Mme. la Baronne de Rothschild.

Chopin's nationality shows more clearly in this valse than in any of the others.   There is in it more of the Slav temperament.   Repeatedly the time sways from the valse rhythm to that of the Mazurka, and in contrast of moods it is strikingly Polish.

This dance poem might represent the feelings of an unhappy lover at a ball.   The first section is wildly melancholy, full of sadness and yearning.   At the *più mosso* the whirling dance urges him to forget his sorrow.   The third section (*più lento* in D flat) is tender and consoling, but the last three bars indicate despairing doubts, and again there is the whirl of the dance ; then a resumption of the first mood, and though once more there is the anodyne of the valse, the lover's doubts are only half stilled as the music dies away.

The recurring valse section should be taken in fairly strict time and rapidly whilst the lyric quality of the other sections demands a slower *tempo* and considerable *rubato*.

Niecks thinks that tender lovesick longing cannot be depicted more truthfully, sweetly and entrancingly than in this valse, whilst Huneker says ; "it is the most poetic of all. The first theme has never been excelled by Chopin for a species of veiled melancholy. It is a fascinating lyrical sorrow, a space of clearer skies : warmer more consoling winds are in the D flat interlude, but the spirit of unrest, *ennui* returns. The elegiac imprint is unmistakable in this soul dance."

No. 3.   Valse in A flat.   Moderato.
Dedicated to Mme. la Baronne Bronicka.

It is difficult to believe when listening to this exquisite, graceful, and apparently light-hearted composition, that it was almost the last that issued from Chopin's pen at a time when the shadows of a fatal illness were closing in upon him. The feverish melancholy of the preceding number has disappeared entirely, and in its place we have a fascinating dance which, as Huneker says, is "for superior souls who dance with intellectual joy, with the joy that comes of making exquisite patterns and curves. Out of the salon and from its brilliantly lighted spaces the dancers do not wander, do not dance into the darkness and churchyard, as Ehlert imagines of certain other valses."

Niecks evidently thinks it inferior to the two preceding ones in spite of its "exquisite serpentining melodic lines, and other beautiful details."

Willeby thinks the middle section in C major the most notable and virile portion, and rightly finds a suggestion in it of the informing genius of the Polonaise. The time should be moderate throughout, with towards the end increasing animation." The middle section is decidedly a conversation in the pauses of the dance, and the two voices must be kept distinct.

OPUS 65.—Sonata for piano and violoncello in G minor.

Dedicated to Mr. C. Franchomme.
Published October, 1847.

THIS was the last composition published during Chopin's lifetime. Niecks calls it one of his most strenuous efforts in the larger forms, and, although written at a time when he was very weak and ill, it shows no falling off in power. Sir Charles Hallé gives an interesting account of his hearing Chopin and Franchomme play this Sonata soon after it was written.

" Chopin grew weaker and weaker to such a degree that when we dined together at Leo's or other friends' houses, he had to be carried upstairs, even to the first floor. His spirits and his mental energy remained nevertheless unimpaired. . . . On our arrival we found him hardly able to move, bent like a half-opened penknife, and evidently in great pain. We entreated him to postpone the performance, but he would not hear of it ; soon he sat down to the piano, and as he warmed to his work, his body gradually resumed its normal position, the spirit having mastered the flesh."

Karasowski considers the first movement to be of surpassing beauty, and yet an account given by a contemporary of Chopin's, Madame Dubois, shows us that even by artists and intimate friends this movement was not understood. " It appeared to the hearers obscure, involved by too many ideas, in short it had no success. At the last moment Chopin dared not play the whole Sonata before so worldly and elegant an audience, but confined himself to the Scherzo, Adagio and Finale." Moscheles, who never really understood or appreciated Chopin's true greatness, wrote of this Sonata : " In composition Chopin proves that he has only isolated happy thoughts which he does not know how to work up into a rounded whole. In this Sonata I find often passages which sound as if some one were preluding on the piano and knocked at all the keys to learn whether euphony was at home."

He subsequently arranged the Sonata for four hands, and called it a trial of patience.

" To me it is a tangled forest, through which now and then penetrates a gleam of the sun."

Niecks is very unsparing in his criticism. He says that " Liszt's dictum, ' *plus de volonté que d'inspiration*,' applies in all its force to this Sonata, in which hardly anything but effort, painful effort, manifests itself. The first and last movements are immense wildernesses with only here and there a small flower. The middle movements do not rise to the dignity of a Sonata, and moreover lack distinction, especially the slow movement, a Nocturne-like dialogue between the two instruments."

He admits certain beauties, *e.g.*, the first subject of the first movement at the entrance of the 'cello, the opening bars of the scherzo, &c. ; but " they are merely beginnings, springs that lose themselves in a sandy waste."

Huneker speaks of the 'cello Sonata as a task for whose accomplishment Nature did not design Chopin. " He must touch the keys by himself without being called upon to heed the players sitting next him. He is at his best when without formal restraint he can create out of his inmost soul."

Elsewhere he says : " I fancy the critics have dealt too hardly with this work. Robbed of its title of Sonata, though sedulously aping this form, it contains much pretty music. And it is grateful for the 'cello. Tonal monotony is the worst charge to be brought against this work."

Finck, however, in his whole-hearted and generous fashion when a work pleases him, says : " The 'cello Sonata was the last of his larger works, and in my opinion it is superior to any of the 'cello Sonatas of Mendelssohn, Brahms, and even Beethoven and Rubinstein."

Had we only the youthful C minor Sonata to put beside this, there might be some shadow of an excuse for the repetition of the parrot cry that Chopin could not write Sonatas ; but with the masterpieces of the B flat minor and B minor Sonatas before us, it is astonishing how this legend seems to have blinded both critics and performers to the obvious merits of this most interesting work. Barbedette speaks most appreciatively of it : " *Sa belle Sonate . . . page rémarquablement écrite en point de vue scientifique appropriée au génie des deux instruments, remplie de détails d'une exquisite délicatesse, sensibilité el grace touchante."*

It is true that Kleczynski professes to find in it evidence of a broken spirit, but this is probably because he started with a preconceived idea that he ought to find this in Chopin's latest works.

OPUS 66.—Fantaisie Impromptu in C sharp minor.

Composed 1834 ; published posthumously 1855.

EVEN Niecks, who is so against the publication of works which Chopin himself withheld from publication, admits that he would not like to have lost this Fantaisie-Impromptu, and he styles it the most valuable of all the compositions published posthumously by Fontana. He asks, " Why did Chopin keep it in his portfolio ? " and answers himself thus : " I suspect he missed in it, especially in the middle section, that degree of distinction and perfection of detail which alone satisfied his fastidious taste."

Barbedette, however, prefers it to all the other impromptus ; he calls it a *chef-d'œuvre*, and is at a loss to imagine why Chopin " left in his portfolio this piece so worthy of publicity."

Huneker is sarcastic about the saccharine and mawkish quality of the trio, but properly handled there should be only sweetness and beauty in this lovely melody. The opening is as fresh as anything in Chopin ; its rhythmical difficulties require beautifully clear playing. The trio is a little over long and can be brought to a better balance by omitting the last twelve bars before the return of the first movement.

The *coda*, where the melody of the slow movement is taken up in the bass under a *pianissimo* accompaniment of semiquavers, brings this delightful work to a most satisfying conclusion.

OPUS 67.—Four Mazurkas.

No. 1 in G major, 1835 ;* No. 2 in G minor, 1849 ;* No. 3 in C major, 1835 ; No. 4 in A minor, 1846.
Published posthumously by J. Fontana, 1855.

IT is a puzzle why Fontana, when deciding to publish the eight Mazurkas of Chopin which make up this and Opus 68, did not arrange them in chronological order of their composition. This would seem the only logical course to pursue, as their chief interest lies in the aid they give us in tracing Chopin's development.

There is little to be said about these four. Niecks thinks Fontana should not have published the manuscripts that Chopin had deliberately withheld from publication. Of all the posthumous works this set of Mazurkas might best be spared.

The first in G major, dated 1835, is not specially distinguished, and if we compare it with the four forming Opus 24 of the same date, we shall see at once why Chopin rejected it. Huneker calls it " jolly and rather superficial."

The second in G minor, which is assigned to the year of Chopin's death, 1849, is very pretty, but Chopin does not seem to have taken much trouble over it.

The third in C major is also of 1835, and the same remarks apply as to the first of the same date.

The fourth in A minor of 1846 is much the best of the set, and possibly Chopin might have included it when next publishing a book of Mazurkas. It would not have added to his reputation, but it would have done it no harm.

* Apparently some copies of Klindworth's edition have the dates of these two Mazurkas transposed. Those given agree with Niecks' dates, but Huneker would seem to have an edition where the dates are reversed.

OPUS 68.—Four Mazurkas.

No. 1 in C major, 1830 ; No. 2 in A minor, 1827 ; No. 3 in
F major, 1830 ; No. 4 in F minor, 1849.
Published posthumously by J. Fontana in 1855.

THIS Opus contains three youthful efforts, and the very
last composition Chopin wrote.

The first is, as Huneker justly remarks, commonplace.

The second is the best of all the posthumous Mazurkas.
Niecks says of it : " It is simple and rustic, and at the
same time graceful.   The trio (*poco più mosso*), the more
original portion of the Mazurka, reappears in a slightly
altered form in later Mazurkas.   It is these foreshadowings of future beauties that make those early works so
interesting."

Huneker refers to it as much better than No. 1, " being
lighter and well made."

No. 3 he dismisses as weak and trivial.   This is not
undeserved, although the trio is interesting with its drone
bass and curious countrified effect.

To the fourth Fontana affixed the following pathetic
note : " *Cette Mazurka est la dernière inspiration que
Chopin ait jetée sur le papier peu de temps avant sa mort ;
il était déjà trop malade pour l'essayer au piano.*"

Huneker says : " It is certainly morbid in its sick insis-
tance in phrase repetition, close harmonies and wild
departure—in A—from the first figure."

Here we may echo, without any savour of Liszt's con-
descension or Von Lenz's irony, " *Pauvre Frédéric !* "

In his " greater Chopin," Huneker refers again to this
Mazurka : " Its singular idea, almost a fixed one, its
gaiety and astounding gloom, show us the sick brain of
the dying man."

Karasowski says : " It is sad, very sad, like the last
days of the great master.   He showed by this swan-song,
and by his yearning after the home of his happy youth,
that in the very last hour of his creative inspiration he
remained faithful to his national music and to his sorely-
tried Fatherland."

Finck refers to this Mazurka as of " heartrending sadness and exquisite pathos," "perhaps it was a patriotic rather than an æsthetic feeling, which led him thus to favour the Mazurka. His love for his country was exceeded only by his devotion to his art."

OPUS 69.—Two Valses.

No. 1 in F minor, composed in 1835 ; No. 2 in B minor, composed in 1829.
Published posthumously 1855.

No. 1 in F minor.

ON the manuscript of this valse appears the inscription "Pour Mlle. Marie," and it is signed F. Chopin. Drezno (Dresden), 1835. (Notwithstanding this clear date, 1836 is given as the date of composition both in Niecks' and Breitkopf and Hartel's catalogue.)

"Mlle. Marie" was the beautiful daughter of Count Wodzinski, with whom Chopin fell deeply in love during one of his holiday trips. In 1836 he proposed and was rejected, as Marie's parents objected to the match. The disappointment does not seem to have affected Chopin very deeply, and the next year the lady married a son of Chopin's godfather, Count Frederick Skarbek.

This is the valse that Camille Pleyel called the history of D flat. Huneker says it has a charm of its own, and is suavely melancholy, though not so melancholy as the one in B minor that follows it. It has more the nature of a lyric poem than of a dance, and Chopin showed his usual judgment in not publishing it. It is slight and far inferior to the next valse of this lyric nature, the A minor Op. 34, No. 1. The second section might almost be a Mazurka.

No. 2.   Valse in B minor.

This is a very early effort, dating from 1829, and it is chiefly interesting as one of the compositions in which Chopin allowed his poetic inspiration full play, and wrote regardless of his position as a virtuoso and without considering the Parisian public, whom he wished to conquer.

Its chief feature is its querulous, pathetic, appealing, helpless melancholy. The middle section seems to indulge in a wan smile, but all through the music seems to indicate a reiterated nervous collapse.

OPUS 70.—Three Valses.

No. 1, G flat major, composed 1835 ; No. 2, F minor, composed 1843.   No. 3, D flat major, composed 1829.

THESE three valses, composed at various dates, differ much in merit. The first is distinctly the weakest, one of the least distinguished of Chopin's works. Huneker describes it as "very gay and sprightly," but there is nothing more to be said of it.

The second is perhaps the most successful of all the posthumous valses ; the middle portion is of great beauty and charm.

The third valse is interesting as containing the germs of ideas subsequently developed in later valses. The first bars should be compared with the opening of Op. 42, in A flat, and the third section with Op. 34, No. 1, third part. It dates from October 3, 1829. In a letter of this date to his friend Titus Woyciechowski, Chopin writes, " While thinking of this lovely being (Constantia Gladkowska, the ideal of his youthful passion), I composed early this morning the valse which I send you. Notice the marked passage ; nobody knows of it but yourself. How glad I should be if I could play my newest composition to you ! In the fifth bar of the trio the bass melody up to E flat dominates, which however I need not tell you, as you are sure to feel it without being told."

Willeby considers this the best of the posthumous valses on account of its easy writing, and the intense amount of movement and life contained in it.

Niecks says, that although by no means equal to any of the valses published by Chopin himself, one may admit that it is pretty.

Huneker says it has no special physiognomy, and that it recalls to him the D flat study in the *Trois Nouvelles Études*.

OPUS 71.—Three Polonaises.

No. 1 in D minor, 1827 ; No. 2 in B flat major, 1828 ; No. 3 in F minor, 1829.
Published posthumously by J. Fontana 1855.
No. 1.   Polonaise in D minor.

IN these three Polonaises dating from Chopin's seven-teenth, eighteenth, and nineteenth years, we have the most important specimens of his youthful work from the point of view of his development as a poetical composer. As Niecks says, it is wonderful, truly wonderful, that a youth of eighteen should have attained such a strongly developed individuality.   Although there are traces of Weber's influence all three numbers are of a striking originality.   " Beside Chopin's peculiar handling we find in them more of his peculiar sentiment.   The *bravura* character is still prominent, but instead of ruling supreme it becomes in every successive work more and more subordinate to thought and emotion.   These Polonaises, although thoroughly Chopinesque, nevertheless differ very much from his later ones, those published by himself, which are generally more compact and fuller of poetry."

Willeby considers that although the last two exhibit no less emotional power, the first is the most spontaneous.

The germ of the opening of the heroic Polonaise can be traced in the first bars of this one in D minor.

Polonaise in B flat major No. 2.

This interesting work foreshadows the melancholy dignity of the C minor, Op. 40, No. 2.

No. 3. Polonaise in F minor.

In one of Chopin's early letters we read : " Princess Elise (Radziwill) was so much interested in my Polonaise in F minor that I could not refuse to send for it. Please let me have it by return of post. You can picture to yourself the character of the Princess from the fact that she makes me play the Polonaise to her every day. The Trio in A flat major always pleases her particularly."

OPUS 72.—Nocturne in E minor (Andante).

Composed 1827. Published posthumously 1855.

THIS Nocturne was composed in Chopin's seventeenth year, the date of the completion of his studies at the Warsaw Lyceum. According to Karasowski it bears evident traces of that youthful period. Huneker dismisses it as weak and uninteresting, and Barbedette finds it wanting in distinction. Niecks says : "It is probably the poorest of the early compositions, but excites one's curiosity as the first specimen of the kind by the incomparable composer of Nocturnes." He draws attention " to the wide-meshed chords and light-winged flights of notes and the foreshadowing of the *coda* of Opus 9, No. 1," as distinctive of Chopin.

As Kullak says, whatever its merits, " a comparison of the first and last Nocturnes (Op. 62, No. 2) will be interesting to the admirers of the great composer. *Ex ungue leonem !*"

The Nocturne is simple and melodious, the figure of the accompaniment unchanged throughout, but slight as it is we would not willingly exchange it for the whole of Field's works bound in full morocco.

OPUS 72b.—Marche Funèbre.   In C Minor.

Composed 1829. Published posthumously 1855.

THIS little known work, which was published posthumously by J. Fontana, must not be confused with the world-famed Funeral March that forms the third movement of the B flat minor Sonata.

" In the legacy of a less rich man the Funeral March in
C minor would be a notable item, in that of Chopin it
counts for little. Whatever the shortcomings of this
composition are, the quiet simplicity and sweet melancholy which pervade it must touch the hearer. But the
Master stands in his own light. The famous Funeral
March in B flat minor eclipses the more modest one in C
minor. Beside the former, with its sublime force and
fervency of passion and imposing mastery of the resources
of the art, the latter sinks into weak insignificance, indeed
appears a mere puerility. Let us note in the earlier work
the anticipation (bar 12) of a motive of the *chef d'œuvre*
(bar 7), and reminiscences of the Funeral March from
Beethoven's Sonata in A flat major, Op. 26." (Niecks.)

Huneker says that this march sounds like Mendelssohn.
" The trio has the processional quality of a Parisian
funeral *cortège*. It is modest and in no wise remarkable."

Had the posthumous works been destroyed we should
have lost in this march a most interesting musical docu-
ment, invaluable in tracing the evolution of Chopin's
musical genius. This work of the youth of nineteen is full
of promise ; a promise which develops in glorious fruition
in a short ten years in the masterpiece of the B flat minor
Funeral March.

OPUS 72c.—Trois Écossaises.

No. 1 in D major ; No. 2 in G major ; No. 3 in D flat major.
Composed 1830. Published posthumously 1855.

THIS is the one work of Chopin's that might, with advantage to his reputation, have been destroyed. They
are merely three little Schottisches, pure dance forms
without any emotional or poetical value, and they have
neither the simplicity or melody necessary to make up for
their deficiency in more serious qualities. Huneker says
" that No. 2 in G is highly popular in girls' boarding
schools," and Niecks considers them the least individual of
Chopin's compositions, " almost the only dances of his
which may be described as dance music pure and simple

—rhythm and melody without poetry, matter with a minimum of soul."

OPUS 73.—Rondo for two pianos in C major.

Composed 1828. Published posthumously 1855.

ORIGINALLY this Rondo * was written for one piano only, but Chopin, in a letter dated September 9, 1828, tells his friend Woyciechowski that he arranged it for two pianos during the summer he spent at Strzyewo : " To-day I tried it with Ernemann, at Buchholtz's, and it came out pretty well."   And later in the year he writes again : " That orphan child, the Rondo for two pianos, has found a step-father in Fontana ; he has learnt it after a month's study."

Huneker says : " It is full of fire, but the ornamentation runs mad, and no tracés of the poetical Chopin are present."

Niecks classes it with the early Sonata Opus 4 and the Duo Opus 8 as student's work : "Granting certain prettinesses, an unusual dash and vigour, and some points of interest in the working out, there remains the fact that the stunted melodies signify little and the too luxuriant passage work signifies less, neither the former nor the latter possessing much of the charm that distinguishes them in the composer's later works.   The original in this piece is confined to the passage work, and has not yet got out of the rudimentary stage."

Any one thinking that owing to the Opus number this must be a late work of Chopin's will necessarily experience a keen sense of disappointment, for it is emphatically of his earliest work, and has none of the poetry, the exquisite style nor deep melodic beauty of his masterpieces.

OPUS 74.—Seventeen Polish Songs.

THESE songs were composed by Chopin at various dates.   Karasowski tells us that if Chopin " met with any new and beautiful poetry in his native tongue, he

* See page 2.

would set it to music, not for publication, but for his own pleasure. Thus these songs gradually accumulated between 1824 and 1844. Many have been lost because, in spite of the request of his friends, the composer constantly put off committing them to paper ; others were sung in Poland without anything positive being known as to their origin, but it is pretty certainly conjectured that Chopin was their composer. Among these must be mentioned the popular and formerly much sung ' The Third of May.' . . . They are simple flowers which do not dazzle, but by their sweet perfume and peculiar delicacy delight sympathetic hearts."

Niecks tells us that the words of most of these songs are by Stephen Witwicki, others are by Mickiewicz, Zaleski and Krasinski; poets with all of whom Chopin was personally acquainted. He considers the "musical settings very unequal, a considerable number of them decidedly commonplace ; several exceedingly simple, and in the style of folk songs. . . . In the symphonies of the songs we meet now and then with reminiscences from his instrumental pieces."

Perhaps the best known are No. 1, " The Maiden's Wish," which has been brilliantly paraphrased by Liszt ; this is in Mazurka form. It is, however, hardly within the limits of this book to describe these songs at length. They are all intensely national and simple. The form of the art-song does not seem to have appealed to Chopin, and these folk-songs must depend for their effect on the pathos and dramatic power with which the simple tunes can be made to express the meaning of the words.

Grand Duo Concertant in E major for piano and violoncello, on themes from " Robert le Diable," by F. Chopin and A. Franchomme.

Composed 1832. Published 1833.

THIS is one of the four works published without an Opus number during the composer's lifetime. Schumann says of this *duo* : " This is a composition for drawing-rooms, in which, behind the lovely shoulders of

Countesses, the head of a famous artist appears here and there ; it is therefore not fitted for tea-parties, at which people play a little in the intervals of conversation. It is essentially a work for the most refined of circles, in which the artist receives the respect and attention his position deserves. It seems to me that Chopin must have sketched it throughout while Franchomme said a gentle ' Yes ' to everything ; for whatever Chopin touches takes his form and spirit, and even in this small *salon* style he asserts himself with a grace and elegance, compared to which all the finish of other brilliant writers is lost on the winds. If the whole of ' Robert le Diable ' were filled with such ideas as Chopin has selected from it for his *duo*, it would need re-baptism, and Chopin's fantastic finger plays hither and thither, veiling, unveiling, so that ear and heart long retain the tones. The reproach of extreme length, which anxious *virtuosi* may bestow on the piece, was perhaps not unjust, for at the twelfth page there is a sort of lameness in the movement ; but already on the thirteenth the strings are grasped with true Chopin-like impatience, and on the music flies again to the end, with a wave-like figure. Is it necessary for us to say that we recommend this *duo* with our very best will ? "

Huneker does not think much of this work. He says : " It is for the *salon* of 1833, when it was published. It is empty, tiresome, and only slightly superior to compositions of the same sort by De Beriot and Osborne. Full of rapid elegancies and shallow passage work, this *duo* is certainly a *pièce d'occasion*—the occasion probably being the need of ready money."

Karasowski also calls it a work without any special merit, written in accordance with the taste of the day.

TROIS NOUVELLES ÉTUDES.

THERE is no means by which we can arrive at the exact date of the composition of these studies.

Niecks thinks that internal evidence shows that they may be regarded as the outcome of a gleaning. It is possible that they were composed about the same time as the studies of Opus 25, but Kullak appears to think that they were written to order about the year 1840, the date in which they were first published in the Pianoforte Method of Moscheles and Fétis.

Niecks thinks they are the weakest of the master's studies, although by no means uninteresting and certainly very characteristic, while Kullak says that although " composed to order and devoted to instructive purposes, circumstances which usually hamper free artistic creation, these Études nevertheless take equal rank with the majority of Chopin's similar works, in which brevity of form is united with wealth of poetic contents."

Huneker says that " the last decade has added much to the artistic stature of these three supplementary studies. They have something of the concision of the Preludes."

No. 1. Étude in F minor.

Kullak compares this study in respect of poetic contents and magical effect with the one in the same key in Opus 25, No. 2, but it is far more emotional than the " magnetic crooning " of the latter.

The technical difficulty consists in playing groups of triplet crotchets in the right hand against eight quavers in the bass.

No. 2. Étude in A flat. Allegretto.

Referring to the time designation Kullak says : " *Allegretto* designates not merely the *tempo*, but at the same time the character of a piece. Composers use the word for compositions in which passion, dazzling antitheses, and deep emotion, are not to find a place, but, instead, cheerfulness, naïveté, harmless idyllic life, or even a light elegiac mood.

Compositions of this *genre* are to be treated like tender plants, and not grasped with rude hands. Thus it is with the present Étude.

This is the best known of the three studies, and so completely is the technical purpose, which is again to overcome the difficulties of rhythm, disguised, that it might have formed part of Opus 28 (the Preludes).

Huneker says of it : " Again the composer demonstrates his exhaustless invention and his power of evoking a single mood, viewing all its lovely contours and letting it melt away like dream magic. Full of gentle spriteliness and lingering sweetness is this study."

Elsewhere he compares it with Opus 119 of Brahms, and says : " But Chopin is so sad, and Brahms so merry, yet the general architechtonic is not dissimilar."

Hadow again uses this study as an example of how Chopin can make unconventional harmonies sound magically correct. He says : " Are consecutive major thirds justly regarded as harsh and dissonant ? Chopin at his dreamiest and most contemplative can employ them with unfailing effect."

No. 3.   Étude in D flat.   Allegretto.

In this study the technical problem is the playing of *legato* and *staccato* simultaneously in one and the same hand. As Huneker says : " The result is an idealised valse in *allegretto tempo* the very incarnation of joy tempered by aristocratic reserve. Chopin never romps, but he jests wittily and always in supremely good taste. This study fitly closes his extraordinary labours in this form, and it is as if he had signed it ' F. Chopin, et ego in Arcady.' "

POSTHUMOUS WORKS.—Variations on a German air in E major.

Composed 1824 :   Published in 1851.

THIS work is distinguished amongst those that appeared posthumously by the fact that Chopin evidently intended to publish it. It was in Haslinger's hands as early as 1830, and it was ultimately published by him at the same time as the Sonata Opus 4.   The theme is a familiar German air known as *Der Schweizerbub*, and according to Szulc the variations were composed between Chopin's twelfth and seventeenth years, in a " few quarter hours."

On account of their greater simplicity and inferior interest, Niecks thinks that they must be of an earlier date than Opus 1, composed in 1825.   He says : " In these variations (which Chopin wrote in his fourteenth year) the treatment of the instrument not only proves that he was already as much in his element on the pianoforte as a fish in the water, but also shows that an as yet vaguely perceived ideal began to beckon him onward." He instances as a weak point the introduction to the variations with their interminable sequences of dominant and tonic chords accompanying a stereotyped run : " Although they leave behind them a pleasurable impression they can lay only a small claim to originality.   Still there are slight indications of it in the *tempo di valse*, the concluding portion of the variations. Chopin's love of widespread chords and skips, if marked at all, is not strongly marked in the variations ; they can hold their own without difficulty and honourably among the better class of light drawing-room pieces."

Huneker calls them " musically light waisted " (whatever that may mean), " although written by one who already knew the keyboard. The last, a Valse, is the brightest of the set," but he thinks they were not worth the trouble of publishing.

Although not difficult they show that their composer even at the early age of fourteen must have been possessed of considerable technique.

Posthumous Mazurkas without Opus numbers.

A MAZURKA in A minor was published in 1842 in No. 2 of a musical periodical called " Notre Temps," a kind of Christmas album of the period.

Another Mazurka in A minor is dedicated "à son ami Emile Gaillard." Of these two Huneker prefers the latter, " it abounds with octaves and ends with a long trill."

Both these two are published by Klindworth and Kullak. The former adds another Mazurka in F sharp, which the researches of Pauer have identified beyond doubt as the work of Charles Mayer. How any amount of forged signatures could ever have led any one to believe this a genuine work of Chopin's is a mystery. In two bars of Chopin's weakest mazurka there is more poetry than in the whole of this common dance tune.

Breitkopf and Härtel's edition gives this Mazurka in the key of F. Also four other Mazurkas, one in G major, dated 1825, "of slight worth" (Huneker), one in B major of the same date, "early as it was composed, it is nevertheless pretty" (Huneker), one in D major, which was written in 1829 or 1830, and remodelled in 1832. "The recasting improves it. The trio is lifted an octave and the doubling of notes throughout gives more weight and richness." The last is in C major of 1833. "There are breadth and decision in it " (Huneker).

The chief interest of these posthumous Mazurkas is to let us see how in his slightest effort, Chopin's individuality stands out, and how even his rejected pieces are better than the admired efforts of lesser men.

Valse in E minor.

Composed 1829.   Published posthumously 1868.

"THE E minor Valse without opus is beloved. It is very graceful and not without sentiment. The major part is early Chopin." (Huneker.)

Henselt has paraphrased this Valse for concert purposes, but it is far more attractive as it is, and distinctly interesting as a forerunner of the two brilliant Valses, Opus 18, and Opus 34, No. 1.

It has a *coda*, and is altogether more ambitious than the other three Valses of the same date.

Valse in E major.

Composed 1829.   Published posthumously 1872.

THIS Valse is not included either in the Klindworth or in Kullak's edition, but appears in No. 11 of the posthumous works without Opus number in Breitkopf and Härtel's catalogue.

Niecks refers to certain rhythmical motives, melodic inflections, and harmonic progressions that occur again in a more perfect form in Valses of later dates. It is just these hints and foreshadowings of later perfection that make a chronological study of these early Valses so fascinating to the intelligent student.

Polonaise in G sharp minor.

Dedicated to Madame Dupont.
Composed 1822.   Published 1864.

OF this Polonaise, said to be of the year 1822, Niecks
says that on account of the *savoir faire* and invention
exhibited in it he holds it to be of a considerably later
time.   " Chopin's individuality, it is true, is here still in a
rudimentary state, chiefly manifested in the light-winged
figuration ; the thoughts and the expression, however, are
natural and even graceful, bearing thus the divine impress.
The echoes of Weber should be noted."

Polonaise in B flat minor.

Adieu to William Kolberg.

THIS Polonaise, which is not included in Klindworth's
edition, but is numbered 10 in the Posthumous Works
published without Opus numbers in Breitkopf and Härtel's
edition, is superscribed as an Adieu to William Kolberg,
while the Trio is headed " Au Revoir ! after an air from
Gazza Ladra."   Of it Niecks says that " it has not less
naturalness and grace than the Polonaise of 1822, and in
addition to these qualities it has also at least one thought
(Part I.) which contains something of the sweet ring of
Chopinian melancholy."   A footnote tells us that the
Polonaise was composed " at Chopin's departure from
[should be ' for '] Reinerz ; " while a second in connection
with the Trio, says that some days before Chopin's
departure the two friends had been present at a performance of Rossini's opera.

VARIOUS.

IN 1837 a charity concert was given in Paris by the
Princess Belgiojoso, at which the chief attraction was
an air from "I Puritani," on which Chopin, Liszt, Thalberg,
Pixis, Henri Herz, and Czerny each wrote a variation.   It
was published in 1841 under the title of Hexameron.   It
is only interesting in so far as it shows Chopin superior
to his contemporaries in grace and style.   " Liszt often
played these variations at his concerts, and even wrote

orchestral accompaniments to them, which, however, were never published." (Niecks.)

Huneker says that "Rosenthal is the only modern virtuoso who plays the Hexameron in his concerts;" and play it he does with overwhelming splendour. Chopin's contribution in E major is in his sentimental salon mood. Musically it is the most impressive of this extraordinary mastodonic survival of the "pianistic" past.

A Polonaise in G flat major exists, but it is of very doubtful authenticity. Niecks says, "Nothing but the composer's autograph could convince one of the genuineness of this piece. There are here and there passages which have the Chopin ring, indeed seem to be almost bodily taken from some other of his works; but there is also a great deal which it is impossible to imagine to have come at any time from his pen—the very opening bars may be instanced."

A piece called "Souvenir de Paganini" in A major was published in the supplement of the Warsaw Echo, *Musyczne*, but neither of these pieces are in any of the collected editions. It was published in facsimile, and was supposed to have been written by Chopin at the age of eleven.

In the Klindworth edition is included a Mazurka in F major, which Mr. E. Pauer has shown conclusively is by Charles Mayer.

"Deux Valses Mélancholiques in F minor and B minor, écrites sur l'Album de Mme. la Comtesse P., 1844," are the same as Opus 70, No. 2 and Opus 69, No. 2.

No. 1 of the Seventeen Polish Songs appeared in the Paris *Journal de Musique* in 1876, with French words by George Sand, under the title of "La Reine des Songes."

M/

[